Advance Praise For Performance-Focused Learner Surveys

Given heavy reliance on surveys to plan and evaluate training programs, an evidence-based approach to construction and interpretation of surveys is way overdue. Kudos to Will Thalheimer for leading the way!

Ruth Colvin Clark
Legendary Learning Researcher & Consultant

It's about time that someone took the ubiquitous but mostly useless end-of-session training feedback questionnaire to task. Will Thalheimer does a great job of telling us why the current practice doesn't work and replaces it with thoughtful and sensible advice for feedback tools that will provide valid and actionable data.

Robert O. Brinkerhoff
Professor Emeritus, Western Michigan University
& Director, Brinkerhoff Evaluation Institute

In our field there can be a lot of hand-waving—general advice without clear application guidelines. Will's book is exactly the opposite. He gives you the deep-dive on training evaluations, including both the how and the why. This is evidence-based practice at the master level.

Julie Dirksen
Author of Design For How People Learn

Will Thalheimer attacks one of the most intractable misconceptions in our field, and does so with authority and humor. His straight-shooter approach to improving learner surveys is a wake-up call for the field. Thalheimer's prescription is easily understandable and makes perfect sense. And, any book that equates learning measurement to pure sex has to be a must read!

Marc J. Rosenberg, PhD
Marc Rosenberg and Associates

In the second edition of his paradigm-busting book, *Performance-Focused Learner Surveys,* Will Thalheimer continues his quest to help learning professionals make training evaluation more valuable—not just for proving training's value, but as decision support for continuous improvement.

Roy Pollock, DVM, PhD
Chief Learning Officer, 6Ds® Company
Co-author of Six Disciplines of Breakthrough Learning

Will Thalheimer, one of our most reputable translators of research into practice, has rewritten his readable treatise on that scourge of learning, smile sheets. The insightful (and inciteful) work that aptly skewered current approaches now provides an even more valuable alternative that both helps us now and educates us to do better going forward. A valuable contribution indeed!

Dr. Clark Quinn
Executive Director of Quinnovation
Author of Learning Science for Instructional Designers

With this book, Will Thalheimer provides an important contribution, particularly in showing how to ensure that learner feedback provides a true gauge of on-the-job success. The book is research-based, comprehensive, and based on real world experiences. If you're spending time and money in using learner surveys, this book will show you how to make them valuable, useful, and relevant to your organization's success.

Jack J. Phillips
Chairman, ROI Institute

Freakin' revolutionary or business smart? Will Thalheimer's position is that learner surveys are a waste unless they're designed to predict a change in job behavior—an idea that's refreshing, worthwhile, and, as the book demonstrates, actionable too! I encourage you to read Performance-Focused Learner Surveys and reflect on how you might improve the feedback your organization captures from its learners.

Judith Hale, PhD, CPT, ID (SEL, ILT, JA+)
Co-founder Institute for Performance Improvement

Will Thalheimer's work is grounded in research, honed through experience, and organized to provide a practical perspective for application. In Performance–Focused Learner Surveys Will dissects the current failure of learner-feedback instruments and provides an alternative perspective on what will work; as well as arguments you can use to change organizational cultures that remain wedded to these inaccurate metrics.

William Coscarelli
Professor Emeritus,
Southern Illinois University

Will Thalheimer, PhD, is one of the definitive myth busters in our field, and he does it with great precision but also humor. It's good that he's explaining the things we need to know about learner surveys, because there are just too many fairytales. We must be held to a higher standard.

Patti Shank, PhD
Author and Learning Analyst
PattiShank.com

Only a few people combine the rigor of a researcher and the usability of a how-to writer. Will Thalheimer is the best among them. He has done it again in his Performance-Focused Learner Surveys. The second edition is a superior version. Will has undertaken an audacious project. This book is the beginning of a radical revolution for professionalizing our field. Sign me up.

Sivasailam Thiagarajan, PhD
Principal and "Mad Scientist"
at The Thiagi Group

It is hard to do, but Will Thalheimer has found a way to make the measurement of learning sexy and exciting in his book Performance-Focused Learner Surveys. You'll find yourself turning the pages and laughing along the way (usually at your own past mistakes, which you won't make again after reading this book).

Ryan Watkins
George Washington University

Finally, a book that acknowledges and addresses the dirty and widespread problem with smile sheets, which typically tell us nothing useful and focus our attention on the wrong things. Will Thalheimer's book provides useful guidance for using this tool correctly, in ways that improve learning and its transfer to the workplace in ways that produce valued performance. Anyone involved in workplace learning and performance will find this book valuable.

Steven W. Villachica, PhD
Associate Professor
Boise State University

Just when I thought it couldn't get any better, this updated version takes the whole concept up a notch (or two) so, if you are responsible for evaluating training, stop right now and read "Performance-Focused Learner Surveys". The insights and ideas will change forever how you create evaluations. Quite simply, the BEST book on learner survey creation and utilization (even better than the first edition), Period!

Karl M. Kapp
Professor of Instructional Technology
Bloomsburg University

What I like most about Thalheimer's updated book on Performance-Focused Learner Surveys is that it still puts the focus where it belongs, on predicting subsequent performance back on the job—the ultimate measure of learning in an enterprise context. This is an excellent guide with many example survey questions for adopting or adapting to nudge the reader to generate better actionable data!

Guy W. Wallace
Performance Analyst &
Instructional Architect, EPPIC Inc.

Thalheimer has replaced the smile sheet beauty pageant with an approach that delivers concretely actionable design insights, reinforces learning, and educates learners and their sponsors about what really matters in learning. He's turned learner surveys into a tool capable of delivering substantial performance impact for both individuals and businesses.

Adam Neaman, PhD
Vice President, Learning & Development
The D. E. Shaw Group

Armed with a lot of heart and incredible insights, this book oozes with mind blowing, radical, myth-busting, research-proven takeaways from the master of learning research, Will Thalheimer. This is a must read, and must apply, for anyone involved in education, learning and evaluation from conferences to workshops to online education.

Jeff Hurt, Chief Epiphany Officer,
Empowered Epiphanies

A must have resource for all L&D professionals who want to lift their game with learner surveys - and in turn, learning effectiveness and transfer. Full of practical guidance, sample questions and rationale. Will makes sure you know what to do (and not do!) and why. An easy and quick guide to radically overhaul this critical component of learning evaluation.

Michelle Ockers
Learning Strategy, Learning Uncut

The familiar four-level taxonomy used for assessing the value of training is fraught with problems; the first level, "smile sheet" reactions from learners, is especially noted as mostly a timewaster. Thalheimer has developed an approach to making this phase of evaluation more worthwhile, as a valuable means of correlating effort with learning, and better informing ways of improving our work. This new edition has several additions, bringing new help for problems that bedevil many of us in the business: asking better questions, getting better feedback, and upping response rates.

Jane Bozarth
Director of Research, The Learning Guild

Let me start with a disclaimer: I am a Will Thalheimer fan. Will's ability to translate scientific research in a way that practitioners can easily apply it in practice is next to impossible to beat. This new book is just one example of his fantastic work. I own the 2016 version of this book and have used it ever since. This 2022 version adds many gems. For example, it shows how learner surveys can be used to nudge—showing training intent or implicitly calling to action. It also includes many new and useful examples (they make it so much easier to redesign your surveys), and a chapter on motivating learners how to respond (data equals power, after all!). Every L&D department needs this book!

Mirjam Neelen
Author of Evidence-Informed Learning Design

PERFORMANCE-FOCUSED
LEARNER SURVEYS

PERFORMANCE-FOCUSED LEARNER SURVEYS

Using Distinctive Questioning to Get Actionable
Data and Guide Learning Effectiveness

SECOND EDITION

Will Thalheimer, PhD, MBA

Work-Learning Press
SOMERVILLE, MASSACHUSETTS

Copyright © 2022 Will Thalheimer

All rights reserved. No part of this publication may be reproduced, distributed or transmitted in any form or by any means, including photocopying, recording, or other electronic or mechanical methods, without the prior written permission of the publisher, except in the case of brief quotations embodied in critical reviews and certain other non-commercial uses permitted by copyright law.

Work-Learning Press
www.worklearning.com

Performance-Focused Learner Surveys / Will Thalheimer. — 2nd Edition

ISBN: 978-1-941577-03-5 (paperback)
ISBN: 978-1-941577-05-9 (hardcover)
ISBN: 978-1-941577-04-2 (ebook)

Library of Congress Control Number: 2022932111

Dedication

For many, many years, I've had the following dedication written down, waiting for my first book to be published. I want to use this chance to honor those who have given me the most.

- To my mom and dad, Kay and Bill, who somehow—in a way that I regret I'll never fully understand—prepared the soil for my growth and learning.

- To my wife, Dorothy, who has allowed me my mission—through the struggle, despair, and joys of the journey.

- To my daughter, Alena, whose young adult explorations and thoughtful skepticism of convention, remind me daily that learning is at the heart of our humanity.

*Let us measure what is important to measure,
not just what is easy to measure.*

*Let us measure to gain insight,
to motivate action,
to enable success.*

Will Thalheimer

Contents

PREFACE VII
WHAT'S NEW IN THE SECOND EDITION IX
WHY THIS BOOK IS WORTH YOUR TIME.. XI
WHO WILL FIND VALUE IN THIS BOOK XIII
ACKNOWLEDGMENTS XV
INTRODUCTION... XVII
CHAPTER 1   WHY LEARNER SURVEYS? 1
CHAPTER 2   YOUR SMILE SHEETS SUCK! 11
CHAPTER 3   MEASURING EFFECTIVENESS... 29
CHAPTER 4   PRODUCING ACTIONABLE RESULTS.............................. 45
CHAPTER 5   SENDING MESSAGES TO NUDGE ACTION 55
CHAPTER 6   LEARNER-SURVEY QUESTION QUIZ 65
CHAPTER 7   CANDIDATE QUESTIONS 79
CHAPTER 8   SPECIAL PURPOSE QUESTIONS.................................... 131
CHAPTER 9   COMMENT QUESTIONS 175
CHAPTER 10   TAILORING YOUR QUESTIONS 181
CHAPTER 11   FOLLOW-UP LEARNER SURVEYS 189
CHAPTER 12   MOTIVATING LEARNERS TO RESPOND....................... 201
CHAPTER 13   PRESENTING LEARNER-SURVEY RESULTS................... 215
CHAPTER 14   MAKING IT HAPPEN 229
CHAPTER 15   MEASURING LEARNER PERCEPTIONS IN OTHER WAYS 237
CHAPTER 16   LTEM: THE BIG PICTURE OF LEARNING EVALUATION 243
EPILOGUE.. 249
WHERE DO WE GO FROM HERE? 249
REFERENCES... RESEARCH INSPIRATION 253
ABOUT THE AUTHOR... WILL THALHEIMER, PHD, MBA 259
INDEX 261

Preface

I've been doing learning since I reached adulthood. I taught emotionally disturbed kids how to act as Boy Scouts. I taught a young woman whose body and mind had been devastated by meningitis—who had almost no control over her arms—how to reach to grab a spoon. It took six weeks. I got into an MBA program so I could find a job, but found that instructional-design courses were much more rewarding. I got work as an instructional designer and designed an "MBA in a box." I built simulations to teach leadership and management skills. I parlayed this into an opportunity to build two simulations to teach at-risk high-school students in Brooklyn about how to run a business. I taught teachers-in-training about educational psychology. They taught me that I knew nothing about schools. I taught leadership courses and change-management courses to managers in Fortune 500 companies. I even taught business strategy a few times with learners polite enough not to laugh at my lack of depth. For twenty-three years, I've been teaching instructional designers, trainers, and elearning developers about the research on learning.

I was lucky. When I started Work-Learning Research in 1998 I had very few responsibilities. No family to help support. No mortgage to pay. I could earn enough money to support myself by selling my skills as a leadership trainer. Most of my time was spent wonderfully lost in the research on learning, memory, and instruction. My aim was to uncover a short list of fundamental learning factors in an otherwise chaotic sea of experimental results. The task was huge—too big for me to succeed in the short term. But, swimming in the vast depths of the research, I began to understand human learning at a deeper level than I could have previously contemplated. I also learned how daunting the task, how impossible! Over the years, I've kept my research going a good portion of the time. It's an important task—bridging the gap between research and practice; but, unfortunately, it's one that the world doesn't easily support in the learning field. Still, I'm grateful I've had the time.

I took this path because I believed strongly—and still believe—that learning is a noble cause. It is learning that has enabled human civilization and growth. It is learning that enables individuals to excel and thrive. It is learning that holds the promise of the future.

If learning is so important and our task is such a noble one, don't we, as learning professionals, have an almost sacred responsibility to do our jobs well?

The way I see it, there are two lynchpins to our performance. First, scientific research must guide our starting assumptions. Second, we must use good learning measurement to get valid feedback so we can refine our understandings, improve our learning designs, and live up to our promise—so we can maximize learning's benefits.

This book focuses on the second imperative. It examines the popular (yet down-trodden) learner survey and attempts to elevate it to full effectiveness. While learner surveys should never be the only way we get feedback on learning, by improving them, we can get significantly better information about how we're doing. With better information, we can create virtuous cycles of continuous improvement. We can build more effective learning interventions and meet our obligations as learning professionals.

What's New in the Second Edition

I finished writing the first edition in 2015, published it in 2016, and, since then, I have helped hundreds of organizations build radically improved learner surveys. I have learned a huge amount along the way and have improved my learner-survey methodologies. Also, since then, I've continued my study of learning evaluation. Doing a rough facsimile of investigative journalism, I found out that Donald Kirkpatrick was NOT the originator of the Four-Level Model of learning evaluation—Raymond Katzell was. I built—with the help of others—a new learning-evaluation model to replace the Kirkpatrick-Katzell Four-Level Model. The new evaluation model is LTEM, the Learning-Transfer Evaluation Model. It is pronounced "L-tem." It has begun to transform learning evaluation and the whole infrastructure of learning and development in organizations throughout the world.

I've also begun to envision learning evaluation in a radically new way. The premise of the new way is simple—and obvious once it is stated out loud. We in the learning field have missed it completely, however—our thinking handcuffed, and our vision diminished by the Four-Level Model. I call the new approach *LEADS* (pronounced "Leeds"): Learning Evaluation As Decision Support. I will talk more about this in my forthcoming book, *The CEO's Guide to Training, eLearning & Work: Reshaping Learning into a Competitive Advantage*.

In this second edition, though, there is not enough time to delve deeply into LTEM and LEADS. However, their DNA is integrated throughout, and I include a chapter on LTEM as a brief introduction.

The following specific updates have been made in this second edition:

1. The book is retitled: Performance-Focused Learner Surveys. The term "learner survey" replaces "smile sheet" because it is more descriptive. Also, "learner survey" is less freighted with derision.

2. The subtitle has changed: *Using Distinctive Questioning to Get Actionable Data and Guide Learning Effectiveness.* The new subtitle is more descriptive, helping people find the book.

3. After years of nudging from readers, I've coined a term for the unique question methodology recommended in this book. *Distinctive Questioning.*

4. I've improved the wording and design of many of the questions presented in the original book. I have been working with organizations to build improved learner surveys for over six years and I've learned a ton through pilot testing and feedback. I've also continued to study survey design and learning and have incorporated new wisdom I've picked up along the way.

5. I added a new chapter with more than a dozen special-purpose survey questions. Altogether, this second edition has about twice as many candidate questions as the first edition.

6. I added a new chapter on how to use open-ended questions.

7. I added a new chapter introducing LTEM.

8. I added a new chapter on how to tailor questions to make them more engaging, more relevant, and more powerful.

9. I added a new chapter on how to get higher response rates from our surveys—whether they are online or in the classroom.

10. I added a new chapter on other ways to get feedback from learners.

11. I included insights and lessons learned from people who have used performance-focused learner survey approaches in their organizations.

12. I've reconceptualized the benefits of learner surveys, and now offer a list of twenty benefits rather than the original nine from the first edition.

Why this Book is Worth Your Time

1. The methods presented in this book will help you create learner surveys that provide you and your stakeholders with truly valuable data and information—of the kind that enable you to create virtuous cycles of continuous improvement and, thus, significantly improve learning outcomes for your learners and your organization.

2. This book is research-based. It draws its recommendations from the world's best learning research from the preeminent refereed scientific journals on learning, memory, and instruction.

3. This book is comprehensive. It offers a complete system for developing learner surveys.

4. This book is born of real-world experience. It acknowledges that research alone is not worth anything without practical wisdom.

5. This book is designed to help you learn. It will support your learning as much as the book format allows.

6. This book is a "call to arms." It takes an honest look at the learning-and-development field and our poor measurement practices. It celebrates sound ideas. It fumes angrily at bad practices.

7. This book follows the aphorism often attributed to Albert Einstein, "Everything should be made as simple as possible, but no simpler."[1] It simplifies complex realities into workable recommendations.

---

[1] Ironically, these words were probably not actually stated by Einstein, but are rather a simplification of the sentence, "It can scarcely be denied that the supreme goal of all theory is to make the irreducible basic elements as simple and as few as possible without having to surrender the adequate representation of a single datum of experience," as described at https://quoteinvestigator.com/2011/05/13/einstein-simple/.

Who Will Find Value in This Book

This book will benefit workplace-learning professionals who want to improve the design and delivery of their learning interventions.

1. **Learning measurement professionals**—practitioners responsible for learner surveys, assessments of learning and performance, and learning-based organizational results.

2. **Creators of learning interventions**—instructional designers, trainers, elearning developers, teachers, professors, and other educators.

3. **Managers of learning**—chief learning officers, learning executives, training managers, conference-education professionals, and instructional-development managers.

4. **Graduate students and faculty**—in learning measurement, assessment, instructional design, instructional technology, elearning, performance improvement, and adult learning.

Performance-Focused Learner Surveys is ideal for experienced practitioners who want to (1) energize their current practices with research-based recommendations, (2) challenge themselves with unique and provocative perspectives, and (3) prepare for the future of the learning-and-performance field.

Acknowledgments

First Edition:

Books don't get written or published by themselves. I am grateful to my wife, Dorothy, and my daughter, Alena, who have allowed me time to write and think. I am indebted to thousands of research scientists, journal editors and publishers, libraries, and database creators for enabling me to learn from the research. I am thankful to my clients who have made it possible over the past seventeen years for me to make a living and continue my work.

Specific thanks go to Doug Holt and Russ Spaulding for enabling me to share some of the underlying concepts of Performance-Focused Learner Surveys before they were fully formed. Thanks to all the folks who gave me advice on book publishing, including Mark Klein, Chad Udell, Clark Quinn, Julie Dirksen, Michael Allen, Ruth Clark, Allison Rossett, Roy Pollock, and various members of the Maine Writers and Publishers Alliance.

Thanks to Kate Ankofski and Katherine Pickett for their incredibly helpful editing. I had no idea that so many improvements could be made.

Special thanks go to Jack Phillips, Rob Brinkerhoff, Bill Coscarelli, Clark Quinn, Adam Neaman, and Julie Dirksen, for giving me in-depth feedback on the initial draft of this book—helping me improve it immeasurably.

Second Edition:

Thanks go out to my wife and daughter again for their forbearance, especially when my consulting practice hit hard times.

Thanks to those in the learning-and-development industry who have seen the transformative value of the ideas in this book, who have advocated for these ideas, and who have supported my work. I am truly grateful!

Thanks to Ross Edwards (FreelanceScribe.com) for providing expert copyediting.

Thanks to my research-to-practice family who have been a source of inspiration and comfort throughout the years: Ruth Clark, Patti Shank, Clark Quinn, Julie Dirksen, Mirjam Neelen, Guy Wallace, Jane Bozarth, and Karl Kapp. Thanks to Matt Richter for our many efforts at supporting the learning-and-development community, including the Truth In Learning Podcast, the Learning Development Conference, and the Learning Development Accelerator professional community and for encouraging me to keep at it when times were difficult. Thanks to Patti Shank for encouraging me to publish in a different way, a faster way, a way with less friction! Thanks to my TiER1 colleagues who thrill me every day with their compassion and commitment to helping people do their best work.

Introduction

For over two decades I've exhaustively reviewed research on how people learn—reading an average of more than two hundred articles every year from scientific refereed journals. Doing the research enabled me to build a consulting practice where I could provide workplace learning professionals with research-inspired insights. It has also compelled me—and I really can't help myself—to think about the state of the learning profession. This is not always a happy endeavor.

One thing I noticed a few years ago was that we, as workplace-learning professionals, often work in darkness. We get most of our feedback from learner surveys—also known as smile sheets, happy sheets, postcourse evaluations, student-response forms, training-reaction surveys, and so on. We also get feedback from knowledge tests. Unfortunately, both learner surveys and knowledge tests are often flawed in their execution, providing dangerously misleading information. Yet, without valid feedback, it is impossible for us to know how successful our learning designs have been. I've written this book to help you get better feedback and to help your organization produce more effective learning initiatives. I focus here on learner surveys because they are so central to our work in today's workplace-learning industry.

We, as workplace learning-and-performance professionals, often see learner surveys as a small thing when they are, in fact, a huge, dark, and demonic colossus. More than any other tool in the training-and-development industry, learner surveys control what we do. They are a self-inflicted form of mind control, warping our thoughts from learning's essential realities. Learner surveys—as typically designed—do not just tell us nothing. They tell us worse than nothing. They focus our worries toward the wrong things. They make us think our learning interventions are more effective than they are. More than any other practice in our field, they have done the most damage.

In brief, here are the problems with traditional smile sheets:

1. They are not correlated with learning results.
2. They don't tell us whether our learning interventions are good or bad.
3. They misinform us about what improvements should be made.
4. They don't enable meaningful feedback loops.
5. They don't support learner-survey decision-making.
6. They don't help stakeholders understand learner-survey results.
7. They don't educate stakeholders about important learning truths.
8. They provide misleading information.
9. They hurt our organizations by not enabling cycles of continuous improvement.
10. They create a culture of dishonest deliberation.

This book aims to stop the bleeding.

My hope for this book is simple: to help you get significantly better insight into the factors that drive your learning results—so you can improve your current learning practices. By reading this book, you will learn how to create performance-focused learner surveys using the Distinctive Questioning approach. You will look at your current learner surveys in a whole new light—as if seeing them for the first time. With newfound wisdom, you'll know how to radically improve your learner surveys, providing you and your stakeholders with a unique and enlightening vision of your learning outcomes! The learner surveys you will build will be inspired by the learning research, will help your learners produce more useful information, and will focus not just on the learning event but also on the situations and factors that enable the learning to culminate in successful real-world accomplishments.

Chapter 1
Why Learner Surveys?

Imagine yourself as the chief learning officer of a global corporation. You've been with the company seven years, working your way up, reveling in the success of the workplace learning-and-performance function. Suddenly, your CEO retires and a new CEO, Julie Sendirk, is hired. Julie is known as an innovator and a straight shooter. After a month or so and several meetings, Julie calls you into her office and asks you to help her understand the annual report your department created.

Julie: "Hey, welcome! Here's what I'm interested in, and I need your help. In general, I want to understand how you learning folks operate. Today, I want to drill down on the learner-survey results from the past year. If I read this report right, it says that, overall, our training courses have an average rating of about 4.1? Is that accurate?"

You: "Yes, and 82% of our courses are rated at 4.5 or better. We're very proud of our results. We've worked hard to improve our ratings over the past three years."

Julie: "But what does a 4.1 actually mean?"

You: "It means that we're doing well, that the training is well received. It's a 4.1 on a 1-to-5 scale, so we can't get much higher."

Julie: "But what does the 4.1 actually mean?"

You: [controlling the urge to talk louder] "Well, at the end of every training class, we give learners a set of questions about their perceptions of the training."

Julie: "And each question has a 1–5 scale?"

Performance-Focused Learner Surveys

You: "No, actually. Each question is really a statement, and the learners select one of five answer choices, from 'strongly disagree,' which gets a 1, to 'strongly agree,' which gets a 5."

Julie: "So a 4.1 means that most people 'agree,' and, if they don't select 'agree,' they likely selected 'strongly agree,' and, if not, then they've probably chosen 'neither agree nor disagree?'"

You: "Yes, that's exactly right. Pretty simple, really."

Julie: "Hmm. But what does a 4.1 mean? It certainly can't mean that our employees tend to be agreeable?"

You: "Well, no. . . ."

Julie: [cutting you off] "So the 4.1 is an average of the dozen or so questions you ask?"

You: "Well, no; in the annual report we just share the results of one question, our main question."

Julie: [now looking skeptical] "So you collect more than 10 times the data than you share with senior management?"

You: [starting to sweat] "Well, in our experience—and let me apologize for saying this—most senior managers just want the overall scores."

Julie: "So what is this overarching question you ask, your main question as you call it—the one that answers the question I asked earlier, 'What does 4.1 mean?'"

You: "We ask the learners to rate the overall value of the course. The question statement reads, 'This training provided valuable job-relevant information that supports on-the-job performance.'"

Julie: "Hmm. And what evidence do you have that the learners are good at evaluating the value of training? What evidence do you have that your main question is associated with actual on-the-job performance?"

You: "It's a learning-industry standard."

Chapter 1—Why Learner Surveys?

Julie: "And this standard is based on trusted scientific research?"

You: "Well, I haven't actually seen the research, but I'm sure the learning-measurement experts rely on the best research."

Julie: "Have we done any studies to show that this one question is valid with our learners and the content areas in our organization? So, for example, if we get high scores on this question, do we know whether our employees are more likely to be successful on the job than if they've been in a course that gets a low rating?"

You: "We've seen that this question is correlated to our other smile-sheet questions, so we're pretty confident."

Julie: "But that's not what I'm asking. Of course, the questions are correlated—probably because people just circle the same numbers down the smile sheet. What I want to know is whether our smile-sheet results—the ones you show management every year—are related to on-the-job performance. Do we know that?"

You: "They should be." [Here you go into a long discussion of the Kirkpatrick-Katzell Four-Level Model of training evaluation.]

Julie: "Has this model been tested? Does it show that learner surveys are correlated with learning results? And, even if it has been tested generally, how do we know our learner surveys are correlated with our learning results?"

You: "The Kirkpatrick Model has been around since the 1960s."

Julie: [acting highly skeptical] "All right! Thank you! Here's what I want. I want a way to measure how effective our training courses are in helping our employees understand the concepts and skills they're being taught. I also want to know whether our employees are able to remember the concepts and skills and whether they're successful in applying them to their jobs."

You: "We can do that, but it costs more money to measure learning and application. We occasionally do some of this kind of measurement, but most previous senior leaders didn't want to pay for it."

Julie: "Make a business case, and I'll definitely pay for it. I don't know how you guys can operate in the dark, without getting any feedback on how you're really doing. But what about these learner surveys? Can't you improve them to at least give you some idea of how effective the training has been?"

Okay, this is Will again. Let me apologize for putting you into the role of an almost-clueless chief learning officer. Just like I tell my daughter, you'll thank me for it later. SMILE. The truth is that Julie, our savvy new CEO, asked some damn good questions—questions we in the learning-and-development field don't always ask ourselves. I'm starting the book with this example to show how our traditional approach to learner surveys may have a few chinks in its armor—and also to get your blood flowing a bit. We'll go into more depth about the issues this case presents but, first, let me cover some basics to make sure we're on the same page.

What Is a Learner Survey?

A learner survey is a set of questions provided to learners after a learning event—or after a portion of a learning event—asking for learners' perceptions of the value of the learning experience. I use the words "learning event" and "learning experience" to signal that learner surveys can be used for training, education, elearning, self-directed learning, peer learning, coaching, mentoring, learning from reading books, watching movies, going to church—any type of learning event!

Learner surveys are also known as smile sheets, smiley sheets, happy sheets, student-response forms, trainee reaction surveys, and so forth. In fact, the terms "smile sheet," "smiley sheet," and "happy sheet" are often considered to have a derogatory connotation. The feeling among many practitioners is that learner surveys have minimal value or provide misleading results. Despite these concerns, learner surveys are the most popular way to get evaluative feedback about the success of workplace training—and the same is true in higher education as well.[2]

Learner surveys are often placed within a framework of other learning-measurement methods. By far the most popular of these frameworks is the Kirkpatrick-Katzell Four-

---

[2] In some recent research I conducted with Jane Bozarth and the Learning Guild (Thalheimer, 2019), we found that learning professionals reported that attendance and completion rates were slightly more popular than learner surveys. Still, because most of us don't see attendance or completion as related to learning outcomes, it seems fair to say that learner surveys are by far the most popular method used to validate learning success.

Level Model of learning evaluation. It has traditionally been called the Kirkpatrick Model, but I've renamed it here and elsewhere as the "Kirkpatrick-Katzell Four-Level Model" because, while Donald Kirkpatrick popularized it and brought the four-level idea to light, Donald Kirkpatrick himself attributed the four levels to Raymond Katzell, a highly-honored industrial-organizational psychologist.

The four levels are:

1. Learner Reaction
2. Learning Results
3. On-the-job Behavioral Results
4. Organizational Results

Learners' reactions are almost always measured through learner surveys. Learning can be measured in many ways, including tests, skill demonstrations, scenario questions, and more. On-the-job behavioral results are often measured with self-report data, but can be measured through observations of actual performance, ratings from others, and objective performance measures such as time-on-task completion. Organizational results are usually measured with organizational data that is already collected by the organization, such as sales revenue, costs, and customer satisfaction. While the Kirkpatrick-Katzell Model is widely used, it is also widely criticized for its shortcomings. We will touch on these shortcomings in Chapter 2. In Chapter 16 I'll introduce you to a new learning-evaluation framework that is a significant upgrade over the Kirkpatrick-Katzell Model. The new framework is called LTEM, pronounced "L-tem." For now, it's critical to understand that, for many people, the Four-Level Model signifies that learner surveys are related to the other four levels.

Learner surveys can be utilized for many reasons.[3] In the first edition of the book, I presented a list of nine reasons, which I'd modified slightly from learning-measurement expert Rob Brinkerhoff. In this second edition, I'm providing a twenty-item list and I've divided the list into conceptual categories to highlight key ideas:

Supporting Learning Design Effectiveness

1. Red-flagging training programs that are not sufficiently effective.
2. Gathering ideas for ongoing updates and revisions of learning programs.
3. Judging the strengths, weaknesses, and viability of program updates and pilots.

---

[3] Special thanks to Rob Brinkerhoff for reminding me of this truth.

Performance-Focused Learner Surveys

4. Providing learning architects and trainers with feedback to aid their development.
5. Judging the competence of learning architects and trainers.
6. Judging the contributions to learning made by people outside of the learning team.
7. Assessing the contributions of learning supports and organizational practices.

Supporting Learners in Learning and Application

8. Helping learners reflect on and reinforce what they have learned.
9. Helping learners determine what (if anything) they plan to do with their learning.
10. Nudging learners to greater efforts in learning and application.

Nudging Action Through Stealth Messaging

11. Guiding learning architects to create more effective learning by sharing survey questions with them prior to the design phase and sharing survey results after data is gathered.
12. Guiding trainers to more effectively facilitate learning by sharing survey questions with them before their training preparations and sharing survey results after data is gathered.
13. Guiding organizational stakeholders to support learning efforts more effectively by sharing survey questions and survey results.
14. Guiding organizational decision makers to better appreciate the complexity and depth of learning and development—helping the learning team gain credibility and autonomy.[4]

Supporting Relationships with Learners and Other Key Stakeholders

15. Capturing learner satisfaction data to understand—and make decisions that relate to—the reputation of the learning intervention and/or the instructors.
16. Upholding the spirit of common courtesy by giving learners a chance for feedback.

---

[4] I was going to use the word "power" instead of "autonomy" but, sadly, we learning professionals don't seem confident enough to make "power" seem like a reasonable request. We will get there! Autonomy helps us do what we know we should do—work to maximize learning effectiveness. But power gives us more of what we need to be fully effective—resources and stakeholder inclination toward obligatory support.

17. Enabling learner frustrations to be vented—to limit damage from negative back-channel communications.

Maintaining Organizational Credibility

18. Engaging in visibly credible efforts to assess learning effectiveness.
19. Engaging in visibly credible efforts to utilize data to improve effectiveness.
20. Reporting out data to demonstrate learning effectiveness.

Traditional smile sheets were pretty good at supporting relationships with learners and other stakeholders (numbers 15, 16, and 17 above)—getting learner satisfaction data, providing a feedback mechanism out of common courtesy, and enabling learners to vent their frustrations. Smile sheets have also played a role in helping the learning team maintain organizational credibility (numbers 18, 19, and 20). But just doing these few things is simply not good enough! Especially now when we know how to do better.

I'm on my high horse in this book to help us realize the full promise of learner surveys. We should develop better feedback loops so we can create virtuous cycles of continuous improvement. We should better support our learners in learning and application. We should do a better job in utilizing our learning evaluation practices to educate our stakeholders and get their help in supporting learning and development.

That's my hope, but you and your organization are going to have to determine for yourselves what you want to get out of your learner surveys. Indeed, one key to successful evaluation is to first figure out why you're doing what you're doing. I recommend you get your team together to reflect on the above twenty-item list and see what you want to accomplish with your learner surveys. Only then should you start your learner-survey design work.

Let me add one more note about terminology. You might have noticed that I'm using two terms almost as synonyms: "smile sheets" and "learner surveys." In this second edition of the book, I will use the term "smile sheet" to refer to *poorly designed* learner surveys. I will use the term "learner survey" as a general term, encompassing both the good and the bad.

Learning Measurement Is Pure Sex!

I received a call, as I wrote the first edition of the book, asking me to speak at an industry meeting. The caller said she loved my work and anything I wanted to talk about would be great. Because of all the love and goodwill I was hearing, I brimmed with warm fuzzies as I recited half a dozen topics I could speak on. When we got to the topic of "performance-focused learner surveys" I practically oozed with elation. I talked about their importance and how recent audiences—even of learning executives—trembled in delight when they learned that traditional smile sheets could actually be dangerous. The person I was speaking with got fired up, too, but finally said this: "Learning measurement just isn't sexy enough to draw people to our meeting, so I think we should go with another topic."

What the heck? Learning measurement isn't sexy enough? Let me start this book by saying that learning measurement is pure sex—with titillating foreplay (evaluation work begins before the main event), naked truth (powerfully useful data), and the dangerous rapture of the potential for new life (evaluation feedback gives birth to learning innovation and improvement). Seriously! Learning measurement is one of the most important topics in learning and development—not only because most learning measurement is frustratingly impotent—but more pointedly, because simple improvements can help us take back control of our learning outcomes and learning designs!

I've been on the warpath on learning measurement for over a decade. I've written articles on learning-measurement bias. I've done numerous keynote addresses, featured sessions, invited masters presentations, and workshops on learning measurement. I almost always bring up the need for better learning measurement with my consulting clients. Why am I—a research-guzzling learning consultant—so crazy about learning measurement? Because learning measurement gives us feedback! It gives us feedback so we can improve what we're doing. It is one of the most important things we do! Without adequate feedback loops, we simply can't know whether we're doing any good at all. We can't know what to improve—or whether to improve.

Without getting good feedback we frankly aren't worthy of the title "professional."

In the diagram that follows, you'll notice the tried-and-true instructional-design process. In it, feedback loops show how the instructional-design process is supposed to work. We are supposed to get routine feedback so we can improve our current efforts and also improve our knowledge and wisdom, while reducing our biases. Rarely does it work as diagrammed.

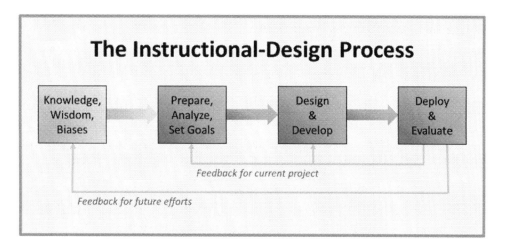

We tend to measure learning at the end of learning events. This seems sensible, but it doesn't account for eons of research on human learning and forgetting. When we measure at the end of learning, we are measuring only our learners' *understanding* at that point in time; we are *not* measuring their ability to *remember* after the learning event. Look at the next diagram—of the learning and forgetting curves. You can see that, if we measure at the end of the learning event, the learners are at their highest level of memory retrieval. Of course! Everything at the end of a learning event is top-of-mind. Things are easy to recall. When we measure at the end of learning, we are getting biased results. We are getting results that make us—and our learning interventions—look a whole lot better than the truth.

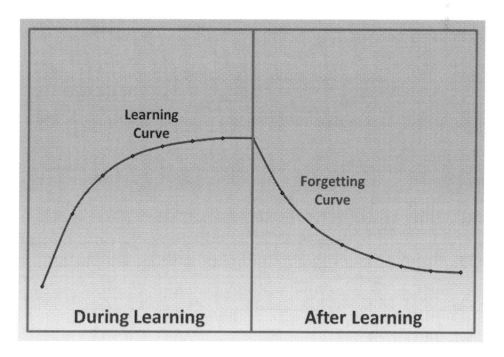

Performance-Focused Learner Surveys

Similarly, when we measure in the learning context, we are also biasing our results. People aren't like computers. We don't just retrieve perfect packets of information from memory; we access a full range of associated memories. When a person is in the same context in which they learned, the stimuli in that context will remind them of what they learned. If the learning context is not the work context, then measuring learning in the learning context will produce more and better memory retrieval than the work context will—again producing biased learning-measurement results.

A third learning-measurement bias entails how we are measuring. As Sharon Shrock and Bill Coscarelli have pointed out in their brilliant book on criterion-referenced test development, the best measure of performance competence is actual performance.[5] If we're teaching someone to drive a forklift, the best way to measure their competence will be to have them drive a forklift—preferably in the same conditions they'll face on the job. If we can't measure real-world performance, we can simulate or have the learners make authentic scenario-based decisions as reasonable proxies for performance. What we don't want to do is just test learners on their knowledge of simple facts. Unfortunately, because it is a lot easier to measure simple knowledge than to measure deeper performance-focused know-how, most learning measurement is biased toward the retrieval of facts—even though such metrics are extremely poor predictors of real-world performance.

Just like these more direct assessments of learning, learner surveys should likewise be relevant to actual performance and as unbiased as possible. But, alas, most learner surveys suffer from the same issues as the three biases mentioned above. They are deployed only at the end of learning, only in the learning context, and only with poorly designed, irrelevant questions.

---

[5] Shrock & Coscarelli (2007).

Chapter 2
Your Smile Sheets Suck!

Most people I talk with don't really like learner surveys but see them as a necessary requirement in their organizations—and at least somewhat valuable. I will admit to the same feelings. I spent several years as a leadership trainer, helping managers become effective leaders. At first, I didn't do well on my learner surveys; but, over time—partly by taking learner-survey comments seriously—I got reasonably good as a leadership trainer.

That being said, in this chapter, I'm going to prove to you, as effectively as I can, that your learner surveys suck! My apologies for using such a harsh word. Some of the people I respect most in my life will certainly bristle at the word "*suck*"—but I'm going to break with protocol here because I want to leave no doubt in your mind. Your smile sheets suck![6]

Research on Traditional Smile Sheets

I'll start with the research. Do smile sheets relate to learning results? Are learners' responses on smile sheets related to their ability to understand, remember, or apply what they've learned? Presumably, we are providing learner surveys because we—being wise and honorable learning professionals—want to know how effective our learning interventions are in producing benefits. We certainly wouldn't want to waste people's time giving them training that wasn't fully effective, would we?

Fortunately, there has been a ton of top-flight scientific research on this very question. In 1997, George Alliger, Scott Tannenbaum, Winston Bennett, Holly Traver, and Allison Shotland meta-analyzed the results of thirty-four scientific studies on the potency of smile sheets. They found that smile sheets were basically uncorrelated with learning results! To be specific, they were minutely correlated with learning-test results (at a correlation of .09). To explain, correlations go from -1 to 1, and correlations between -.30 and .30 are considered weak—so having a correlation of .09 means there is practically *no correlation at all* between

---

[6] Of course, some who read this book will undoubtedly use great learner surveys. If you're one of them, I applaud you and ask your forgiveness for painting with such a broad stroke.

smile sheets and learning results. It would be like correlating the household level of peanut butter use with the household level of television use.

This 1990s meta-analysis should have stopped us from relying so heavily on smile sheets. Yet, somehow, we could not help ourselves, and the popularity of smile sheets continued. More recently, to put a wooden stake through the heart of this blood-sucking vampire (the traditional smile sheet), another set of researchers did their own meta-analysis. In 2008, Traci Sitzmann, Kenneth Brown, Wendy Casper, Katherine Ely, and Ryan Zimmerman looked at 136 studies and found the exact same thing. Smile-sheet results were correlated with learning results at .09—practically no correlation at all.

But wait! There's more bad news! In 2016, a team of researchers focused on health care training did another meta-analysis and found that smile sheets were correlated at .03![7] And again, in 2017, a team of researchers focused on university teaching found a correlation of .20.[8] All these meta-analyses showed weak correlations between traditional smile sheets and learning!

These four meta-analyses covering hundreds of studies from the scientific research tell us that traditional smile sheets are not predictive of learning results. Instead of wasting time, money, and energy in using smile sheets, we'd be just as well off if we flipped a coin to determine whether a training course was good or bad. Seriously!

The bottom line is that traditional smile sheets are not predictive of important learning outcomes. Indeed, by relying on them we are exhibiting superstitious behavior unbecoming of a true professional.

Neil Rackham—famous for his research on the sales process and discovering that the best salespeople are not those who have the strongest closing technique, but are those who listen the best—tells a cautionary tale about smile-sheet ratings.[9] He was asked by a company what to do with two sales trainers who consistently got the worst smile-sheet ratings. The company wondered whether to fire them, coach them, or punish them in some way. Rackham asked the company if he could look more deeply. He decided he had to look beyond the smile-sheet ratings and look at the after-training success of the learners. What he found was that the learners for the two "failing" sales trainers sold the most—they had the best performance as salespeople! These instructors received the worst smile-sheet ratings, but their learners actually learned the most! These black-sheep sales trainers used

---

[7] Hughes, Gregory, Joseph, Sonesh, Marlow, Lacerenza, Benishek, King, & Salas (2016).
[8] Uttl, White, & Gonzalez (2017).
[9] Somewhere, many years ago, I heard Neil Rackham tell his story. Later, in 2006, Sarah Boehle wrote a *Training Magazine* article about that story (Boehle, 2006).

more rigorous training methods than their peers, and they got the best results—except on the smile sheets.

In Rackham's real-world example, smile sheets did not show a strong positive correlation with performance. They showed exactly the opposite. As the meta-analyses show, the reverse happens too: For some training programs, the highest smile-sheet ratings can be associated with the best learning results. Unfortunately, however, we can't tell when traditional smile sheets will be predictive and when they won't.

Just so you don't think I'm the only one who has pointed out that smile-sheet ratings tell us nothing, let me quote from Richard Clark and Fred Estes's book, *Turning Research Into Results*. They wrote this about learner surveys:

> *People often give very positive ratings to ineffective performance programs. Reaction forms [smile sheets] ask people what they liked the most. What they like, however, is not always what helps them perform better. . . . The reverse can also happen. A successful program can be judged to be ineffective because it asks participants to change something very basic about their beliefs, expectations, and behavior. (p. 8)*

And, because many of us have been raised on the nipple of the Kirkpatrick-Katzell Four-Level Model of training evaluation and can't imagine that the model and its Level 1 learner-survey recommendation might be flawed, let me share with you a quote from a recent review article from the top-tier scientific journal *Psychological Science in the Public Interest*:

> *Historically, organizations and training researchers have relied on Kirkpatrick's [four-level] hierarchy as a framework for evaluating training programs. . . . The Kirkpatrick framework has a number of theoretical and practical shortcomings. [It] is antithetical to nearly 40 years of research on human learning, leads to a checklist approach to evaluation (e.g., 'we are measuring Levels 1 and 2, so we need to measure Level 3'), and, by ignoring the actual purpose for evaluation, risks providing no information of value to stakeholders. (Salas, Tannenbaum, Kraiger, & Smith-Jentsch, 2012, p. 91)*

Performance-Focused Learner Surveys

Later, in Chapter 13, we will explore the strengths and weaknesses of the Kirkpatrick-Katzell Four-Level Model in more depth, and I will share with you a new learning-evaluation model.

The research I've cited so far is pretty damning of the learning-measurement practices we in the learning-and-development industry employ. It not only reflects appallingly on our field but also shows that what we are doing has to change.

Let me offer one final example of how learner surveys provide inaccurate information—this time from my own work evaluating training programs. I was doing work for an organization that created training materials used by instructors to help learners become entrepreneurs.

Previously—before I'd been called in—the organization had measured success by asking instructors to rate the course. That's all they measured. They had never tested actual learning results. Typically, they found that instructors rated the course at about 4.5 on a 5-point scale—an excellent result. I found similar results. But I dug deeper. I found that learners rated the course significantly lower, giving the online portion of the course a rating of 3.3 and the classroom portion of the course a 3.8 rating.

Here's the kicker: Actual objective measures of the course's impact showed no improvement—pretest to posttest—on realistic scenario questions. That is, when they answered scenario questions on the posttest linked to similar questions on the pretest, learners showed zero improvement. Zero! Indeed, on the posttest, they averaged 31% correct on four-item multiple-choice questions that would have been answered with pure guessing at 25% correct! Moreover, the business plans created by the learners as part of the course were some of the worst business plans ever seen by the expert reviewers! Two of the reviewers were so alarmed that they made a special effort to contact me and implore me to let the poor quality be known.

Now imagine if the organization had decided only to use smile-sheet ratings, which you'll remember produced an overall average rating of 3.3 and a classroom-only rating of 3.8. They would have concluded that the course outcomes were average to slightly above average. Or, what if the organization had relied only on the results from the instructor version of the smile sheet, which produced a rating of 4.5? They would have been thrilled with an excellent result. But the truth is that the course produced terrible outcomes. It created no improvement on well-designed scenario questions and terrible work products—not the stuff of successful training. Again, traditional smile sheets failed to predict important learning outcomes.

Perhaps your learner surveys are different from the hundreds of learner surveys evaluated by the research. Perhaps you've devised learner surveys that go beyond what most learning-measurement books and learning-measurement gurus recommend. But I'm betting that, just like most traditional learner surveys, your smile sheets suck!

Autopsy of the Traditional Smile Sheet

Let me draw on Charles Dickens to imbue my next point with a bit of gravitas.

Today, I declare to the entire world that the traditional smile sheet is dead. It was dead to begin with. There is no doubt whatever about that. Let us register its burial with the clergyman, the clerk, the undertaker, and the chief mourners. Let me sign my name to it. The traditional smile sheet is as dead as a door-nail. This must be distinctly understood, or nothing wonderful can come of the arguments I am going to convey herein (with sincere and loving apologies to Charles Dickens).

Just as Charles Dickens's Scrooge is often seen as a metaphor for institutionalized greed among the most powerful and the possibility that even wayward souls can find redemption if only they are shown the light, the story of the smile sheet in today's workplace learning-and-performance industry can be borne in a similar illumination. Without Dickens's skill, but with conviction, let me raise the ghost of Marley for this good purpose. Let me note, in passing, that powerful mourners will likely attempt to raise the dead corpse of the smile sheet—and perhaps have Marley slain doubly and decisively, chasing off the three specters: truth, effectiveness, and professionalism.

The traditional smile sheet is dead from many fatal blows—not merely one or two. I will highlight them in turn.

But first, let me remind you, dear reader, of one of the most fundamental principles of measurement. There is no perfect measurement instrument! Our efforts in learning measurement should be aimed at producing measurement instruments that are as good as they can be. For our learner surveys, we should aim to increase validity, reliability, and effectiveness. We should aim to improve the decision making of our learner-survey respondents—increasing their attention, minimizing bias, and focusing on the most relevant aspects of the learning intervention and the learning ecosystem. The results will not reach perfection, but they can produce meaningful results.

Subjective Inputs

First and foremost, learner surveys are based on subjective inputs of learners—and subjective assessments made by human beings are often flawed. This does not mean that subjective judgments can't have value. They can.[10] But, before we look to learner-survey results as gospel, we must recognize the problems inherent in subjective opinions. Then, we must minimize the deleterious effects of such weaknesses. Finally, when we're looking at learner-survey results, we must view and reconcile the results in light of the weaknesses inherent in subjective inputs. The ideas in this book will help us minimize the subjectivity penalty but will not eliminate it.

"But, Dr. Thalheimer, aren't we dishonoring our learners by not trusting their intuitions?" Nonsense! Certainly, we should honor our learners' intuitions, but only after we help surface those intuitions in a way that doesn't bias them. *"But is this really necessary? Aren't learners knowledgeable enough about their own circumstances to respond accurately to our questions?"* No, they are not!

Learners, like all humans, have many accurate perceptions and many inaccurate ones. Moreover, all human beings can be swayed by situational cues toward and away from accuracy and precision. Did you know that, if a woman touches your shoulder when you are making a risky decision—whether you're a man or a woman—you will be more willing to take the riskiest option? Did you know you're more likely to be influenced by a better-looking person than an average-looking person? (Not in writing, fortunately for me.) Did you know you are more likely to drive slowly if there are trees alongside a road than if there are no trees? We, as human beings, are nudged this way and that by contextual cues in every situation we face. It's the same for our learners. As we will discuss, the learner survey context often nudges learners toward bias.

Finally, learners are not always accurate in assessing their own learning. For example, learners are overly optimistic about their ability to remember what they've learned, so they tend to fail to give themselves enough repetitions.[11] Learners fail to utilize retrieval practice to support long-term remembering.[12] Learners don't always overcome their incorrect prior knowledge when reading.[13] Learners often fail to utilize examples in ways that would foster deeper learning.[14] These scientific findings don't mean learners are always wrong about their own learning, but they do show that learners are often inaccurate.[15] Therefore, if we are counting on learners to give us accurate appraisals of the success of a learning

---

[10] But we have to be sensitive to when and how subjective inputs have value.
[11] Zechmeister & Shaughnessy (1980).
[12] Karpicke, Butler, & Roediger (2009).
[13] Kendeou & van den Broek (2005).
[14] Renkl (1997).
[15] For two recent reviews that show that learners don't always know best, see Brown, Roediger & McDaniel (2014); Kirschner & van Merriënboer (2013).

intervention, we are asking more of them than they can deliver. We simply must be skeptical of subjective inputs. We also must do whatever we can to limit the problems inherent in subjective inputs. As you will see below, traditional smile sheets fail in numerous ways to support learners in making unbiased learner-survey responses.

Likert-Like Scales Create Poor Learner-Survey Decision Making

Likert-like scales are ubiquitous on smile sheets—but they are very problematic and should be avoided in most circumstances. I know I'm going completely against most training-industry practices in saying this, but it's the truth. Likert-like scales create poor data on learner surveys!

Likert-like scales provide a statement and ask learners to choose between answer choices representing a range. For example:

- Strongly Agree
- Agree
- Neither Agree nor Disagree
- Disagree
- Strongly Disagree

Or, they provide a question and ask learners to choose among answers:

- Extremely Satisfied
- Very Satisfied
- Somewhat Satisfied
- Somewhat Dissatisfied
- Very Dissatisfied
- Extremely Dissatisfied

Likert-like scales are especially problematic because they don't give learners clear distinctions between the answer choices. This creates three issues: (1) it nudges learners away from taking their responses seriously; (2) it creates indecision that can make biased responding more likely, and (3) it produces cognitive fatigue that can lessen the attention learners give to their responses.

Performance-Focused Learner Surveys

One of the most critical things to understand about learner surveys is that learners are making decisions when they answer learner-survey questions—and such decisions can be swayed by lack of attention and by contextual cues (and by the combination of the two). Therefore, we as learning professionals must do everything in our power to improve learner-survey decision making! Likert-like scales harm decision making and so should be avoided as much as possible. It's a lot tougher to decide between "Strongly Agree" and "Agree" than between two more-concrete answer choices. Of course, there may be some circumstances when a Likert-like scale is the perfect methodology, but these situations will be few and far between.

Sharon Shrock and Bill Coscarelli, authors of the classic text, now in its third edition, *Criterion-Referenced Test Development*, offer the following wisdom on using Likert-like descriptive scales:

> *The resulting scale is deficient in that the [response words] are open to many interpretations. (p. 188)*

"But, Dr. Thalheimer, why do so many surveys and personality diagnostics use Likert-like scales?" Answer: Because it's easy, it's the tradition, and these tools—unlike learner surveys—can create psychometric advantages by repeating the same concepts in multiple questions and then comparing one category to another category.

In most instances, however, Likert-like scales are ineffective at best. They don't allow learners to make good decisions. A person deciding between "Strongly Agree" and "Agree" will create less precision than a person deciding between two more descriptive statements.

"But, Dr. Thalheimer, don't Likert-like scales have the advantage of placing all our questions on the same continuum—so we can compare them one to another?" No, they don't. This is a silly fantasy—as if the question stems themselves had no bearing on whether the responses are comparable! Let me give an example. Suppose I use the question stem, "Chunky peanut butter tastes better than smooth peanut butter," and provide the Likert-like scale, "strongly agree, agree, neutral, disagree, strongly disagree." Can we compare the results to the question stem, "Einstein was a great scientist" even if we used the exact same Likert-like scale? Obviously not! So what makes us think we are creating perfectly comparable question stems on our learner-survey questions? We are not and cannot! It is impossible!

Numeric scales are just as fuzzy and problematic as Likert-like scales. Replacing a Likert scale with the numbers 1 through 5 does not make things better! This is true too for the

NPS (Net Promoter Score), which uses an 11-point scale from 0 to 10. The Net Promoter Score should not be used for learner surveys. More about this later.

The bottom line is that, in most cases, we can help our learners make good decisions by avoiding Likert-like scales and numeric scales—and using more descriptive answer choices.

Learner Survey Timing

In a research study I led with the eLearning Guild (now the Learning Guild), we found that 90% of learning measurement occurred at the end of the learning event. Indeed, in the many workshops and conference presentations I have given over the years, this is the standard response of audience members. Most learner surveys are given immediately at the end of learning. Recently, this trend seems to be reversing slightly. With the increase in digital learner surveys delivered to learners soon after learning, more learner surveys are delivered after a short delay. Still, most learner surveys are delivered just before learners leave the classroom or exit their elearning program.

Is this a problem? Yes, very much so! When learning is top-of-mind, learners can easily remember what they've learned and imagine themselves implementing their learning back on the job. Unfortunately, such intentions are rarely transferred back to the workplace, so learners' responses on end-of-training learner surveys are biased. Learners may think the training they received was effective—even when it was not.

We've already talked about the research showing that learners are overly optimistic about their ability to remember what they've learned. They are likely to shun needed practice and repetitions because they can't think beyond the learning situation. They can't imagine what it will be like—cognitively—when their learning is not top-of-mind. As researchers Dina Ghodsian, Robert Bjork, and Aaron Benjamin point out:

Trainees' performance during training is an unreliable indicator of posttraining performance. [Training designs] that enhance performance during training can yield poor long-term post-training performance, and other [training designs] that seem to create difficulties and slow the rate of learning can be optimal in terms of long-term performance. (1997, p. 63)

Both learners and those who facilitate learning can be fooled by this paradox. When we're in a learning situation, we might feel we have learned fully—or it might seem like our learners have learned fully. But those feelings are poor indicators of whether the learning will carry through to future situations. Learners may feel a high level of confidence during learning, but their perceptions during learning can fool them into thinking they will always have the learned information at the top of their minds. Alas, our cognitive machinery is simply not set up to allow us to imagine what our future cognitive states will feel like. Here's why: The state of our working memory is dependent on the environmental and cognitive cues influencing it in every moment. The cues during learning will always be different from the cues during a later performance—at the very least, they will be sufficiently different to elicit different working-memory states. Learners cannot predict their performance futures with enough specificity to predict whether they'll be able to remember or not.

Earlier, I argued—rather vociferously—that we need to help our learners make unbiased decisions when they complete our learner surveys. Unfortunately, almost nothing adds to learner-survey bias more than deploying our learner surveys when learning is top-of-mind. When we give learners surveys immediately after learning, much of what they learned is highly accessible in memory; therefore, much of their perspective will be biased at that time toward what they recently learned.

But let's be careful here! While this top-of-mind condition makes it more difficult for learners to imagine their future cognitive states, measuring learners soon after learning does make it easier for learners to remember their recent state of mind. They are more likely to recall the feelings they had within training, their sense of comprehension, the difficulty they had in understanding new material, and their current levels of confidence and conviction. This is why it would be a mistake just to give learners surveys after a delay. We would miss a ton of rich information.

Let me be specific about the forgetting that can come with the timing of learner surveys. Even short delays of a few hours may produce enough forgetting that learners can't make good decisions on their learner surveys. For example, if learners are taught ten key concepts in a one-day workshop, by the end of the day—when they are answering learner-survey questions—they may need a reminder about the topics they learned in the morning. For multiple-day training events, failing to remember can be even worse. Learner surveys delivered a day or more after learning should include some mechanism to remind the learners of the topics they learned and the methods used in the training.

In essence, the timing of learner surveys is open to two potent forces. One of these forces controls what learners remember—and hence what insights they can bring to learner-survey decision making. The other influences learners' predictions of the future, also affecting decision making on learner surveys. To be clear, these forces are the following:

- Learners will tend to remember and think about the most recent learning experiences and forget to consider earlier learning experiences.

- Learners will be overconfident that they will be able to remember. They'll also be overconfident that they will remain motivated to apply what they've learned.

In balancing these competing forces in regard to the timing of learner surveys, we can help our learners make good learner survey decisions by doing the following:

- Provide learner-survey questions *soon after each topic area* to ensure learners can give us good feedback about their within-learning thoughts and feelings.

- Provide learner-survey questions *after a delay* to ensure that learners can give us good feedback about how well the learning prepared them to remember.

- Provide learner-survey questions *after learners have attempted to apply* what they've learned so we get information about job relevance.

- Provide *reminders to learners about the details of the topics* they've learned before asking them to respond to learner-survey questions—especially when there is some likelihood the learners may have forgotten aspects of the learning.[16]

When we analyze our learner-survey results, we should also put into perspective the kinds of information we can get from different timings of learner-survey deployment. The timing of learner surveys dictates what information we will be able to capture. If we only measure immediately at the end of learning, we will fail to get good information about remembering and application. If we measure only after a delay, we will fail to get good information about immediate comprehension, confusion, enjoyment, and confidence. When we analyze our results, we must take learner-survey timing into account so we draw valid conclusions.

---

[16] One caveat: If you are also testing memory or decision making directly, you will want to do this before you remind the learners of what they learned.

Performance-Focused Learner Surveys

The Learner-Survey Context

Another bias inherent in learner-survey practice involves the contextual cues present when learner surveys are delivered. When people are questioned at the end of a learning event, they are being questioned within the same context in which they learned. Unfortunately, as huge amounts of research have shown, memory retrieval is influenced by the contextual cues in one's environment.[17] In short, it is easier for us to remember something if we attempt to retrieve it in the same situation in which we learned it than if we attempt to retrieve it in another situation. The cues in our environment will either support correct retrieval or push us toward inappropriate retrieval processing.

This concept can be difficult to grasp, but all of us have experienced context-dependent memory in our lives. When you meet someone you know—but meet them in a strange situation and can't remember their name or you can't remember where you know them from—you've experienced context-dependent memory. If you can't remember your ATM code until you see the ATM keypad, you've experienced context-dependent memory. But context-dependent memory happens all the time, not just in these most obvious situations. We are being primed and triggered every minute of every day by the contextual cues in our environment.

For classroom training events, the learning context is not the work context—so we have a mismatch between the two. While our learners may be able to retrieve a key concept in the learning context, they may not be able to retrieve it in the work context. This is why—from a learning design perspective—it is critical to present learners with realistic situations and prompt decision making of the kind they'll have to use on the job.

But we're not talking learning design here. We're talking learner-survey design and deployment. In terms of learner surveys, we want the cues (while learners are completing their learner surveys) to support valid learner-survey decision making. We want cues from the learning situation to remind learners of the full extent of the learning context. We also want cues related to learners' worksites to support learners in deciding how well the training facilitates actual on-the-job performance.

If you're new to the concept of contextual triggering, this may all seem strange at first. Have no worries. I'll make the repercussions of this obvious as we go forward.

---

[17] Research reviews of context-dependent memory: Bjork & Richardson-Klavehn (1989); Smith (1988); Smith & Vela (2001); Eich (1980); Roediger & Guynn (1996); Davies (1986). Context alignment is so fundamental that it has been codified in the "encoding-specificity" principle (Tulving & Thompson, 1973) and in the notion of "transfer-appropriate processing" (Bransford, Franks, Morris, & Stein, 1979) and "context-dependent memory" (Smith, 1988).

Likert-Like Scales Create Ambiguous Learner-Survey Results

We've already seen how Likert-like questions don't allow learners to make good learner-survey decisions. Now we'll see how they produce less-than-meaningful results.

Learner surveys that utilize Likert-like scales are almost always transformed into numbers—for example:

- Strongly Agree = 5
- Agree = 4
- Neither Agree nor Disagree = 3
- Disagree = 2
- Strongly Disagree = 1

Then, these numbers are averaged over learners. So, for example, a training class with 20 people might produce the following results on one of its questions: 5, 5, 5, 5, 5, 5, 5, 5, 5, 5, 4, 4, 4, 4, 4, 3, 3, 3, 2, 1. These numbers average 4.1.

It's time for reflection. Take a deep breath. Breathe in. Breathe out. Inhale fresh air. Exhale the impurities. Let's examine the airbrush blurring we just witnessed.

We first start with the fuzzy adjectives from the Likert-like scale. "Strongly agree" is already removed from the statement it has judged. Next, we transmortify[18] the fuzzy adjective into a number. Next, we average the number—removing even more information. Finally, we may remove all but one of the questions that were asked. "The course achieved an overall score of 4.1." Again, we are leaving out significant amounts of information.

It's hard to breathe out all the impurities from this appalling transmortification. The end result bears little relationship to the question originally asked. Yet somehow, without even a hint of regret, we boldly share our averaged learner-survey results with our senior stakeholders. You might remember our earlier discussion with CEO Julie. When she closely examined what her chief learning officer was telling her, she not only found that the numbers didn't add up, but also that the whole logic of learner-survey data handling was built on a faulty foundation. It's bad enough that we share this data with our senior leaders; it's perhaps even more scandalous that we believe in our numbers—and make decisions based on them.

---

[18] "Transmortify" is an intentional misspelling of the word *transmogrify*, which means "to transform, especially in a surprising or magical manner." It's mortifying that we work in a profession that does this!

Performance-Focused Learner Surveys

What the hell does a result of 3.7, 4.1, or 4.2 mean? With all our transmortifications, it means almost nothing. And let's remember: These numbers were proven by our four meta-analyses *not* to be correlated with learning! But, even if we could trace our blurry averages up the chain to the source of meaning, we are still looking at an isolated number. Let me try to make this clear using a sports analogy. Just like in sports, our numbers don't really mean anything if we can't compare those numbers to some other comparator—to some other number.

Our numbers are not like numbers in sports or business that actually mean what they say they mean. Our 4.2 isn't the same thing as a baseball pitcher with a 4.20 earned run average or a rugby player with 4.2 yards per carry. Those numbers have inherent meaning. Pitchers try to get lower earned run averages. Rugby players (and American football players) try to average more yards per carry. But even these numbers don't have full meaning unless they are compared to some other numbers. Is a pitcher with a 4.20 earned run average doing well, doing okay, or doing poorly? We simply can't know unless we compare those numbers to some other standard. If the league average is 4.30, then our pitcher's 4.20 is about average. If the league's top five pitchers average 3.10, then our 4.20 pitcher is not close to being the best.

One final point about drawing averages from our smile-sheet data—and this is somewhat technical. While most smile sheets are reported out as averages, or "means" as statisticians call them, it's actually a statistically questionable practice to use the mean when the data doesn't follow a normal distribution (the typical "bell curve" distribution). The problem is that an average tells us nothing about whether the data is skewed up or down or not at all. So, again, we see that traditional smile-sheet practices leave out valuable information.

Numbers—indeed all results—attain full meaning only when they are compared to something. They can be compared to previous results, to other current results, or to some standard. Learner survey results are often compared to the following:

- To our previous same-course results
- To our other current-course results
- To other companies' course results
- To some standard (for example, a 4.0 course-rating threshold)

Our comparisons give the illusion that our numbers have meaning, but, again, we fool ourselves and our stakeholders. We've seen how these Likert-derived numbers have fuzzy meaning to begin with—so comparing our current numbers to our previous numbers (or to our other current numbers or to other companies' numbers) is an exercise in magical thinking. The alternative—comparing our numbers to some standard—may seem enticing, but how can we select an arbitrary standard based on fuzzy numbers? Is a 4.0 acceptable, but not a 3.9? If so, why is a 4.0 acceptable? Why? Why? Why?

What makes these comparisons even worse is that many training courses are poorly designed—lacking in support for remembering and lacking in support for on-the-job application, among other deficiencies. Yes, yes, yes, there are excellent training courses. But most training courses can be more effectively designed. Comparing our courses to typical, poorly designed courses—even if our courses get seemingly good smile-sheet ratings—is deeply flawed and warrants a torrent of tears for our profession—and for our credibility as well.

The bottom line is that Likert-like scales on smile sheets produce information that is not only inherently meaningless, but also inherently dangerous when taken seriously. It is dangerous because we are likely to make decisions based on the information—and our decisions will then be untouched by the factors that really matter for learning.

I've seen the danger of faulty smile-sheet data many times in my work as a consultant. Here's how it typically goes. I'm called in by a chief learning officer (or other senior learning leader). For this example, we'll make the person a CLO named Eugene. Eugene knows that a lot of his company's training is not nearly as effective as it could be. Eugene calls me in to do a learning audit, and I too find that, by and large, the training is poorly designed—so Eugene isn't imagining the problems. He'd like to make big changes, but his stakeholders—including his company's senior managers and, sadly enough, a large group of his own training staff—do not see the need for improvement. They point to the smile-sheet results that show the training routinely averages 4.5s on a 5-point scale. *"But, Eugene, we're getting excellent smile-sheet ratings, so our courses are clearly working!"* Eugene is stuck! He's absolutely immobilized. He can nibble around the edges, making minor improvements, but he can't get the political support or organizational resources to make his company's training effective. Is there a way out for Eugene? Yes! He can fix the learner surveys!

Remember Julie, the CEO in my first example? If she had learner-survey results that showed that her company's training courses were not supporting on-the-job performance, do you think she'd be satisfied with the status quo? If Eugene worked for her, you could bet he'd get the resources and support he'd need to create effective learning interventions.

Performance-Focused Learner Surveys

Questions that use Likert-like scales or numeric scales are not the only ones that produce fuzzy information. Regardless of the types of answer choices we use, we must do everything in our power to avoid questions that produce bogus data.

Traditional Smile-Sheet Questions

Perhaps the most important biases in smile-sheet design are the questions themselves. Let's do a thought experiment. If we asked only about the quality of the room, breaks, and food of a training session, learners would be biased toward providing data on those criteria. Even if we added open-ended questions after these triggering questions, learners would focus more on the room, breaks, and food than on other aspects of the training. That's probably obvious, but what isn't so obvious is that the questions we ask aren't always the ones that target the most important factors. Most learner surveys simply ask the wrong questions. They don't ask questions related to learning factors of importance. They don't account for the latest research on how learning should be designed. They don't parlay that knowledge into a learner-survey design that would index training on the factors that matter most. In the next chapter, we'll look in depth at the factors that learner surveys should be assessing.

Summary: The Stink of Traditional Smile Sheets

On our learner surveys, we want the learners to be able to make good decisions, and we want to send clear messages about what they have decided. Anything that fuzzes things up hurts the validity of the learner-survey data. We've seen that Likert-like scales fail to provide meaningful data, that our transmogrifications distort reality, that our traditional methods are prone to bias. To put it simply, we must do better than this.

Our final autopsy report on traditional smile sheets reads as follows:

1. Death by a thousand cuts.

2. Research on traditional smile sheets finds they are unrelated to learning results.

3. Subjective responses are not carefully analyzed to minimize their most damaging effects.

4. Likert-like responses hurt learners' decision making as they respond.

5. Likert-like responses are transmogrified inappropriately, losing information.

6. Likert-like responses produce unclear guidance for action.

7. Numerical averaging of smile-sheet data is inappropriate and conveys results in a way that hurts stakeholder decision making.

8. The timing of learner surveys introduces bias.

9. The context of learner-survey deployment introduces bias.

10. Smile-sheet questions focus on factors that are only weakly related to learning.

Chapter 3
Measuring Effectiveness

Traditional smile sheets are failing us. It's time we change that and design a learner survey that works. To do that, we must determine what a learner survey should do and then build it from the ground up.

Before we begin, however, we must answer an important question. *"Dr. T, if learner surveys are not correlated with learning—and if they have so many design flaws—shouldn't we just avoid learner surveys altogether?"* Well, that's a very good question. Let me answer it in four ways. First, even poorly designed learner surveys can occasionally produce valuable insights—especially if open-ended comments are allowed that provide deeper insights than multiple-choice questions. Second, let's be real. Just because smile sheets are obviously flawed doesn't mean they will be quickly replaced with better evaluations. In the near future, the weight of tradition and expectations will keep most organizations using learner surveys of some sort. Given this, we'll probably have more success in improving learner surveys than in proselytizing their abandonment. Third, learner surveys don't just gather data; they also enable us to send messages about what's important. Finally, if we start from scratch—using research-inspired wisdom about learning—we can certainly design a more effective learner survey. In this chapter, I aim to prove that to you.

Many of the most venerated thinkers in learning measurement have argued that, in the Kirkpatrick-Katzell Model, Level 1 reactions are like a customer-satisfaction survey: They tell us whether people are satisfied with their learning events. They further argue that Level 1, learner satisfaction, is related to Level 2, learning; Level 3, behavior-change; and Level 4, organization results. This equates to the following: If learners aren't happy with the learning event, they won't learn anything—and learning will not have a positive impact. But, as we saw from the four research meta-analyses, this argument is wrong. Sometimes satisfaction is related to learning. Sometimes it isn't. We must go beyond the notion of customer satisfaction to look at the factors that enable learning. It is simply not enough for a learner survey to focus on learner satisfaction—or other less-critical learning goals.

Performance-Focused Learner Surveys

What, then, should learner surveys do? They should do three things. First, learner surveys should give us a good gauge of the likelihood that the learning has utilized factors that are actually essential to learning. Second, learner surveys should produce actionable results that clearly communicate the success or failure of the learning design and deployment. Third, learner survey questions should nudge the thinking and actions of key stakeholders in ways that benefit learning effectiveness. Let me highlight these three key goals for an effective smile sheet.

A Maximally Effective Learner Survey

1. **Gauges the effectiveness of the training design**
   Answering the question, "Will the training be effective in supporting work performance?"

2. **Enables reporting that is actionable**
   Answering the question, "Will the learner-survey results communicate with clarity and urgency to guide action?"

3. **Sends messages that nudge action**
   Answering the question, "Will the learner survey help educate or remind key stakeholders (including ourselves) of important considerations?"

Measuring the Inputs and Outputs

Before we go on to see how we can redesign our smile sheets, it's important that I share a fundamental concept in learning measurement. Learning interventions can be evaluated based on their outputs and their inputs. The following lists should give you a good idea of the difference.

Examples of Inputs:

- Costs of development
- Instructional-design methods used
- Supervisor support for training and on-the-job learning
- Senior-management support for learning
- Time spent in learning

Examples of Outputs:

- Number of people trained
- Learner satisfaction levels
- Results of multiple-choice tests
- Results of scenario-based decision making
- Results of simulation exercises
- Job-performance improvements
- Organizational results (examples: lower costs, higher productivity)

Ultimately, what we care about is whether our learning interventions produce results—that their outputs provide benefits at a reasonable benefit/cost ratio. But not all outputs are equally important. The number of people trained and the levels of learner satisfaction are not very useful. What is critical is (1) whether learners have understood what we taught them, (2) whether they remember what we taught them, and (3) whether they've successfully applied what we taught them.

Learner surveys don't capture—and can't fully capture—these important learning outcomes. Thus (and this is extremely critical), learner surveys should not be used in isolation. They must be augmented with outcome measures that get at (1) learner understanding, (2) learner remembering, and (3) learner application. This doesn't mean every implementation of every course requires our most careful measurement methods, but it does require that we measure important outcomes enough to be getting good feedback.

Learner surveys can't fully capture these important outcome measures, but they can be designed to give us better predictions about these outcomes than have traditionally been available from smile sheets. By the end of this chapter, you'll have clear ideas about how to do this.

Gauging the Effectiveness of Training Design

You'll remember that three factors are critical to the design of a learner survey: (1) gauging the effectiveness of the training design; (2) enabling reporting that is actionable; and (3) sending messages that nudge action. This chapter covers the first of these aspects—gauging the effectiveness of training design.

Performance-Focused Learner Surveys

What does effective training look like? Effective training creates improved work performance.[19] It does *not* just create awareness or increased knowledge! Given this truism, it's helpful to distinguish between training that is meant to provide awareness and training that is meant to support actual performance improvement. The following three-level taxonomy makes this clear.

Levels of Training

1. Awareness training
2. Performance training
3. Performance training with performance assistance

Awareness training conveys information to learners but doesn't provide sufficient support for remembering or on-the-job application. Awareness training does not ensure learning will be applied on the job.[20] *Performance training* provides remembering and application support—and aims specifically to improve on-the-job performance. By augmenting performance training with *performance assistance* at the worksite, we can accelerate the journey to full performance proficiency.[21]

---

[19] For those of you in education who aren't immediately concerned with learners' on-the-job performance—but do want to create better student surveys—I'm using the word "work" so we can think beyond job performance. Students who learn algebra can later do *work* in calculus. Students who learn writing can later do the *work* of crafting a persuasive message. You don't teach just to educate. You teach so your learners will do something different at some later time. What do you want them to be able to do? In what situations will this behavior be utilized? Once you answer those questions, you'll know what "work" you are preparing them to perform. No matter what kind of learning professional we are, we should all focus on preparing our learners for some specific work-performance situations.

[20] Awareness training also includes read-and-acknowledge training, where learners are presented a document and are asked to read and acknowledge that they understand it and/or will comply with it.

[21] I use the term *performance assistance* rather than *performance support* because many people view performance support as tool-based support and I want to include human-based support as well.

Here's how a course on the same topic might look at each of the three levels. As an example, let's take a one-day course on how to provide good customer service in a hardware store.

1. *Example of awareness training*

    The awareness training course is composed mostly of lecture. It talks about the importance of good customer service to the hardware store business. It tries to motivate learners to engage the learning with attention. It reviews the rules of good customer service. It provides examples. It asks the learners to reflect on the examples and discuss bad customer service experiences they might have had as a customer. It encourages learners to create action plans—listing what goals they have for customer service when they return to the job.

2. *Example of performance training*

    The performance-training course comprises one-third lecture and two-thirds practice, feedback, and more practice. It provides many of the same topics as the awareness training course but shortens them by more than half. It provides learners with a two-page job aid of sixteen critical customer service situations and suggestions for how to handle those situations. Each of the sixteen situations is first role-played using the job aid and is followed by peer feedback and discussion. Learners then write their own set of actions for each of the situations in the spaces provided on the job aid form. Learners role-play each of the sixteen situations—referring to their job aid only if they need it. They get feedback and revise their action plans if warranted. Learners are then presented with more complex customer service scenarios and act out their responses, get feedback, and reflect on what they've learned. Finally, learners learn to handle common obstacles they may face in implementing their new learning.

3. *Example of performance training with performance assistance*

    For this version of the course, learners receive performance training as described above; but, in addition, their workplace is prepared for their posttraining application of the course material. This is done by (1) preparing the hardware store managers to model and coach the desired behaviors, (2) encouraging learner-manager discussions before the course even starts, (3) providing an after-training application plan for the learner and a coaching plan for the manager, (4) evaluating actual customer service results in a manner that gives both managers and learners corrective feedback, (5) reminding learners and managers of the key points of the program periodically after the training ends, and (6) acknowledging effort and success as learners and managers apply what they've learned.

Awareness training is not very effective from a learning standpoint. It simply doesn't provide enough support to ensure that learners can remember or apply what they've learned. In their recent research review in the top-tier scientific journal *Psychological Science in the Public Interest,* Eduardo Salas, Scott Tannenbaum, Kurt Kraiger, and Kimberly Smith-Jentsch (2012) reviewed the research on training and development and highlighted the weaknesses of awareness training.

> *Recent reports suggest that information and demonstrations (i.e., workbooks, lectures, and videos) remain the strategies of choice in industry. And this is a problem [because] we know from the body of research that learning occurs through the practice and feedback components... It has long been recognized that traditional, stand-up lectures are an inefficient and unengaging strategy for imparting new knowledge and skills. (p. 86)*

Our goal as training professionals, then, should be performance training or performance training augmented with on-the-job performance assistance. Certainly, some circumstances warrant awareness training, but these are few. After all, if we're not impacting performance, what have we achieved? In almost all cases, we should target performance training as our minimum standard.

Okay, let's take a breath here. I just took time to digress into a discussion of the three levels of training. I did this for two reasons:

- This three-tier distinction is one of the most important distinctions in training and development (not that many people think about it this way), and I wanted to make sure you could become one of the enlightened ones. Do you feel enlightened?

- I want to highlight the main point of this chapter—that one of the goals of learner-survey design is that we ought to be gauging the effectiveness of our training. Awareness training is generally *not effective,* performance training *is effective,* and performance training with performance assistance *is maximally effective.*

Chapter 3—Measuring Effectiveness

Two Models of Training Effectiveness

Now, I'm going to introduce two models that will take us deeper into the discussion of what makes training effective.

The Learning Maximizers model offers a good way to begin thinking about what effective performance training looks like.

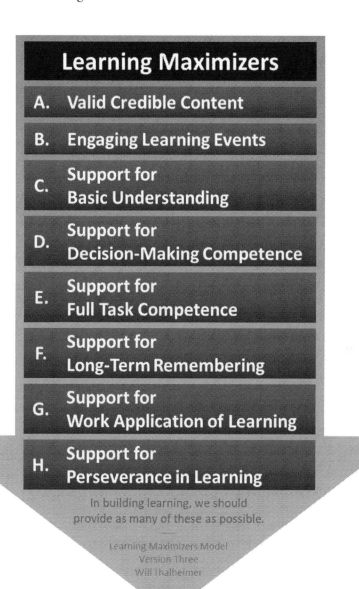

Performance training requires all the Learning Maximizers listed in the figure, whereas awareness training tends to focus only on B (creating engaging learning events) and C (providing support for basic understanding of the concepts to be learned). The Learning Maximizers[22] model is based on years of research of the kind I have compiled from top-tier, refereed scientific journals in building the Decisive Dozen, a list of the most important learning factors.

The Decisive Dozen are worth exploring in more depth so you can see the kinds of factors that really matter in learning.[23] I like to think of the Decisive Dozen in terms of the way biologists think of DNA. The human genome consists of twenty-three pairs of chromosomes with approximately 23,000 protein-coding genes and slightly more than three billion DNA base pairs.

The human genome enables us to live, but some parts of the genome are more important than others. Consider that chimpanzees and bonobos share 99% of the same genome as humans. Clearly, that 1% difference is everything to us! Indeed, scientists have used the term *junk DNA* to indicate that a large portion of DNA has little or no purpose.

The learning genome is the same. Of the thousands of learning factors we might consider, some are *sine qua non* essential. Some have moderate importance. Most have little importance. I spent more than a decade sifting through the scientific research on learning, memory, and instruction—trying to discover the most important factors in the learning genome. I ended up with twelve indispensable factors.

Certainly, there may be others I've missed, or other ways to present the factors I've compiled, but my commitment to these twelve factors rests on this assurance: When we use these twelve factors to design learning interventions, we will create learning interventions that are better than 95% of those deployed today.[24]

I started my research and consulting practice, Work-Learning Research, in 1998 because I saw us as an industry jumping from one fad to another and holding on sanctimoniously

---

[22] This is the latest version of the Learning Maximizers model.

[23] To learn more about the Decisive Dozen, see www.is.gd/ddResearch.

[24] Such a bold statement demands evidence. But this is easy. Most workplace learning interventions do not utilize very many repetitions of key learning points—yet research shows that just a few repetitions can increase learning by 100% or more. Most workplace learning interventions do not utilize very many realistic practice opportunities—yet research demonstrates that retrieval practice is better than simple repetitions by up to 100% or more, and aligning the learning context with the retrieval context can improve results up to 50% (the context alignment is what we mean by "realistic" practice). Because most learning interventions don't give enough retrieval practice, they don't give enough feedback—and the feedback they do give is often poorly designed to be too lengthy, too immediate, and not corrective enough. Giving learners feedback properly can improve learning results easily by 50% or more. Of course, my 95% prediction is a quick-and-dirty estimate, but I hope my point is clear: Most workplace learning interventions are not currently well designed—you can easily do better by following the Decisive Dozen learning factors.

to learning approaches that didn't work well or at all. If you've been in the learning field for any amount of time—whether workplace learning or K–12 education—you certainly must have noticed how learning fads come and go with the breeze. The Decisive Dozen is my answer to this—an anchor to keep us from flying hither and thither in the wind.[25]

Here are the elements of the Decisive Dozen:

Basic Enablers

1. *Content*
   When learners learn, they ought to learn from content that is correct and true and relevant to their future needs.
2. *Exposure*
   When learners need to learn, they must be exposed to relevant or targeted learning content or learning events.

Creating Engagement and Understanding

3. *Guiding Attention*
   When we guide learners' attention to the most critical information or contextual stimuli, their learning improves.
4. *Creating Correct Conceptions*
   When we structure learning so learners can quickly build correct understanding, they learn more effectively and more efficiently.
5. *Repetition*
   When we provide repetition (in a manner that engages), learners more effectively understand and remember.
6. *Feedback*
   When we utilize feedback appropriately, we correct learners' misconceptions and support correct retrieval.
7. *Variation*
   When we vary the learning materials, proper contingencies are learned, future memory retrieval is improved, and learners stay more engaged with the learning content.

---

[25] I'll credit Edgar Allan Poe for this use of "hither and thither." "The Conqueror Worm," http://www.poetryfoundation.org/poem/178359.

Supporting Remembering

8. *Context Alignment*

   When we integrate workplace cues (or other task-relevant cues) in our learning events, future memory retrievals are more likely to be triggered (and triggered when needed).

9. *Retrieval Practice*

   When we provide practice in memory retrieval, learners are more likely in future circumstances to have successful memory retrieval of the information learned.

10. *Spacing*

    When we space repetitions of content and instructional events over time, future memory retrieval is improved.

Enabling Future Application

11. *Persuasion*

    When we persuade learners, they will be more likely to reinforce the concepts learned—and engage in attempts to use what they have learned in their work and in their lives.

12. *Perseverance*

    When we support our learners in persevering in both learning and subsequent learning application, we enable them to engage with goal-directed metacognitive effort.

When we focus on these twelve factors first, we will create better learning interventions. These factors are supported by hundreds—if not thousands—of scientific research studies. Of course, just like the human body needs more than its DNA to function, human learning needs us as learning architects to build on these Decisive Dozen Learning-DNA elements. Let's take Guiding Attention as an example. There are many ways to guide attention. Among other ways, we can:

- Use focusing objectives.
- Use white space to make visual elements pop out into salience.
- Use words or tone of voice to emphasize importance.
- Tie our content to relevance for our learners.
- Connect content to emotionally-important considerations.
- Repeat information to designate its importance.

My point here is that the Decisive Dozen provide a critical framework from which we can use our creativity to make learning-design decision.

"But, Dr. Thalheimer, aren't we talking about learning measurement, not learning design?" Damn right! It's time to get back to learning measurement!

The point I'm trying to reinforce by sharing the Decisive Dozen and the Learning Maximizers model is that, when we create a learner survey, it should give us an idea of whether the training program will be effective in improving on-the-job performance—and, when we're doing that, shouldn't we base our learning-measurement designs on learning research? While the Decisive Dozen is a list of learning factors, the Learning Maximizers model is a goal model—one that aligns with the research underpinning the Decisive Dozen. Whereas each of the eight Learning Maximizers items provides you, as a learning designer, a specific goal to achieve (for example, supporting remembering), the Decisive Dozen learning factors provide you with the ingredient list you can use (for example, retrieval practice) to achieve those goals.

The bottom line here is that, before we start thinking about how to design our new learner survey, we must begin with an understanding of what we're trying to accomplish in terms of our learning. Both the Decisive Dozen and the Learning Maximizers model are offered here to make us sensitive to what good learning looks like.

Four Pillars of Training Effectiveness

Now that we've reflected on what good training looks like, what's the next step in creating an effective learner survey? My recommendation begins below. First, it may be helpful to remind you of the three primary goals of performance-focused learner surveys, the first of which is the focus of this chapter:

- Gauge the effectiveness of the training design.
- Enable actionable reporting.
- Send messages that nudge action.

If one of our primary goals in creating a learner survey is to determine whether a learning program creates on-the-job performance, our secondary goals should be the following—which I will refer to as the four pillars of training effectiveness.

Performance-Focused Learner Surveys

1. Do the learners understand?

2. Will they remember?

3. Are they motivated to apply?

4. Are there after-training supports in place?

If a training program achieves all four of these goals, it is extremely likely to create on-the-job performance. Of course, this assumes the content is valid and relevant.[26]

We will now look at each of the four secondary goals in turn.

Learners Understand

Obviously, learners must correctly comprehend the content they are learning. While the best way to measure such comprehension is with tests of learning—not with learner surveys—learner surveys can give the learners' perceptions of whether they understand the material, which, in general, is a reasonable proxy for their understanding.

Third-level (or tertiary) goals related to learner understanding include such things as making sure learners are (1) engaged in the learning and (2) provided with the cognitive supports they need to fully comprehend the information. Cognitive supports can include such things as advance organizers, aligning to prior knowledge, animations, examples, use of white space, clear writing, and comprehension testing and feedback.

Fourth-level (or quaternary) goals related to learner understanding include such things as ensuring learners are motivated to learn; the classroom environment is conducive to learning; the instructors are credible, engaging, and supportive; the learning is well organized; and the learners are satisfied with the learning experience. Note that these quaternary goals—a long way removed from the actual effectiveness of the training—are typically what smile sheets target. While often smile sheets do ask about the tertiary goals of learners' engagement and belief in the value of the concepts, all too often traditional smile sheets focus on quaternary goals such as instructor competence, the learning environment, the organization of the learning, and overall learner satisfaction—failing to look at other key tertiary goals and completely ignoring secondary goals that actually indicate

---

[26] The question of content validity and relevance—as portrayed in both the Decisive Dozen and the Learning Maximizers model—is not one of the secondary goals because smile sheets can't get at the truth of content validity and relevance. Although learners can give their perceptions of these factors, learners are not always reliable sources on these issues.

meaningful impact. It is no wonder our traditional smile sheets are ineffective in providing us with good feedback.

Learners Remember

Having learners understand is good, but insufficient. If we don't help our learners remember what they've learned, then we have failed them. Too many learning interventions fall short in this regard. Our learners can't apply what they've learned if they can't remember it.

The best way to measure remembering is with delayed tests of learning—not with learner surveys—but our learner surveys can be designed to give us indications of whether the learning is likely to lead to remembering.

Tertiary goals related to remembering include whether the learners have received realistic practice, repetitions spaced over time, and situation-action triggers to spur spontaneous remembering. As laid out in the Decisive Dozen, long-term remembering is supported by aligning the learning and performance contexts by providing learners with significant levels of retrieval practice, and by spacing repetitions of key learning messages over time. Without these supports, learners are unlikely to remember what they've learned.

Learners Are Motivated to Apply What They've Learned

Mostly, when we learning professionals think of motivation, we think of the learners' motivation to engage in learning. Equally important is our learners' motivation to apply what they've learned. Let's face the truth. Learning that truly changes behavior usually requires substantial motivation and metacognitive effort. Learners not only have to remember what they've learned but also need to initiate actions in their jobs—in between the flow and bounce of regular practices. Getting started may be the biggest obstacle, but learners then have to persevere in the face of obstacles, other priorities, and the deadening weight of tradition and culture. Learners have to race time before they forget what they learned—or they have to remind themselves of what they learned. They have to ensure they prioritize the application of their learning—and reprioritize it as other demands take precedent. To navigate these many issues, learners have to go back to their jobs with substantial motivation and maintain their motivation over time.

Tertiary goals related to motivation to apply include whether the learners have a belief in the concepts they learned, whether they have a sense of self-efficacy in being able to apply their new skills successfully, and whether they feel they can continue to learn and improve their new skills on the job. Training that doesn't address these motivational imperatives is unlikely to lead to successful transfer to the job.

After-Training Supports Are in Place

Not only do learners need to be motivated to apply what they've learned but concrete supports should be available to learners to help them navigate the flotsam of implementation. While some rare learners will rise up and implement their learning without support, a large majority will be successful only if they have additional resources and guidance.

Tertiary goals related to after-training support include whether the learners have been inoculated (while in training) to the obstacles they might face, whether they've been given sufficient practice (while in training) regarding what can go wrong, whether they've been given job aids (and practiced using them while in training), and whether supervisors are likely to follow up with resources, encouragement, and guidance.

Chapter 3—Measuring Effectiveness

Summary: How to Gauge Training Effectiveness

One of the primary goals of a learner survey is to assess whether a training program is likely to be effective. Training programs should go beyond awareness training to performance training, ideally augmented with performance assistance. The Learning Maximizers model does a nice job of conveying—without a level of complexity that might overwhelm—much of the research regarding what makes training effective. These factors can be distilled—for the purpose of learner-survey design—into the four pillars of training effectiveness, which I outlined above: (1) understanding, (2) remembering, (3) motivation to apply, and (4) after-training supports. These secondary learner-survey goals are aligned with tertiary goals that can also be targeted for learner-survey measurement. If our learner survey is going to provide reasonable information about whether a training program is going to be successful, it must ask questions that get at the secondary and tertiary goals outlined above. It won't always be easy to do that, but it is possible.

Because these new learner surveys are specifically designed to assess the likelihood of on-the-job performance improvement, I have labeled them performance-focused learner surveys[27]. They won't be perfect in ascertaining whether a training program can lead to performance, but they will be significantly better than traditional smile sheets.

Finally, let me remind you of one of my main points. Learner surveys are not perfect and should not be used alone. However, given that most organizations will continue to use them, we should at least use learner surveys that are effective in providing us with performance-relevant information.

---

[27] In the first edition of the book, I called them "performance-focused smile sheets"—hoping to reclaim the term "smile sheet" and make it less pejorative. This helped somewhat, but not enough, so I'm using "learner survey" as a term that is both more positive and more descriptive. Its descriptive message should enlighten us as well—these questions we provide learners are surveys of learner perspectives. They are nothing more and nothing less.

Chapter 4
Producing Actionable Results

In the previous chapter, we covered the first imperative of a learner survey—gauging the likelihood that training will be effective in producing on-the-job performance improvement. In this chapter, we will cover the second imperative of learner surveys: that they produce actionable results. When our learner-survey results are actionable, they communicate with clarity and urgency about whether a training program should be kept, modified, or discarded; moreover, they help us see which design elements should be improved.

Three sets of guidelines will enable us to create actionable results:

1. The quality of learners' learner-survey decisions

2. Whether learner-survey results distinguish between different levels of success

3. Whether we are measuring the things that matter

Each will be discussed in turn.

Quality of Learners' Learner-Survey Decisions

First and foremost, our learner-survey design and deployment methods should help learners make good decisions in answering the learner-survey questions. It is critical that we prevent the garbage-in, garbage-out problem. If learners' survey-question decisions produce poor data, then any reports we create will be garbage. If learners don't take learner-surveys seriously, if they are rushing through the questions, if they are overly fatigued, they won't give their full attention to answering the questions, and their responses won't reflect their most accurate judgments. If learners can't remember what they learned or can't remember the specifics of the learning events, they won't be able to make accurate assessments of their learning. If learners are guided to unimportant criteria and distracted from critical learning factors, their responses won't fully reflect the most important factors. If answer choices don't provide clarity or enough granularity to help learners make distinctions between the options, then accuracy will be harmed. If leading questions—or other biasing questions—are included, then learners' responses will be biased.

As you can see, there are many ways learners' learner-survey decisions can be biased or inaccurate. Here are some recommended guidelines for avoiding these dangers:

1. ***Remind learners of the learning experience.***
   Unless the learning event is very short (less than an hour) and learner surveys are presented soon after learning, learners should be reminded of the topics presented and the learning methods employed. Otherwise, the learners will be making learner-survey decisions based only on the most salient aspects of the training—ignoring the bulk of the training experience. Reminding learners of what they learned can be a tricky proposition because it can lengthen the learner survey and make it feel unwieldy. Reminding can consist of a list of the learning topics presented to learners before they answer learner-survey questions. Or, the topics themselves can be integrated into the learner surveys as questions. For example, questions could ask the learners to rate each topic on its relevance to their job or ask them to pick out the three most important topics. Of course, reminding need not be incorporated into the learner survey. If learners review the material in some way, or are given a test on the training concepts immediately before the learner survey, such events can serve as reminders as well. The one caveat is that, if these reminders are not hard-wired into the process, then comparing the learner-survey results from one class to another will not be a fair comparison, as different instructors will likely provide different levels of reminding.

2. ***Increase learner attention.***
   To improve learners' attention as they answer learner-survey questions, a persuasive and personal appeal should be made to learners about the importance of the learner-survey results. Learner surveys should not be too long or too short. If they are too long, learners will become fatigued and uninterested. If they are too short, learners will get the message that the learner surveys are not important. Within a few weeks after the training, trainers or instructional designers should follow up with learners to let them know how the training course has been improved (or at least evaluated) with the recent learner-survey results. Learner-survey questions should be carefully designed. By using well-designed questions, learners are more likely to take learner surveys seriously. Questions should use descriptive answer choices—not Likert-like scales, nor numeric scales. Likert-like scales just don't feel

very important. Neither do numeric scales. Ample time should be given for learner-survey completion. Moreover, it can be valuable to offer a learning interaction after the learner surveys are completed so the learner surveys are not the very last thing to be completed as learners run out the door.

3. *Avoid biasing questions.*

    Care must be given not to lead learners in one direction or another with the question stems or with the answer choices. For example, avoid affirmations such as the following: "My skills and abilities improved as a result of this training." These types of affirmations push learners to answer in the affirmative. Similarly, avoid answer choices that lead to bias. This is obvious for some sets of answer choices, but not for others. You'll want to ensure you provide answer choices that are equally positive and negative, and/or that encompass the full range of possibilities that might be expected. If you have doubts about whether your learner-survey questions are creating bias, seek a measurement expert. In fact, you probably ought to seek a measurement expert anyway, because you're unlikely to see your own biases—unless you're incredibly experienced.

4. *Ask clear and relevant questions.*

    One of the rules of measurement is never to ask a question whose answer can't or won't be used to actually make some kind of improvement. For example, don't ask about the quality of the diagnostic instruments used in a course if your organization is unlikely to change them. Similarly, don't ask questions about low-priority issues—for example, the quality of the food or the cleanliness of the restrooms. If low-priority topics are a real issue, learners will write about them in open-ended questions. Finally, make sure the wording is crystal clear. Fuzzy wording makes it hard for learners to interpret. For example, the following question stem could be worded more clearly: "I was well engaged during the learning event." The problem is that "well engaged" could have many meanings. It could connote attention, enjoyment, activity, or something else. To be more specific we might write, "My attention did not wander during the training session."

5. *Ask questions that learners can answer knowledgeably.*

    Sometimes we ask questions with good intent, but without asking ourselves whether the learners are likely to be good judges of the issue queried. Here's an example of a question that learners are unlikely to answer with insight: "My learning was enhanced by the course structure." Learners are unlikely to be aware of how the course structure affects their learning. Here's another one: "I was able to relate each of the learning objectives to the learning I achieved." This question will not only be difficult to answer, but it's largely irrelevant to whether the learning event was successful. It makes little difference whether learners relate their learning to a learning objective or not. This issue falls within the junk DNA of the learning genome.

6. *Provide descriptive and easily understood answer choices.*
Learners will make better decisions if we use descriptive answers rather than Likert-like response choices. Of course, our descriptive answers have to be well crafted, which is not always easy. Shorter answers are more easily comprehended, but sometimes more words are required to be precise. The right balance is needed. In short, answer choices should be distinctive—easily distinguishable from each other. To highlight the importance of this—and because people have been bugging me to coin a term for this new approach to survey questions—I am now labeling questions that have descriptive answer choices "*distinctive questions,*" and the new approach to survey questions, "*distinctive questioning.*"

7. *Provide follow-up learner surveys.*
Learner surveys delivered to learners in their worksites two to four weeks after the training can provide information that end-of-training learner surveys cannot provide. Specifically, follow-up learner surveys help learners see whether they've actually implemented the new material or not. Moreover, they can help provide information about the obstacles and success factors that hurt or helped learners implement the learning. This doesn't mean that immediate learner surveys should be avoided—a point I'll expound on in Chapter 11, which focuses on follow-up learner surveys.

Distinguishing Between Different Levels of Success

Learner-survey results should distinguish between different levels of success. In other words, when someone reviews the learner-survey results, those results should clearly differentiate between success and failure of the training and between different levels of success. Without clear lines of demarcation, we as learning professionals won't know what to do with the learner-survey results. We won't know whether we need to keep things as they are, improve the current training methods, or do a complete rethinking of the training design. Similarly, our stakeholders won't really know what to make of the learner-survey results either. Given that one of our responsibilities is to clearly convey our results to our organizational stakeholders, we have a responsibility to ensure those results are actionable.

Here are some recommended guidelines:

1. ***Don't transform results into numbers.***

    Learner-survey results should not be transformed into numbers, because numbers don't distinguish between success levels. There is no clear demarcation between a 3.8, 3.9, 4.0, 4.1, 4.2, and so on.

2. ***Avoid meaningless answer-choice labels.***

    Results that have relatively meaningless labels, such as "Strongly Agree," also provide no clear demarcation between levels of success. For example, it isn't clear whether "Strongly Agree" is the only acceptable result or whether "Agree" should be considered sufficient.

3. ***Delineate standards for each answer choice during question design.***

    One way to help you design your questions to enable different levels of success is to delineate the standards as you design each question. Let's examine the following question as an example:

	Now that you've completed the learning experience, how well do you feel you understand the concepts taught? CHOOSE ONE.
A	I am still at least SOMEWHAT CONFUSED about the concepts.
B	I am now SOMEWHAT FAMILIAR WITH the concepts.
C	I have a SOLID UNDERSTANDING of the concepts.
D	I AM FULLY READY TO USE the concepts in my work.
E	I have an EXPERT-LEVEL ABILITY to use the concepts.

Performance-Focused Learner Surveys

Most organizations using learner surveys do not have standards for responses; so, if they used the question presented above, they would wait until they received learner responses before deciding what results would be acceptable and what results would not be acceptable. This after-the-fact analysis lends itself to bias, to multiple and conflicting interpretations, and to confusion about what to do.

The alternative is to specify the standards when the question is being designed. For example, the answer choices might have the following standards associated with them.

	Now that you've completed the learning experience, how well do you feel you understand the concepts taught? CHOOSE ONE.	*Proposed Standards* not shown to learners
A	I am still at least SOMEWHAT CONFUSED about the concepts.	Alarming
B	I am now SOMEWHAT FAMILIAR WITH the concepts.	Unacceptable
C	I have a SOLID UNDERSTANDING of the concepts.	Acceptable
D	I AM FULLY READY TO USE the concepts in my work.	Superior
E	I have an EXPERT-LEVEL ABILITY to use the concepts.	Superior/ Overconfident?
	Note: Learners are NOT shown the text in the gray cells of this table.	

Let's examine standards in more depth.

More on Standards

By having standards associated with each answer choice, we enable ourselves to make decisions, to find meaning in gray splashes of data, to share truths in stories that resonate. We unleash the power of learner surveys when we use standards!

How do we start developing standards for a question? I've found it useful to limit the standards to a small set—at least for most questions. I use these five:

- Alarming
- Unacceptable
- Acceptable
- Superior
- Superior/Overconfident?

The "Superior/Overconfident?" option is used for "over-the-top" answer choices. It recognizes that we can't know for sure whether a person is deciding with realism or overconfidence. Usually, this five-item set will suffice but, sometimes (rarely), I've found other standards are appropriate given unique situations. I've used "useful" and "wasteful" in one context. I've used "exceptional" to add a superlative higher than "superior," and "extremely problematic" to add a negative worse than "alarming." I've used "borderline acceptable" to add a shade of gray. In general, I'd recommend you stick to a short list—only using different standards where necessary.

Standards can change depending on the type of learning being evaluated. The same answer choice might be "acceptable" for one type of learning and "unacceptable" for another. That sounds really weird, so let me provide an example. In the question above, the following answer choice was used: *I am now SOMEWHAT FAMILIAR WITH the concepts.* This would be "unacceptable" for a performance training course (for example, a one-day workshop on how to create effective PowerPoint slides. In such a course—a full-day course on a narrow topic—we would expect more from the learning. On the other hand, for a short awareness course—say a one-hour high-level overview of PowerPoint tricks and tips—creating familiarity with the concepts seems perfectly "acceptable."

In this book, I will recommend standards for each answer choice. Whatever you do, don't just accept my standards! You can see from the example above that standards must be tailored to the learning intervention being evaluated, but there's more. Standards are a golden opportunity to engage our stakeholders—to get their buy-in and educate them about our work. By negotiating our answer-choice standards with key stakeholders, we bring them in as partners.

Standards should also be reality-checked after the data comes in. We don't want to lower our standards just because we don't achieve enough acceptable responses, but we may want to raise our standards or modify our answer choices if we originally made things too easy.

Performance-Focused Learner Surveys

Finally, note that standards enable us to create acceptability indexes—a quantitative methodology that enables us to make comparisons from one learning intervention to another. I'll share the details of this later.

Measuring Things That Matter

While I hinted at this in the previous section on the quality of the questions, this issue is worth highlighting separately. The simple principle is that we should measure things that matter—and we should avoid asking questions about things that are low priority or are of less relevance to actual training effectiveness.

The best way to measure things that matter is to commit to measuring the four pillars of training effectiveness: (1) understanding, (2) remembering, (3) motivation to apply, and (4) after-training supports. We've already covered this in the previous chapter, so there is no need to go into more depth here. One critical point, however, is that measuring training effectiveness—as much as the learner survey format allows—is one of the central guiding principles of performance-focused learner surveys.

Summary: How to Produce Actionable Results

Traditional smile sheets often leave us in an unconscious state of indecision. We are lulled into a mesmerizing complacency, not even knowing that we ought to be making improvements to our learning interventions. In short, too many of today's learner surveys do not (and cannot) guide action. They do nothing to help us create virtuous cycles of continuous improvement. They leave us in the dark.

Fortunately, we can take a number of actions to ensure our learner surveys produce actionable results. At the highest conceptual level, we need to help our learners make better learner-survey decisions, we must design our questions to distinguish between success and failure, and we have to measure factors that relate to learning effectiveness. In the next chapter we'll add another criterion—designing our learner surveys to send appropriate stealth messages to our key stakeholders.

To summarize the ideas from this chapter in a list, we highlighted the following design and deployment recommendations:

Chapter 4—Producing Actionable Results

1. Remind learners of the content and the learning experience to ensure they consider the full learning experience.

2. Persuade learners to attend to learner surveys with full engagement.

3. Ensure learner surveys are not too long and are not too short.

4. Follow up with learners to let them know that the learner-survey results were reviewed and utilized in redesign.

5. Use descriptive answer choices. Do not use numbers, fuzzy adjectives, or other vague wording.

6. Avoid using affirmations in your questions.

7. Use answer choices that have a balance between positive and negative responses.

8. Use answer choices that offer the full range of choices that might be expected.

9. Seek a measurement expert to check your question wording to help you avoid biases and unclear language.

10. Never ask a question you can't or won't be able to use to make an improvement or make a decision.

11. Don't ask learners questions they won't be good at answering.

12. Balance the length and precision of your answer choices—keeping the answers as short as possible, but lengthening them as needed to make them precise enough that learners will know what they mean.

13. Provide follow-up learner surveys in addition to in-the-learning learner surveys.

14. Do not transform learner-survey results into numbers.

15. Delineate standards of success and failure—acceptable results versus unacceptable results—in advance of training.

16. Ensure your learner surveys measure factors that are aligned with research-based recommendations for learning effectiveness—for example, the four pillars of training effectiveness: (1) understanding, (2) remembering, (3) motivation to apply, and (4) after-training supports.

Chapter 5
Sending Messages to Nudge Action

As workplace learning-and-performance professionals, our primary responsibility is to help people excel in their jobs. To meet this demanding responsibility, we must parlay resources and know-how in a manner that coordinates among a vast number of people across our organizations. To manage this coordination, we must persuade others. With severely limited touch points, we often find it difficult to persuade. Our efforts at educating our stakeholders often fall short—and, when we fail to persuade, often learning and performance suffers.

Indeed, the most astute learning leaders make regular attempts to build relationships and educate key stakeholders about how learning can be used to bolster organizational performance. But even the best learning leaders can have difficulty in educating stakeholders. First, it's difficult to educate people in complex topics like learning. It takes time, multiple touch points, and savvy messaging. Second, in educating people about learning we often find ourselves fighting preconceived notions that are wrong or incomplete. Finally, if we do succeed in educating key stakeholders, we often find them being promoted, recruited, or retired—replaced by new people who require the whole damned education process all over again.

One of the reasons we haven't been successful is that we rely too much on making good arguments. We rely too much on conscious channels of perception, even though these are less potent than unconscious channels and can easily be filtered out or ignored. Let me give you an example. If we want drivers to drive more slowly on city streets, we have two options: We can try to reach them with conscious messaging like speed-limit signs, or we can use subconscious triggers that prompt them to slow down. As traffic engineers have found, speed-limit signs don't work as well as subconscious triggers. For example, narrowing traffic lanes, planting trees close to the road, and getting rid of center lane lines send subconscious messages to drivers that prompt them to slow down. Trees, for instance, send an unconscious message that you're driving through a residential area where there might be pedestrians, dogs, and children playing.

Performance-Focused Learner Surveys

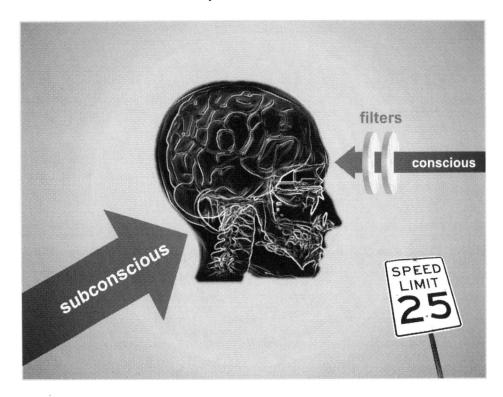

Fortunately, we have another option besides overt messaging. We can use "stealth messaging" to persuade and educate. Stealth messages are messages conveyed during our routine practices and procedures. For example, suppose we are serious about being performance focused and we want to create more training programs that are performance focused. We could try to educate our stakeholders through ordinary means, by creating well-designed slide presentations, by stating our case in meetings, and/or by writing memos and reports that convey our performance-focused message. Alternatively, we could use stealth messages within our recruiting, evaluation, reporting, and other standard operating procedures.

Learner surveys are one of the most important practices we engage in—in terms of sending messages to key stakeholders in our organizations, that is. The results are seen by senior managers of all sorts and by trainers, instructional designers, and learning leaders. Traditional smile sheets send weak and confusing messages, but performance-focused learner surveys can send critical messages about whether our courses have sufficient support for remembering, after-training follow-through, appropriate job aids, supervisory support for learning, and so forth. By designing better learner surveys, we can send stealth messages that are potent and are less likely to be filtered out.

Being able to send potent stealth messages requires us to follow the recommendations discussed so far—and it requires us to do an effective job of developing reports and presenting them to our key stakeholders. Chapter 13 will focus on how to report out the learner-survey results. For now, let me share some examples of learner-survey questions and the stealth messages they can send.

The following question sends a very strong message that training is not enough; that after-training supports are critical as well. What specific messages does it also send?

	After-Training Support	
	After the course, when you begin to apply your new knowledge at your worksite, which of the following supports are likely to be in place for you? **SELECT AS MANY ITEMS** as are likely to be true	*Proposed Standards* not shown to learners
A	MY MANAGER WILL ACTIVELY SUPPORT ME with key supports like time, resources, advice, and/or encouragement.	Acceptable
B	I will use a COACH OR MENTOR to guide me in applying the learning to my work.	Acceptable
C	I will regularly receive support from a COURSE INSTRUCTOR to help me in applying the learning to my work.	Acceptable
D	I will be given JOB AIDS like checklists, search tools, or reference materials to guide me in applying the learning to my work.	Acceptable
E	Through a LEARNING APP or other means, I will be PERIODICALLY REMINDED of key concepts and skills that were taught.	Acceptable
F	I will NOT get much direct support but will rely on my own initiative.	Unacceptable
	Note: Learners are NOT shown the text in the gray cells of this table.	

Performance-Focused Learner Surveys

The question also sends the following messages, all of which are aligned with the research[28] on learning transfer:

- Learners' managers can provide important after-training supports.
- Coaches or mentors can provide helpful guidance.
- Instructors should not just disappear after training but can provide important supports in helping learners apply what they've learned.
- Job aids can provide important support in helping learners in their work.
- Reminders sent to learners after training can produce benefits.

Wow! Haven't we as learning professionals known these things for years? Haven't we spent time educating stakeholders—including members of our learning team—about the value of these after-training supports? Yes! We have! Are we providing these after-training supports? Not as much as we should!

What is our problem? One, we don't have the political clout in our organizations to get permission or resources to provide these supports. Two, in the face of these brick walls, we don't have the guts to stand up and do what we know is right. Three, we ourselves—probably because the cognitive dissonance hurts too much to bear—have forgotten or ignored these supports. We on the learning team have pushed them out of our minds.

I'm not saying these things are easy. I'm saying they're worth doing. Most importantly, I'm saying there's a new tool we can use to advocate for these proven learning supports—stealth messages sent through our standard practices. Specifically, here, I'm advocating for using our learner-survey questions and answer choices to send stealth messages. But, beyond learner surveys, we can also send stealth messages in the evaluation model we use, in our training-request process, in our learning strategy models, etc. For now, let's focus on learner surveys.

Let's look at the question above and think about who it sends messages to. It sends messages to our learning architects—that they might think about enlisting learners' managers, finding coaches, providing job aids, creating after-training reminders. It sends a message to our trainers that they should not consider their job done when the training workshop is over. It may nudge a trainer to have learners use job aids in the training, so they'll use them in their work. It may push a trainer to have after-training office hours to support people in applying what they've learned. The learner-survey question above may

---

[28] Thalheimer, W. (2020).

send messages to management that managers should be more involved in supporting training; that the learning team could use resources to create reminders, coaching programs, job aids; and that training alone is not sufficient. And what about the learners themselves as they answer the question? They may be woken up to ideas that may benefit them. *"Maybe I should seek out my manager for advice or resources to help me in applying the learning? Maybe I should find a mentor. Maybe I should remind myself of what I learned or use the job aid provided in the training."*

Now imagine the responses come back from this question and show that virtually no managers are offering support. Sometimes, this will be fine and appropriate. Managers have important duties and certainly aren't needed to support every training. On the other hand, some training programs are so strategic or so important, and some direct reports have very large gaps or blind spots that need focus and attention—when these circumstances are in place, managers should be involved.

Imagine a strategically important program is run to help a company pivot to a new business model—one that will help the company survive in a newly competitive market landscape. Imagine further that the results from the above question show that only 10% of managers supported the learners? Wouldn't this send ripples of horror throughout the organization? Senior management would likely freak and make it a priority to get managers involved in supporting their teams. Managers themselves, on hearing that they've been negligent, would likely get to work, get involved, and figure out how to support their learners.

What messages does the following question send to employees at the non-profit Good-For-All Foundation?

	We at Good-For-All strive to be a values-driven organization in all that we do—and this is important in our learning activities as well. How did this workshop exemplify or fail to exemplify Good-For-All's values? Choose one answer.	*Proposed Standards* *not shown to learners*
A	Significant aspects of the workshop WERE DIRECTLY CONTRARY to Good-For-All's values.	Alarming
B	The workshop WAS NEUTRAL in regard to Good-For-All's values—it neither encouraged nor discouraged such values.	Unacceptable
C	Significant aspects of the workshop DIRECTLY EXEMPLIFED Good-For-All's values.	Acceptable
D	The workshop WAS EXCEPTIONAL IN EXEMPLIFYING Good-For-All's values.	Superior
	Note: Learners are NOT shown the text in the gray cells of this table.	

By asking the question, the organization highlights that it is a values-driven organization. It sends a message to learning architects and trainers that they'd better create learning exemplifying the organizational values. It sends a message to learners that the organization is serious about the values. Indeed, a variation on this question could go further and explicitly highlight the values of the organization.

> **We at Good-For-All strive to be a values-driven organization in all that we do—and this is important in our learning activities as well. Our most important values are formalized as follows:**
>
> - To be stewards of the environment in all we do.
> - To embrace people of all varieties, to treat everyone fairly.
> - To work productively and passionately in support of our clients/benefactors.
> - To work as a team, supporting each other as we support our work.
>
> **How did this workshop exemplify or fail to exemplify Good-For-All's values? Choose one answer.**

Our learner-survey questions can send all types of messages, including brand messages. For example, at the L&D Conference 2020, which I co-organized, we used conference-session questions to support our brand concepts, including the importance of research-based practices.

Performance-Focused Learner Surveys

	STRENGTHS OF THIS SESSION. For this session, what benefits did you get, if any? SELECT ALL THAT ARE TRUE FOR YOU! And PLEASE, do NOT just select them all unless they are all definitely true for you!	*Proposed Standards not shown to learners*
A	I learned NEW INFORMATION I can USE WITHIN THE NEXT MONTH.	Acceptable
B	I was exposed to ideas that significantly DEEPENED MY UNDERSTANDING of important learning and development topics.	Acceptable
C	I was provided with information that was aligned with SCIENTIFIC RESEARCH or supported with other compelling evidence.	Acceptable
D	I am confident in what I learned because the SPEAKER(S) WERE HIGHLY CREDIBLE.	Acceptable
E	UNFORTUNATELY, the information conveyed will NOT BE SUFFICIENTLY USEFUL to me.	Unacceptable
	Note: Learners are NOT shown the text in the gray cells of this table.	

This question was paired with a question about the negatives of the session. The question stem for the negative question was: ***"IMPROVEMENTS NEEDED.*** *To ensure our sessions are respectfully and effectively conducted, we'd like your feedback to point out areas of concern. PLEASE SELECT ANY THAT WERE TRUE about this session!"* Together, these two questions enabled us to send messages—and collect data—related to the brand we wanted to convey in our conference sessions. Specifically, we wanted to focus on: (1) providing evidence-aligned information, (2) enabling and nudging attendees to use what they've learned in their work, (3) providing effective learning experiences, and (4) creating an environment that is enjoyable, inspiring, and respectful. We designed the questions in our conference surveys based on these overall goals.

What's the brand image you want to convey as a learning team? This is a very important question! As learning professionals our reputation enables our success. A good reputation gains us resources, time, and permission to do what is most effective. A brand image can also convey our values, our mission, our purpose. When we ask questions about work performance, we gain an image as a team who cares about organizational success. When we ask questions about after-learning follow-through, we gain an image as a learning team that augments training with additional supports. When we ask meaningful questions about how well we've supported our learners, we gain an image as a team who really cares and looks after our fellow employees.

But watch out! Our survey questions can tarnish our image as well. When we focus on the quality of the food, the cleanliness of the bathrooms, and the number of breaks we give, we gain an image as a group who wants to pander, who cares more about comfort than learning, who subjugates itself instead of asserting itself as professionals. When we use Likert-like scales and numeric scales we brand ourselves as unserious, as beholden to traditions more than effectiveness, as going through the motions.

Most learning teams fail to consider how their learner surveys impact their reputations—their organizational brand. It's an opportunity lost.

Summary: How to Use Stealth Messages to Nudge Action

One of the most important contributions in this book is the notion of stealth messaging and the idea that learner surveys can be used *not only* to measure learning but also to directly drive thoughts and actions. This is truly a revolutionary concept![29] Nowhere before—at least as far as I can tell—has anyone made this recommendation. Normally, I would urge caution knowing that I might have a bodacious blind spot—that I might be crazy or wrong about this recommendation. But I have seen how this works in real life. Let me provide one example.

Ian Blake, senior learning portfolio manager at TetraPak—a global innovative packaging company headquartered in Switzerland—rolled out a new learner survey and shared it in one-to-one meetings with trainers before deploying it. The idea was to get their feedback so as not to surprise them with a new set of learner survey questions. Also, Ian wanted input to co-create some of the questions—tailoring the question stems and fine-tuning some of the answer choices. One of the key questions on the learner survey involved after-training follow-through. One of the answer choices asked whether the learners had been invited to engage in Yammer as part of the learning experience and afterward for ongoing support. Yammer is collaboration software with some similarity to Slack.[30] In one of the one-on-one meetings with trainers, Ian—acting in his role as a learning evaluator—was stunned when

---

[29] In the first edition of this book stealth messaging was discussed, but in the second edition I moved it into a separate chapter because of its revolutionary importance.
[30] Yammer was recently bundled into Microsoft Teams.

Performance-Focused Learner Surveys

the trainer strongly rejected the Yammer idea as ridiculous and not worth doing. A day later, however, the trainer wrote a note apologizing.

"...I have also pondered your idea about a Yammer group. After my rant yesterday it dawned on me that I would be an idiot NOT to start such a group. So, I have set up a meeting [with my IT representative] later this week and hopefully she can help me get started. I also know what information and tips I want to share in that group. Thanks for showing me the light. (Smiley Face)"

Stealth message sent and received! And successful in nudging action! And note that action was taken even before any data was collected! Learner surveys can certainly capture important data, but they can also act directly to generate action! And isn't that what evaluations are supposed to do anyway? When we evaluate, we gather data to help us make decisions so we can improve the actions we are taking—so we can achieve improved results. Stealth messages in our learner surveys simply add another pathway to action and results! Our learner surveys can nudge actions and promote results with stealth messaging at the same time they gather data to support decision-making to nudge action and promote results.

Chapter 6
Learner-Survey Question Quiz

Okay, dear reader, it's time to see if you can distinguish a good learner-survey question from a bad one. This chapter consists entirely of questions for you to critique—with my critical reflections of those questions. First, I'll present the questions. Then you'll analyze them and I'll give you feedback on each question.

Question 1
I learned new knowledge and skills from this training.
A. Strongly Disagree
B. Disagree
C. Slightly Disagree
D. Neutral
E. Slightly Agree
F. Agree
G. Strongly Agree

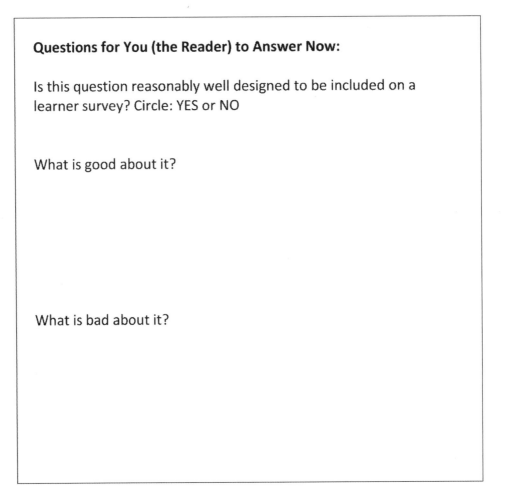

Yo, reader! What the heck are you doing? You must write down your responses. Really! There's good research showing that, if you take this kind of exercise seriously, you'll think more deeply about the issues, you'll learn more, and you'll remember what you learned for a longer period of time.

I know. You don't want to scar this beatific book. But truly, you will scar it by not writing in it.

Feedback on Question #1

This question is terrible!

First, it uses a Likert-like scale, making it hard for learners to calibrate their answers and hard for stakeholders to understand the meaning of the outcomes reported.

Second, the statement, because it is conveyed as an affirmation, is likely to bias results toward positive outcomes.

But here is the most telling thing about Question 1. It is used and has been recommended for use by one of our industry's most popular learning-measurement consultancies. Seriously! Many of our learning-measurement "experts" simply don't know what they're doing.

Question 2
The training will have a significant impact on (check all that apply):
A. Increasing Quality
B. Decreasing Costs
C. Decreasing Cycle Time
D. Increasing Productivity
E. Increasing Sales
F. Decreasing Risk
G. Increasing Employee Satisfaction
H. Increasing Customer Satisfaction

> **Questions for You (the Reader) to Answer Now:**
>
> Is this question reasonably well designed to be included on a learner survey? Circle: YES or NO
>
> What is good about it?
>
> What is bad about it?

Feedback on Question #2

Wait. Wait. Wait. Do yourself a big favor and write down your answer first before reading this well-crafted feedback! And let me give you a hint. This question has both strengths and weaknesses. Go back and write down both the good and the bad.

Here's the feedback. Despite good points and bad, overall this question cannot be recommended.

First, what is good about it? Well, it uses descriptive answer choices (for example, "Increasing Quality"). This gives learners something specific to analyze. So that is one thing in its favor.

Unfortunately, there isn't much else going for this question. For example, all the choices are positive, severely biasing the results. This question begs for at least one of the answers to be chosen. When we report out on the data, there will then seem to be positive results, even though the data will reflect the question's influence, not the actual results. Go back and look at the question so you can see its absurdity!

In addition, we should ask whether our learners are good judges of whether these types of changes occur because of training. It seems doubtful that learners have accurate insights about whether a training program will decrease risk, increase customer satisfaction, and so forth.

I would not recommend this question for use on a learner survey. Again, this question is taken directly from another of the top learning-measurement companies in our industry. That chief learning officers would fall for such an obviously biased question speaks to one of two things: Either they just don't understand learning measurement, or they want to look good regardless of the truth.

Question 3

Regarding the topics taught, how motivated WILL YOU BE TO USE these concepts/skills in your work? CHOOSE ONE.

A. I will NOT MAKE THIS A PRIORITY when I get back to my day-to-day job.

B. I will make this a PRIORITY—BUT A LOW PRIORITY when I get back to my day-to-day job.

C. I will make this a MODERATE PRIORITY when I get back to my day-to-day job.

D. I will make this a HIGH PRIORITY when I get back to my day-to-day job.

E. I will make this ONE OF MY HIGHEST PRIORITIES when I get back to my day-to-day job.

Questions for You (the Reader) to Answer Now:

Is this question reasonably well designed to be included on a learner survey? Circle: YES or NO

What is good about it?

What is bad about it?

Feedback on Question #3

This question is a good one!

First, it directly focuses on one of the four pillars of training effectiveness, that is, whether learners are motivated to apply what they've learned.

Second, the answer choices give learners a choice between real alternatives—specifically, between different levels of priority they may have in applying the learning back on the job.

Finally, because of the way the answer choices are worded—and especially because of the capitalization of the key differentiators between the choices—when the results of this question are reported, it will be possible to highlight clear distinctions to stakeholders. Specifically, we will be able to report how many learners will make application of the learning a low priority, a moderate priority, a high priority, and so on.

Question 4

Using job aids, checklists, or other prompts can be an effective way to ensure you properly apply skills to your job. Which of the following are true?

SELECT ALL that apply.

A. We did NOT RECEIVE ANY WORTHWHILE job aids, checklists, or similar prompts to direct our on-the-job actions.

B. We RECEIVED ONE OR MORE WORTHWHILE job aids, checklists, or similar prompts.

C. During the course, we USED ONE OR MORE WORTHWHILE job aids, checklists, or similar prompts in REALISTIC PRACTICE EXERCISES.

D. Between sessions of the course, IN OUR WORKSITES, WE UTILIZED one or more WORTHWHILE job aids, checklists, or similar prompts IN A REAL-WORLD JOB TASK.

> **Questions for You (the Reader) to Answer Now:**
>
> Is this question reasonably well designed to be included on a learner survey? Circle: YES or NO
>
> What is good about it?
>
> What is bad about it?

Feedback on Question #4

This question is a good one, although it can seem a little awkward for those of us accustomed to traditional smile sheets.

First, it focuses on one of the four pillars of training effectiveness, that is, whether there are after-training supports in place. Indeed, job aids provide great benefits in support of actual on-the-job performance. They are even more potent as supporters of remembering when they are utilized within a training program.

Second, the answer choices give learners a choice between real alternatives, specifically, between qualitatively different levels of job-aid use—levels based on research.

Third—and also because the answer choices provide clear alternatives—this question can be reported out to stakeholders with enough clarity to drive action (the stealth messaging idea).

Question 5

Overall, how satisfied are you with this learning experience?

A. Not at all satisfied.

B. Not very satisfied.

C. Somewhat satisfied.

D. Very satisfied.

E. Extremely satisfied.

Questions for You (the Reader) to Answer Now:

Is this question reasonably well designed to be included on a learner survey? Circle: YES or NO

What is good about it?

What is bad about it?

Feedback on Question #5

This question is a poor one.

First, it focuses on learner satisfaction, which is not one of the essential factors in learning effectiveness. Remember, traditional smile sheets that use questions regarding learner satisfaction have not been correlated with learning results.

Second, while it doesn't use a full-bore Likert-like scale, the distinctions between the different levels of satisfaction still may be difficult for the learners to differentiate. Certainly, "extremely satisfied" is more descriptive than "strongly agree," but even more concreteness would be beneficial. Moreover, if we think ahead to how the answers will be reported out—and what the standards might be for each answer choice—it is unclear where the dividing line between acceptable and unacceptable levels of satisfaction would lie.

The question is also not actionable. Even if you learn that people aren't satisfied with the learning experience, the question doesn't tell you what's wrong.

To reiterate, the big problem with this question is that it is focused not on a primary goal of learner surveys (like training effectiveness), not a secondary goal (like learner understanding), and not even a tertiary goal (like whether the learners were engaged and attentive to the learning). It is focused on learner satisfaction, which is a quaternary goal—far removed from whether the training is effective or not.

Question 6

How likely is it that you would recommend this training course to a friend or colleague?

A. NOT AT ALL LIKELY to recommend

B. VERY UNLIKELY to recommend

C. SOMEWHAT UNLIKELY to recommend

D. SOMEWHAT LIKELY to recommend

E. VERY LIKELY to recommend

F. EXTREMELY LIKELY to recommend

Questions for You (the Reader) to Answer Now:

Is this question reasonably well designed to be included on a learner survey? Circle: YES or NO

What is good about it?

What is bad about it?

Feedback on Question #6

This question is also a poor one. It does not focus on any of the most important factors that relate to training effectiveness. As stated earlier, learners don't always know what makes good learning, so their recommendations are not likely to be related to training effectiveness. This is the key thing wrong with this question.

It can be argued that asking for this type of customer satisfaction data helps us determine whether our training course is meeting the expectations of an important stakeholder constituent—our learners. This does seem reasonable on the face of it; but, since we've seen that such satisfaction data is uncorrelated with learning results, shouldn't we do more than encourage these inappropriate expectations? Shouldn't we nudge our learners to expect more from their time and effort? Why can't we threshold their expectations to the level of improved on-the-job performance?

Some of you will notice that the question stem above—asking people whether they would recommend the training to others—is similar to the popular NPS (Net Promoter Score). As we will see in greater detail, a Net-Promoter-Score type of question cannot be recommended for learning measurement.

Chapter 7
Candidate Questions

Hopefully, most of the arguments I've made now resonate with you—and we can agree that learner surveys should target training effectiveness and actionable results, while also nudging action through stealth messaging. I, of course, will leave open the possibility that you have some quibbles—and that's okay; it's important that we all think for ourselves. Still, I'm guessing I've been at least somewhat persuasive if you're still reading. No matter; it's time to look at candidate questions you might consider for your learner surveys.

Let me reiterate a key point. There are no perfect learning-measurement instruments, nor are there any perfect learner-survey questions. Every word added or subtracted from a question implies trade-offs and a change in meaning. People will read questions differently. We are not creating exactitude. Instead, our aim is to be as true and effective as possible and to always look for improvements. I've been working to improve my own learner surveys for years and years, and I'm sure I will continue seeing improvements I can make.

I'm going to offer some damn good questions here, but certainly you may see improvements you could make—for example, better ways to phrase something for your audience and your content areas. That's great! I highly recommend that you use the candidate questions based on your own wisdom and that you modify them when you think you can improve them. Of course, you might want to get other folks' feedback as well.

One final note before we jump in. This is the second edition of the book. The questions I am offering here are almost all improved significantly from the first edition. Also, I've added a whole chapter after this one that introduces new questions you may find useful for special purposes. The practice of learner survey questioning has undergone an intense transformation over the past five years.

In this chapter and next, I share the best state-of-the-art questions—questions I am confident will stand the test of time—but, still, I encourage you not just to use my questions without your own reflection and contextualization. First, they are written in a generic way and can be improved by tailoring them to your specific learning goals and contexts. I have added a chapter—Chapter 10—to show you how to tailor your questions. Second, my wording may not convey the same meaning to all learners—to all people in an organization, a region, a country. The wording of the questions as written will certainly work, but slight changes in wording might make them more precisely convey the necessary meaning. Similarly, translating my questions to another language will require going beyond literal translations, as each word conveys weight and meaning. Finally, even though these questions have been fine tuned exhaustively over time and experience, there are likely to be at least a few improvements that can be made.

My main point is this—wording matters! I recommend you maintain a balance. Don't just mindlessly change the wording of the questions, but don't just mindlessly use the questions as written either. Writing survey questions is a serious discipline. To get the best results, we need to honor it as such!

Learner-Survey Training-Effectiveness Taxonomy

The questions in this chapter will be indexed based on what we might call the learner-survey training-effectiveness taxonomy, based partially on the four pillars of training effectiveness. More simply, this is a reiteration of the training-effectiveness goal structure I presented previously.

Learner-Survey Training-Effectiveness Taxonomy

Learner-Survey Primary Goal—Training Effectiveness

   Secondary Goal—Understanding

     Tertiary Goal—Learners Engaged

         Quaternary Goal*—Learners Motivated to Learn

         Quaternary Goal*—Instructors Credible and Engaging

         Quaternary Goal*—Environment Conducive to Learning

     Tertiary Goal—Cognitive Supports Effective

         Quaternary Goal*—Course Well Organized

         Quaternary Goal*—Materials Signal Attention Hot Spots

         Quaternary Goal*—Content Aligned to Prior Knowledge

Learner-Survey Training-Effectiveness Taxonomy
(continued)

Secondary Goal—Remembering

   Tertiary Goal—Realistic Retrieval Practice

   Tertiary Goal—Spaced Repetitions

   Tertiary Goal—Situation-Action Triggering

Secondary Goal—Motivation to Apply

   Tertiary Goal—Belief in the Value of Concepts

   Tertiary Goal—Self-Efficacy

   Tertiary Goal—Resilience

Secondary Goal—After-Training Follow-Through

   Tertiary Goal—Reminding Mechanisms

   Tertiary Goal—Job Aids

   Tertiary Goal—Supervisor Follow-Up

* Quaternary goals are included for completeness (on the previous page), but generally you won't want to create learner survey questions for them because they are at too low a priority for inclusion.

Ideally, each of the primary, secondary, and tertiary goals would have at least one question that examines how well the course targets it. Of course, if your learner surveys had one question for each of these goals, you would have too many questions to maintain your learners' attention and interest. Quaternary goals—those at the fourth level of priority—are included in the taxonomy too; however, please note—these goals are a low priority for learner-survey questions because they are far removed from the primary goal.

The rest of this chapter introduces candidate questions indexed to the taxonomy above.

Learner-Survey Primary Goal—Training Effectiveness

Our primary goal in performance-focused training is to create improved on-the-job performance. Given that, we can ask our learners whether they feel they will be able to utilize the training concepts on the job.

The following question is a powerful way to get feedback about the effectiveness of a learning intervention to produce improvements in work performance:

Question 101	
Question Rationale: Used to determine how prepared learners feel in being able to take what they've learned and use it in their work.	
HOW ABLE ARE YOU to put what you've learned into practice in your work? CHOOSE THE ONE OPTION that best describes your current readiness.	
A	My CURRENT ROLE DOES NOT ENABLE me to use what I learned.
B	I AM STILL UNCLEAR about what to do, and/or why to do it.
C	I NEED MORE GUIDANCE before I know how to use what I learned.
D	I NEED MORE EXPERIENCE to be good at using what I learned.
E	I CAN BE SUCCESSFUL NOW in using what I learned (even without more guidance or experience).
F	I CAN PERFORM NOW AT AN EXPERT LEVEL in using what I learned.
Note: Learners are NOT shown the text in the gray cells of this table.	

The question is aimed specifically at training effectiveness. It asks learners for their impression of their ability to put the training concepts into practice on the job. This question is written so that, in addition to being relevant at the end of training, it can also be deployed on a follow-up learner survey given to learners two to four weeks after the end of training.

Given that each question should be written with standards for acceptable results, here's my list of proposed standards for this question:

	Question 101 (With Standards)	
	Question Rationale: Used to determine how prepared learners feel in being able to take what they've learned and use it in their work.	
	HOW ABLE ARE YOU to put what you've learned into practice in your work? CHOOSE THE ONE OPTION that best describes your current readiness.	*Proposed Standards* Not shown to learners
A	My CURRENT ROLE DOES NOT ENABLE me to use what I learned.	Alarming
B	I AM STILL UNCLEAR about what to do, and/or why to do it.	Alarming
C	I NEED MORE GUIDANCE before I know how to use what I learned.	Unacceptable
D	I NEED MORE EXPERIENCE to be good at using what I learned.	Acceptable
E	I CAN BE SUCCESSFUL NOW in using what I learned (even without more guidance or experience).	Superior
F	I CAN PERFORM NOW AT AN EXPERT LEVEL in using what I learned.	Superior/ Overconfident?
	Note: Learners are NOT shown the text in the gray cells of this table.	

This question's inherent message—one designed to reverberate as a stealth message—is that the focus of training is on-the-job performance. Moreover, the question pushes us to see that we can have differing levels of success. We can give people general awareness of a concept, but not adequately prepare them to act. We can support our learners so they can take tentative steps toward competence but leave them needing more guidance or experience.

Performance-Focused Learner Surveys

As I mentioned earlier in Chapter 4, note that my suggestions for standards should be taken as somewhat flexible. I recommend standards, but you should adjust them in negotiations with your key stakeholders. You should also adjust them upwards or downwards depending on the goals of your training. If you're aiming for improved work performance, you will have higher standards than if you are aiming only to give your learners general awareness of a topic. Similarly, a course that teaches conflict-resolution skills might warrant a different set of standards than a course teaching how to use a piece of software.

If you are creating a performance-training course—one where your goal is to prepare your learners from improved performance in their work—then the standards in the above question make sense. But what about for a course where your goal is only to give people general awareness of a topic—so they can learn more on their own if they choose? Then, Choice C might become "Acceptable" instead of "Unacceptable." It might be acceptable that they would need more guidance before they knew how to use what they learned.

Note that Option F in the question above will almost always be unrealistic to achieve. It says, "I CAN PERFORM NOW AT AN EXPERT LEVEL in using what I learned"—a very unlikely occurrence. Adding "over-the-top" options helps slow down respondents so they think critically about the answer choices. Given the tendency of learner-survey respondents to circle the "best" answer for every question without giving the answer choices much thought, this tactic may help limit people's ingrained uncritical responses. Of course, you'll need to show some wisdom about your organizational culture. Some organizational cultures—usually highly dysfunctional ones—expect to achieve the highest "grades" on everything. The over-the-top "expert" answer choice may not work as intended in these contexts.

Note also that the question above—which targets training effectiveness—also partially covers the secondary goal of learner understanding, at least in its "B" and "C" answer choices. Choice B asks whether learners are clear about what to do. Choice C asks whether they need more guidance. But beware! Just because a question partially covers another goal doesn't mean it fully covers it. Indeed, without a question that specifically targets understanding, we haven't really covered understanding. We need to provide a question that gives learners options with different levels of understanding—as we will see in the next section. If we don't have different levels, we don't have the granularity that enables accurate decision making.

Here's another example of a question that directly targets training effectiveness:

Question 102 (NOT Recommended for Use)	
From your perspective, how valuable are the concepts taught in the course? HOW MUCH WILL THEY HELP YOU IMPROVE YOUR WORK OUTCOMES?	
A	Will NOT HELP ME to improve my work outcomes.
B	Will HELP ME SLIGHTLY to improve my work outcomes.
C	Will HELP ME A MODERATE AMOUNT to improve my work outcomes.
D	Will HELP ME SIGNIFICANTLY to improve my work outcomes.
E	Concepts taught are NOT RELEVANT to my work.

Question 102 is NOT as good as Question 101 because its answer choices are not as descriptive. Indeed, these choices are similar to Likert-like answer choices in that we are asking learners to calibrate using fuzzy words like "slightly," "moderate," and "significantly." Of course, we should remember that perfection is not necessary or likely—we are always dealing with shades of acceptability. One question you can ask yourself to give you insight about a question's acceptability is whether you can clearly delineate standards for the answer choices. This question, in my mind, passes that test, but just barely. I can see choice A as alarming, B unacceptable, C acceptable, and D superior—with choice E as alarming. Still, I would strongly recommend against using Question 102, because we can easily do better.

Here is another question that can be used to gauge overall results. It may be more appropriate to use when the learning is focused on deeply personal content. In the question below, I use sexual-harassment prevention as an example, but this type of question could also be valuable in anti-bias training, diversity-equity-inclusion training, and ethics training.

Question 103

Question Rationale: Used the assess how learners perceive the impact of the learning session on their thoughts and behavior.			
What impact, if any, will the learning session have on your future actions? Choose as MANY ANSWERS AS ARE TRUE for you.			*Proposed Standards* Not shown to learners
A	The session REINFORCED MY PREVIOUS THOUGHTS on [[sexual harassment]].		Acceptable
B	The session made me MORE SENSITIVE to issues related to [[sexual harassment]].		Acceptable
C	The session will likely CHANGE HOW I ACT AT WORK.		Acceptable
D	The session will likely CHANGE HOW I ACT IN MY PERSONAL LIFE.		Acceptable
E	The session DID NOT DO ENOUGH TO PREPARE ME to deal with work situations related to [[sexual harassment]].		Unacceptable
Note: Learners are NOT shown the text in the gray cells of this table. *If calculating an acceptability index, we might consider it acceptable if respondents chose two or more of the acceptable responses, while also avoiding the unacceptable response.* *As always, you should base standards of acceptability on your own circumstances, while also negotiating with your key stakeholders.*			

Secondary Goal #1—Understanding

We've looked at overall effectiveness. Now it's time to drill down on each of the four pillars of training effectiveness. The first is Understanding.

The best way to measure whether learners understand concepts is to test them on those concepts. Not by using learner surveys, but by testing their understanding directly. Using learner-survey questions is a weak proxy for full tests of understanding. Still, it is worth assessing understanding on our learner surveys because it reminds stakeholders that creating comprehension is critical to learning. Also, if we're not adequately measuring understanding in some other way, we will at least have a proxy for understanding.

Another consideration, and one that is usually overlooked, is that, ideally, we should consider using good instructional-design practices to ensure learners have maximum insight into their level of understanding. To generate such insight, shortly before learners complete our learner survey, we should provide learners with exercises, conceptual questions, scenario-based decisions, simulations, or hands-on practice to help them gauge their understanding on key concepts or skills.

Questions such as the following can be utilized to gauge understanding:

	Question 104	
Question Rationale: *Used to determine how well the training helped learners comprehend the concepts taught.*		
Now that you've completed the learning experience, how well do you feel you understand the concepts taught? CHOOSE ONE.		*Proposed Standards* Not shown to learners
A	I am still at least SOMEWHAT CONFUSED about the concepts.	Alarming
B	I am now SOMEWHAT FAMILIAR WITH the concepts.	Unacceptable
C	I have a SOLID UNDERSTANDING of the concepts.	Acceptable
D	I AM FULLY READY TO USE the concepts in my work.	Superior
E	I have an EXPERT-LEVEL ABILITY to use the concepts.	Superior/ Overconfident?
Note: Learners are NOT shown the text in the gray cells of this table.		

This is a nice question because it very simply targets learner understanding—and it offers five graduated options for learners to choose from.

Here is another example of a question that assesses understanding.

Question 105	
Question Rationale: *Used to determine how well the training helped learners comprehend the concepts taught.*	
How well did the course prepare you to understand the concepts? SELECT ALL THAT APPLY	*Proposed Standards* *Not shown to learners*
A — Concepts were CLEARLY PRESENTED.	Acceptable
B — Concepts were REPEATED TO AID CLARITY.	Acceptable
C — Concepts were REPEATED USING A VARIETY METHODS.	Acceptable
D — We were asked to ANSWER QUIZ-LIKE QUESTIONS about concepts/terminology.	Acceptable
E — We were asked to MAKE DECISIONS of the kind we might make IN OUR WORK.	Superior
F — We were asked to COMPLETE TASKS of the kind we might do IN OUR WORK.	Superior
G — We received HELPFUL FEEDBACK on questions, decisions, and/or task practice.	Superior
H — Concepts were NOT WELL PRESENTED.	Alarming
I — Concepts were NOT GIVEN ENOUGH PRACTICE.	Alarming
J — FEEDBACK was NOT GIVEN or was NOT ADEQUATE.	Alarming
Note: Learners are NOT shown the text in the gray cells of this table.	

Note how this type of question—with a select-all-that-apply design—will require a different approach to standard setting. We will discuss later how to determine "acceptability" when using this type of question.

Standards are critically important. Setting standards for each question can drive stealth messaging. Anyone who looks at the standards here will see that presenting concepts is insufficient, that some sort of active practice is important, that feedback is important, and that practice in more realistic situations is best of all. Indeed, nudging people to action—including ourselves as learning professionals—can be one of the primary purposes of learner-survey questions. Please remember this: We do evaluation to make a difference, to help us make decisions, to help us propel action. By using questions to send stealth messages, we are nudging action!

Certainly, if we observed the course ourselves—or we hired a learning consultant to evaluate our course design—it would be obvious whether these "supports for understanding" were in place or not. The benefit of putting this question on the learner survey is twofold. First, it sends stealth messages to trainers, learning architects, and other stakeholders. Second, it gives us continuing feedback on these supports for understanding, in contrast to once-a-year reviews that require significant time and money.

Of course, there's no reason these standards couldn't be used by course designers to design the learning intervention in the first place. However, my experience working in the industry for more than thirty years tells me that these kinds of design-improvement interventions are rarely done—and, even when done, their benefits often fade away with time. Integrating stealth messaging into your learner surveys gives you an opportunity to create a sustainable practice. Initially they drive stakeholder learning. Over time they institutionalize effectiveness.

Understanding—Tertiary Goal: Learners Engaged

I'm not convinced any other questions are needed to assess learner understanding. Specifically, tertiary goals seem less essential here than for some of the other secondary goals. Nevertheless, for completeness—and so you can decide for yourself—here is a question that attempts to get at learner engagement, designed to be used after a webinar, where learner attention is particularly critical.

Question 106	
Question Rationale: Used after webinars or other live online learning sessions, to determine how well learner attention was maintained.	
Compared to most webinars (online meetings), how well did the session keep YOUR attention? Select ONE choice.	*Proposed Standards* Not shown to learners
A — I had a HARD TIME STAYING FOCUSED.	Alarming
B — My attention WANDERED AT A NORMAL LEVEL.	Unacceptable
C — My attention RARELY WANDERED.	Acceptable
D — I was very much SPELLBOUND throughout the session.	Superior/ Overconfident?
Note: Learners are NOT shown the text in the gray cells of this table.	

Understanding—Learners Engaged—Quaternary Goal: Instructors Credible

We could drill down on learner engagement to get to the quaternary level. You might do this if some factor needs special illumination in your situation. For some audiences, the credibility of the instructors is critical. For example, many very experienced people will only take training seriously if the instructors immediately demonstrate the highest levels of credibility.

Given that research shows that human beings tend to evaluate others based on two dimensions—warmth (with a connotation of trust) and competence—we might want our questions about instructors to drill down on these aspects as well as the other learning-related competencies we would normally ask them about.[31]

---

[31] Fiske, Cuddy, & Glick (2007).

Question 107	
Question Rationale: Used to get feedback about the performance of instructors.	
Which of the following are true about your course instructor(s)? **SELECT UP TO THREE ITEMS—THOSE THAT ARE THE MOST IMPORTANT in describing the performance of your instructor(s).**	***Proposed Standards*** *Not shown to learners*
A — Generally DID A GOOD JOB in facilitating the learning.	Superior
B — Too often HURRIED through the content in a SUPERFICIAL manner.	Unacceptable
C — Demonstrated DEEP SUBJECT-MATTER KNOWLEDGE.	Acceptable
D — Was too OFTEN UNCLEAR or DISORGANIZED.	Unacceptable
E — Showed HIGH LEVELS OF REAL-WORLD EXPERIENCE relevant to the topic.	Acceptable
F — Was SOCIALLY AWKWARD or INAPPROPRIATE to an extent that it harmed learning.	Unacceptable
G — Motivated me to ENGAGE MORE DEEPLY IN THE LEARNING than I'd expected.	Acceptable
H — Gave us LITTLE OR NO TIME TO PRACTICE SKILLS we could use in our work.	Unacceptable
I — Is a PERSON I CAME TO REALLY TRUST.	Acceptable
J — I wish he/she/they had PERFORMED BETTER in facilitating the learning.	Alarming
Note: Learners are NOT shown the text in the gray cells of this table.	

The answer choices above have a brutally honest tone to them. This has the benefit of truth telling but may be shocking in some organizational cultures. If you're worried, it might be worth doing a pilot test on a small group of learners before you roll this out to everyone. Alternatively, you might get a group of advocates together—some representing

Performance-Focused Learner Surveys

trainers and some representing learners—to write answer choices both groups can buy into. Remember to have positive and negative attributes along both dimensions—warmth (trust) and competence. On the other hand, you might decide the straightforward nature of the answer choices is just what's needed. Good instructors will exhibit the good behaviors and avoid the bad behaviors.

We must be very careful when we ask for learners' impressions of their instructors. Most of the time instructors are rated very highly. This is partially because most trainers are pretty good at keeping learners engaged and satisfied. But there is also a tendency for us humans to be nice to others—unless they are particularly rude, incompetent, or uncaring. This positivity bias toward instructors causes two fundamental problems. First, we can't differentiate between our instructors because they all get very high scores. If we can't differentiate, then we may be wasting everybody's time by asking a question about instructors. Second, because learners aren't always good judges of their own learning—or of learning design—high instructor scores often hide underlying learning-design flaws. High instructor ratings can give us a false impression that our instructors and our learning designs are good, when the opposite might be true.

What can we do? Well, we could avoid questions about our instructors—and rely instead on all the other questions on our learner survey. Our other questions are essentially proxies for measuring instructor performance. But it's not so simple when instructors are constrained by somebody else's learning design. When instructors are told what and how to teach, it may not be their fault if learning fails—except in not being assertive enough to insist on sufficiently effective learning designs.

I have often suggested to my clients that they avoid questions that directly ask about instructors—to rely on the other questions to grade instructor performance. But I must admit that there is something that compels us to ask about instructor performance. For this reason, I crafted the question above. Please note how the question gives learners permission to be critical of their instructors. It does this by adding an equal number of positive and negative options. On too many learner surveys in the past, instructor questions pushed a positivity bias, for example using question stems like these. *"My instructor was well organized." "My learning was enhanced by the knowledge of the facilitator."* These types of question stems—with their hypnotic Likert-like scales—send a message to learners to rate their instructors highly. And so, with high ratings received, many of us as instructors have been blind to the bias that bolstered our sense of success. We have been shrouded from our own habits of incompetence. We have not even known that we needed to improve.

So, to be practical, if we ask a question about instructors, we must be careful to offer both positive and negative options. In my proposed question, I have offered ten answer choices—to cover a full range of instructor tendencies, both good and bad. Many of you—and/or your stakeholders—will see ten as too many options, but I will argue that we should convey the full range and ask learners to pick a small number of those options. If you do tinker with the options, make sure you keep both positive and negative options. You may also want to push your instructor questions toward the end of your learner survey, after other questions—questions that nudge learners to think about the quality of the learning. Finally, if you have more than one instructor, you will have to either repeat the question for each instructor, or provide an additional open-ended question that says something like this, "For each instructor, please add specifics in the box below—both positive and negative—about his/her performance."

Understanding—Tertiary Goal: Cognitive Supports Effective

Again, tertiary goals are generally less important than higher-level goals, but sometimes they may be needed. Cognitive supports are critical in helping learners build correct mental models of learning concepts. Because learners are unlikely to know what "cognitive supports" are, it may be difficult or impossible to ask about them specifically; instead, quaternary goals may have to be targeted. For example, in evaluating a course on a complicated, non-intuitive software program, it might be especially helpful to drill down on whether the learners received sufficient delayed practice. Often, software learners can perform a task right after they learned it, but not after a delay. If the course doesn't give learners practice after a delay (i.e., one type of cognitive support), then learners are not getting adequate practice.

Performance-Focused Learner Surveys

A question to get at whether such a cognitive support has been provided is presented as an example.

Question 108	
Question Rationale: *Used to measure the amount of delayed practice learners received during the training.*	
Which of the following were true about the opportunities you were given to practice using the software? **SELECT ALL THAT APPLY.**	*Proposed Standards* Not shown to learners
A — We were given NO PRACTICE or ALMOST NO PRACTICE.	Alarming
B — We were given INADEQUATE AMOUNTS OF PRACTICE.	Unacceptable
C — We were OFTEN asked to PRACTICE a task IMMEDIATELY AFTER we learned it.	Acceptable
D — We were OFTEN asked to PRACTICE a task AN HOUR OR MORE AFTER we learned it.	Superior
E — We were OFTEN asked to PRACTICE a task A DAY OR MORE AFTER we learned it.	Superior
Note: Learners are NOT shown the text in the gray cells of this table.	

One interesting aside. Often learners underestimate how much practice they need. Their cognitive machinery is overly optimistic about their ability to remember, so they don't think they need as much practice as they really do. So, it's critical that we are very concrete—as in the answer choices C, D, and E. We are asking about the timing of practice, not whether they thought it was sufficient. We are doing what we can to take subjectivity out of their learner-survey decision making, because we know that, here, learners are particularly open to bias.

Secondary Goal #2—Remembering

It's time to turn to the second secondary goal, Remembering. Here again, the best way to gauge remembering is to measure it directly with concept tests, scenario-based decision making, simulations, hands-on exercises, and so forth—and to measure it after a time delay. To reiterate, measuring these things during learning or immediately after learning can only measure understanding. To measure remembering, we must measure learning after a delay.

Again, dear reader, you might be asking, *"Dr. Willy Boy, why are we trying to measure remembering on a learner survey when it is only a weak proxy for remembering?"* Great question! It's great to have such bright readers—and such familiar ones. Remembering is worth assessing on our learner surveys for two reasons. First, most of us are not going to measure remembering directly—it is sad to say—so it's useful to gauge remembering in some way. Second, because learner surveys send stealth messages—whether we intend those messages to be sent or not—it's helpful to send the message that remembering is a critical goal for learning design. Moreover, by drilling down to remembering's tertiary goals, we can send specific messages about the importance of providing realistic practice, spacing repetitions over time, and using situation-action triggering. These learning methods are usually underutilized, making it unlikely that our learners will remember what they've learned. As a result, it's critical that we highlight these methods for our stakeholders.

If direct tests of remembering are best done after a delay, the principle also has relevance for learner surveys. Indeed, if we take a learner-survey question designed to measure understanding, but we tweak it so we can provide it after a delay, such a learner-survey question can gauge remembering. Here's an example:

Performance-Focused Learner Surveys

Question 109 (a follow-up learner-survey question)

Question Rationale: A follow-up learner-survey question, designed to see if learners have maintained their knowledge of what was learned.

In the training you took two weeks ago, Finance for Non-Financial Managers, you learned about the following topics:

- Topic 1
- Topic 2
- Topic 3
- Topic 4
- Et Cetera…

Now that you've been back in the workplace for several weeks, how well do you feel you understand the concepts that were taught in the course? Select ONE.

Proposed Standards
Not shown to learners

A	I am currently SOMEWHAT CONFUSED about the concepts.	Alarming
B	I am SOMEWHAT FAMILIAR WITH the concepts.	Unacceptable
C	I have a SOLID UNDERSTANDING of the concepts.	Acceptable
D	I AM FULLY ABLE TO USE the concepts in my work.	Superior
E	I have an EXPERT-LEVEL ABILITY to use the concepts.	Superior/ Overconfident?

Note: Learners are NOT shown the text in the gray cells of this table.

One thing about a follow-up learner survey is that it's critical to remind learners of the topics they learned. You could list the topics before the learners answer learner-survey questions, as I did in the question above. Conversely, before you unveil the follow-up learner survey, you could give learners a short booster session, have them take a short quiz, provide them with scenario decisions, or use another means of reminding. Of course, if you're going to go to all that trouble, you'll probably get a better measure of remembering from testing their knowledge and skills directly!

You might be wondering why we can't just ask learners if they remember what they learned. *"How well do you remember how to handle price objections from the workshop?"* First, you'd have to ask them this for each specific topic. You can't just say, *"How well do you remember the concepts taught in the workshop Power Selling for Superstars?"* This prompt is too vague; it covers too much ground. More importantly, though, people aren't that good at recalling how much they've learned. They won't remember what they'd forgotten, so any introspections they have will be fatally flawed. Finally, and maybe this is truly the most important thing, if you're going to go to all the trouble to ask people a series of questions about how much they remember about this topic or that topic, you'd be better off creating a nicely designed set of scenario questions to test people's memory directly. The bottom line is that asking learners how much they think they remember is a terrible idea.

An even worse idea is asking learners to predict how much they think they will remember in the future. You might remember that learners are notoriously overconfident about their ability to remember. Asking them to predict their own remembering is likely to get you highly biased data. Learners will estimate a high proportion of remembering—when in reality they will likely forget a large amount of what they learned.

Because using a learner-survey question to ask for predictions about remembering is so fraught with danger, we are better off looking at the tertiary goals.

Remembering's Tertiary Goals

- Realistic Retrieval Practice
- Spaced Repetitions
- Situation-Action Triggering

We will now look at each of these in turn.

Remembering—Tertiary Goal: Realistic Retrieval Practice

One of the best ways to support our learners in remembering is to provide them with realistic practice, prompting them to retrieve concepts from memory, and, specifically, prompting them to retrieve information in a manner similar to what they will face on the job. I am specifically *not* talking about retrieving low-level, trivial information. As Shrock and Coscarelli (2007) warned us, memorization questions are not acceptable proxies for real-world performance. Realistic practice entails providing learners with realistic background situations and having them make decisions and/or practice skills.

Performance-Focused Learner Surveys

Here's a question that gauges the level of realistic practice given in a training course.

	Question 110	
	Question Rationale: *Used to get a rough estimate of the amount of realistic practice provided to learners.*	
	HOW MUCH OF THE TRAINING WAS DEVOTED TO GIVING YOU PRACTICE working on real job tasks or giving you realistic simulations, scenarios, or exercises related to real job tasks? Choose ONE.	*Proposed Standards* Not shown to learners
A	0% of the training was devoted to realistic practice.	Alarming
B	10%	Alarming
C	20%	Unacceptable
D	30%	Unacceptable
E	40%	Acceptable
F	50% of the training was devoted to realistic practice.	Acceptable
G	60%	Superior
H	70%	Superior
I	80%	Superior
J	90%	Superior/ Exaggerated?
K	100% of the training was devoted to realistic practice.	Superior/ Exaggerated?
	Note: Learners are NOT shown the text in the gray cells of this table.	

I've chosen to give people answer choices at 10% intervals from 0% to 100%. I've done this because my gut tells me that people are better able to calibrate their decision making if they can see a range of responses but not too many responses—but I'm not sure about this, and haven't seen any empirical evidence one way or another. Nevertheless, providing my eleven-item range, instead of using 0–20%, 20%–40%, and so on, or less than 35%, 35%–60%, and so on, seems to me to have another advantage—the advantage of always asking the learners the same question—to enable comparison between different courses. In this way, the question is the same, but the standards for acceptable levels of realistic retrieval practice vary for different types of courses. For example, for a performance training leadership-development course, the acceptable range might be 40–70%, whereas, for a writing course, the acceptable range might be 60–90% (that is, 60–90% of the course should provide realistic retrieval practice).

Let me say this: For any course that aspires to be a performance training course—one devoted to producing on-the-job benefits—the absolute minimum percentage of the course devoted to realistic practice should be 35%. Absolute minimum! Most of us—me included—forget this and try to cram too much content into our training courses. Providing realistic practice in significant amounts is not a luxury; it's a requirement.

Another way to gauge realistic practice is to ask about the specific types of practice we could offer our learners.

Question 111

Question Rationale: *Used to determine the level of realistic practice received by learners.*

In which of the following activities did you spend the most time during the learning? **SELECT UP TO THREE CHOICES ONLY** **(1, 2, or 3 choices please)!**		*Proposed Standards* Not shown to learners
A	VIEWING INFORMATION presented on a screen (example: from PowerPoint)	Acceptable
B	REFLECTING ON HOW I MIGHT USE the ideas presented.	Acceptable
C	Engaging in DISCUSSIONS ON HOW TO USE the ideas presented.	Acceptable
D	Answering QUIZ-LIKE QUESTIONS on the ideas presented.	Acceptable
E	MAKING DECISIONS like those I will face on the job.	Superior
F	DOING TASKS OR ACTIVITIES like those I will face on the job.	Superior
G	Engaging in ACTIVITIES NOT RELEVANT to my job.	Alarming
H	Engaging in RELEVANT ACTIVITIES not listed here, PLEASE SPECIFY BELOW:	Acceptable

Note: Learners are NOT shown the text in the gray cells of this table.

Acceptability indexing will be introduced later, but here are the instructions for this question. If calculating an acceptability index for this question, we might assign one point for an acceptable response and two points for a superior response, and then deem a person's overall response acceptable if the answers add up to four points or more. As always, you should base standards of acceptability on your own circumstances, while also negotiating with your key stakeholders.

Chapter 7—Candidate Questions

Remembering—Tertiary Goal: Spaced Repetitions

The spacing effect is the finding that spacing repetitions over time provides more effective support for long-term remembering than repeating things without a delay or with a shorter delay.[32] Spaced repetitions of two weeks are likely to produce better remembering than spaced repetitions of one week. One day is better than half a day. Two hours is better than one hour. Fifteen minutes is better than five minutes. As Harry Bahrick and Linda Hall once noted in a top-tier scientific journal, the *Journal of Memory and Language*, "The spacing effect is one of the oldest and best documented phenomena in the history of learning and memory research."[33] It is interesting that the spacing effect was, until recently, one of the most underutilized key learning factors in the training-and-development field.

To gauge a training program's utilization of the spacing effect, we might use the following question.

---

[32] Scientific reviews of the spacing literature: Carpenter, Cepeda, Rohrer, Kang, & Pashler (2012); Delaney, Verkoeijen, & Spirgel (2010); Thalheimer (2006); Donovan & Radosevich (1999); Lee & Genovese (1988); Ruch (1928); Cain & Willey (1939); Melton (1970); Crowder (1976); Hintzman (1974); Glenberg (1979); Rea & Modigliani (1988); Dempster (1988, 1989, 1996).
[33] Bahrick & Hall (2005).

Performance-Focused Learner Surveys

Question 112		
Question Rationale: Used to determine the extent to which learners got spaced practice.		
Did you engage in meaningful practice, and if so, how did you receive it? Choose the ONE option that most closely mirrors your experience.		*Proposed Standards* Not shown to learners
A	Meaningful practice was NOT PROVIDED or was RARELY PROVIDED.	Alarming
B	Practice was provided INSUFFICIENTLY, often with only one or two meager practice opportunities.	Unacceptable
C	Meaningful practice was most often provided IMMEDIATELY AFTER a topic was taught.	Unacceptable
D	Meaningful practice was most often provided an HOUR OR MORE after a topic was taught.	Acceptable
E	Meaningful practice was most often provided a DAY OR MORE after a topic was taught.	Superior
F	Meaningful practice was most often provided a WEEK OR MORE after a topic was taught.	Superior
G	Meaningful practice was provided SO OFTEN AND SO ROBUSTLY, that I feel as highly skilled as if I had been doing the work/task for a long time.	Superior/ Overconfident?
Note: Learners are NOT shown the text in the gray cells of this table.		

Note that the granularity in the answer choices could be increased even further by adding the following options, which might be desirable if we are evaluating shorter courses:

- Meaningful practice was most often provided A HALF HOUR OR MORE after a topic was taught.
- Meaningful practice was most often provided TWO HOURS OR MORE after a topic was taught.

Indeed, we could add answer choices to get at micro-spacings—spacings of less than a few minutes—which is a learning design that is often appropriate for intense applications like language learning. Alternatively, if we want to have fewer answer choices, we can easily craft a version of this question with less than seven options.

The question as written does a nice job sending very clear stealth messages about what is really desirable in terms of spaced repetitions. Short spacings are good. Spacings over a day are better. Spacings over a longer time frame are even better. By being very clear about the benefits of longer spacings, we may get our stakeholders onboard with more effective learning designs, including such things as subscription learning applications.

Remembering—Tertiary Goal: Situation-Action Triggers

Situation-action triggers have been shown—in extensive scientific refereed research—to be extremely effective in helping people remember what to do in future situations.[34] Essentially, if we can get people to link situations with actions they plan to take, they'll be much more likely to remember what they were planning to do than if such a link was never made.

Several prominent learning methods parlay this scientific fact. One is triggered action planning. Action planning is well known. It occurs at the end of training when we ask learners what goals they have for taking what they've learned back to the job. Triggered action planning makes it much more likely that action planning will be followed through. Since my original description of triggered action planning, researchers have confirmed its power.[35] In triggered action planning, learners are not only asked what goals they have for learning implementation, but they're asked to think about the situations in which their goals will be realized. For example, in a leadership course, a learner might have the goal of bringing his or her direct reports into decision making. To use triggered action planning, a person might decide that the situation to target is an upcoming staff meeting, and the action to target is asking for input into a particular decision. This situation-action pair becomes the engine for triggered action planning—with the expectation that, when the learner encounters the situation (the staff meeting or the planning for it), he or she will be much more likely to remember to ask his or her direct reports to participate in the decision making.

A second way to utilize situation-action triggering is to prepare learners (through intense practice) to deal with various contingencies—to plan and practice specific actions,

---

[34] Gollwitzer & Sheeran (2006).
[35] Friedman & Ronen (2015).

each aimed at one of multiple situations. A similar methodology can be used specifically to help learners deal with obstacles or problems they might be expected to face on the job. This situation-action type of "inoculation" strategy plans for problem situations and pairs these with both actions and metacognitive strategies for how to deal with the potential emotional blowback from hitting the obstacle.

The bottom line on situation-action triggering is that we are using the natural human tendency to react to stimuli as a way to prepare our learners to respond appropriately when they encounter certain on-the-job stimuli.

Of course, our learners are not going to understand the science or terminology behind this, so writing a learner-survey question is going to be a bit tricky. Here's a question I've come up with.

Question 113

Question Rationale: *Used to determine the extent to which learners were encouraged to set goals and engage in triggered action planning.*

	What types of goal setting and action planning did you do during the learning experience? Choose the ONE option that most closely mirrors your experience.	*Proposed Standards* *Not shown to learners*
A	We did NOT set goals for how we would use what we learned in the future.	Alarming
B	We were GIVEN AN OPPORTUNITY to set goals for using what we learned.	Alarming
C	We were STRONGLY ENCOURAGED to set goals for using what we learned.	Unacceptable
D	We NOT ONLY set goals, but we were also encouraged to PLAN A TIME AND PLACE where we would begin to work toward those goals.	Acceptable
E	We set goals and created plans and BOTH WERE CHECKED by someone in authority (for example, our instructor) to ensure we had a strong set of goals and plans.	Superior

Note: Learners are NOT shown the text in the gray cells of this table.

As you can see from the answer choices, this question can send powerful stealth messages about what should be done with situation-action triggering.

Secondary Goal #3—Motivation to Apply

Learners who don't leave training strongly motivated to apply what they've learned are learners who are unlikely to use what they've learned in their work. Certainly, they are unlikely to bring to bear the energy and metacognitive effort needed to circumnavigate obstacles, marshal resources, and persevere against the wave of normal on-the-job distractions.

Fortunately, measuring our learners' motivation is fairly straightforward. Here is a good question.

Performance-Focused Learner Surveys

Question 114	
Question Rationale: *Used to determine the extent to which learners are motivated to apply what they've learned.*	
Regarding the topics taught, how motivated WILL YOU BE TO USE these concepts/skills in your work? CHOOSE ONE.	*Proposed Standards* Not shown to learners
A — My CURRENT ROLE DOES NOT ENABLE me to use what I learned.	Alarming
B — I will NOT MAKE THIS A PRIORITY when I get back to my day-to-day job.	Alarming
C — I will make this a PRIORITY—BUT A LOW PRIORITY when I get back to my day-to-day job.	Unacceptable
D — I will make this a MODERATE PRIORITY when I get back to my day-to-day job.	Unacceptable
E — I will make this a HIGH PRIORITY when I get back to my day-to-day job.	Acceptable
F — I will make this ONE OF MY HIGHEST PRIORITIES when I get back to my day-to-day job.	Superior
Note: Learners are NOT shown the text in the gray cells of this table.	

Note that only the highest levels of priority—Choices E and F—are deemed at least acceptable. I do this under the assumption that, if people don't prioritize the application of their learning, they are unlikely to follow through. Maybe I'm being too tough here; perhaps you can be more lenient. Still, it's my feeling that we instructors need more encouragement to consider learner motivation, not less.

In addition to targeting Motivation to Apply directly—as in the above question—we can also target its tertiary goals.

Motivation-to-Apply's Tertiary Goals

- Belief in the Value of Concepts

- Self-Efficacy
- Resilience

We will now look at each of these in turn.

Motivation to Apply—Tertiary Goal: Belief in the Value of Concepts

Although we as learning professionals might not like to admit it, learners may not always believe in the concepts we teach them. While this is more likely to be an issue in soft skills training, it can even be true for technical training. I'll never forget sitting in the back of a diversity-training program watching a participant who simply believed that his black colleagues were inferior and that he had every right to treat them as inferiors. Startling, yes!—but a worst-case example of how learners might not believe what we are teaching them. Generally, when people don't believe in the value of the concepts taught, they play along and we don't notice their objections.

We'd be fooling ourselves if we didn't think that beliefs weren't critical to people's motivation. Would you be motivated to put ideas into practice that you didn't believe in? I think not!

Performance-Focused Learner Surveys

Here's a question that can help you assess the strength of people's belief in the concepts taught.

Question 115
Question Rationale: *Used to determine the extent to which learners believe the key principles that were taught.*

	The following five principles provided the basis for this training course.	
	• Principle 1…	
	• Principle 2…	
	• Principle 3…	
	• Principle 4…	
	• Principle 5…	***Proposed Standards*** *Not shown to learners*
	You may believe in these deeply, or not at all. Rate each one on its importance to you.	
A	I BELIEVE DEEPLY in this principle.	Superior
B	I BELIEVE in this principle.	Acceptable
C	I CAN ACCEPT this principle.	Unacceptable
D	I DO NOT ACCEPT this principle.	Alarming
E	I BELIEVE DEEPLY that this principle IS FLAWED.	Alarming
Note: Learners are NOT shown the text in the gray cells of this table.		

Note that this question—because it asks learners to respond to each principle separately—will require a more advanced question type than a simple multiple-choice format. Fortunately, most good survey software can implement this kind of question easily.

If you're using paper-and-pencil learner surveys, you can create a grid with the principles down the left side and the answer choices represented in columns.

Note the standards recommended. It is not enough that people accept a principle. Our job as trainers is to help our learners believe deeply in the principles we teach.

Motivation to Apply—Tertiary Goal: Self-Efficacy

People's motivations are also tied to their sense of self-efficacy about whether they can implement what they want to implement. This is not a generalized sense of self-efficacy, but a self-efficacy tied to specific job skills.

Here's a question to measure self-efficacy.

Question 116 (Not Recommended for Use)		
Question Rationale: Used to determine the extent to which learners are confident that they learned what was taught.		
This training course was designed to teach you skills that you can use on the job. How confident do you feel that you can competently put these skills into practice?		*Proposed Standards* Not shown to learners
A	I AM EXTREMELY CONFIDENT that I can successfully use these skills.	Acceptable
B	I AM CONFIDENT that I can successfully use these skills.	Acceptable
C	I AM PARTIALLY CONFIDENT that I can successfully use these skills.	Unacceptable
D	I AM NOT VERY CONFIDENT that I can successfully use these skills.	Unacceptable
E	I HAVE ZERO CONFIDENCE that I can successfully use these skills.	Alarming
Note: Learners are NOT shown the text in the gray cells of this table.		

Performance-Focused Learner Surveys

Beware! Questions of this type—asking about a person's confidence in their own ability—are likely to suffer from extreme bias. Why? Because people are not always good at knowing what they're able to do—especially if they haven't been given true tests of their ability. The question above also suffers from using "Extremely Confident," "Confident," "Partially Confident," and so on, which are really Likert-like answer choices in disguise. Slightly better because the word "confident" is in the key descriptor, but still potentially too fuzzy for respondents to make clear distinctions. But let's put that aside to focus on the confidence issue.

I remember, as a young man, thinking I might have been a good baseball player if only I had started playing organized baseball earlier. One of the guys on my high school baseball team told me that, although I was the best softball player in our high school, he was a better baseball player. In my mind, I had talent but not enough baseball experience. These delusions of my youthful potential as a star baseball player were fueled by the fact that my skills had never been tested. Being good at stick ball and softball, it turns out, isn't an adequate indicator of one's baseball skills. Indeed, when, several years later, I found I could only throw a baseball at forty-seven miles per hour, when the average big leaguer easily threw over eighty miles per hour, I finally realized that my childhood beliefs in my baseball self-efficacy had been a warm-wash-of-summertime delusion.

Here's the tricky part about measuring self-efficacy and confidence as they relate to training. A training course that really challenges people in attempting new skills is actually less likely to prompt high ratings of self-efficacy than a course that gives minimal challenge—and thus minimal preparation. This is one reason awareness training is so popular even though it doesn't do very much to prepare learners for real on-the-job performance. Awareness training prompts people to believe in their own self-efficacy—even when they are not very skilled.

Are there better ways to measure self-efficacy than the question above? Perhaps; I'm not sure. Certainly, the question above might provide valid data if learners had previously been challenged with realistic job-related tasks. But, based on the question alone, we would have no way of knowing whether such challenges had been offered. If authentic challenges were offered by one instructor and not another, the question would likely produce biased results.

We are left with the question: Is there a way to measure self-efficacy that doesn't suffer from this inherent human bias? Here's my best attempt.

Question 117

Question Rationale: *Used to determine the extent to which learners are confident that they learned what was taught.*

How prepared are you to apply skills from this training to real work situations? Select as many as are true.		*Proposed Standards* *Not shown to learners*
A	I AM CONFIDENT I can successfully use these skills because during training I ACTUALLY USED THESE SKILLS IN DOING REAL WORK.	Superior
B	I AM CONFIDENT because the training challenged me MANY TIMES with practice on DIFFICULT WORK-RELATED TASKS.	Acceptable
C	I AM CONFIDENT because the training challenged me ONCE OR TWICE with practice on DIFFICULT WORK-RELATED TASKS.	Acceptable*
D	I AM CONFIDENT even though the training DID NOT PROVIDE much practice on DIFFICULT WORK-RELATED TASKS.	Unacceptable*
E	I AM NOT VERY CONFIDENT that I can successfully use these skills.	Alarming
F	I HAVE ZERO CONFIDENCE that I can successfully use these skills.	Alarming
Note: Learners are NOT shown the text in the gray cells of this table.		

Note the asterisks on the standards. I add these to remind you that different learning goals demand different standards. If the training were designed for a high-priority situation—for example, training salespeople to handle objections or soldiers how to clear a building—it would be unacceptable to give learners only one or two practice opportunities.

Given the challenge inherent in creating a question on self-efficacy, the question above is a pretty good attempt. Here's what I like about it. It shakes the learner into wakefulness. By hinting that there is a causal relationship between the amount of realistic challenge and one's competence level, learners are likely to be less cocksure of their own ability. Also, the question does a nice job of setting itself up to send valuable stealth messages. It specifically hints at the idea that real-world work challenges and extensive practice on difficult tasks help create skilled competence.

Motivation to Apply—Tertiary Goal—Resilience

Resilience is characteristic of people who will persevere in constructive efforts even when they face difficulties, obstacles, and misfortunes. While the traditional connotation of resilience involves a general long-term state of being, for our purposes, it's more helpful to see resilience as context specific. Indeed, a person might be resilient in applying one type of training to their work and nonresilient in applying another type of training.

The following question is designed to measure a person's sense of their own resilience.

Question 118 (Maybe Acceptable for Use)

Question Rationale: *Used to determine the extent to which learners will persevere in the face of obstacles.*

	Sometimes people—people just like you—will face obstacles or difficulties when they attempt to apply new learning to their jobs. How prepared are you to overcome such difficulties in terms of applying the skills from this training course? SELECT ALL THAT APPLY.	*Proposed Standards* *Not shown to learners*
A	In applying the learning from this course, I will persevere in the face of difficulties BECAUSE I BELIEVE STRONGLY in the ideas and skills taught.	Acceptable
B	I will persevere in the face of difficulties because the training prepared me for MANY OF THE DIFFICULT SITUATIONS I MAY FACE.	Acceptable
C	I will persevere in the face of difficulties because the training prepared me TO BE MENTALLY RESILIENT.	Acceptable
D	I will persevere in the face of difficulties because I HAVE COWORKERS WHO HAVE PLEDGED to support me in doing this.	Acceptable
E	I will persevere in the face of difficulties because MY BOSS HAS PLEDGED to provide guidance, support, and resources.	Acceptable
F	DESPITE NOT HAVING ANY OR MANY OF THESE HELPFUL SUPPORTS, I will persevere in the face of any difficulties I might face.	Unacceptable
G	I will work to apply the learning from this course, but I AM UNLIKELY TO PERSEVERE in the face of difficulties.	Unacceptable
H	I am UNLIKELY TO WORK TO APPLY the learning from this course.	Alarming

Note: Learners are NOT shown the text in the gray cells of this table.

Performance-Focused Learner Surveys

Note how this question uses the same strategy as the question immediately before it on self-efficacy. That is, it primes the respondent to think deeply about what causes—or what can influence—resilience. This design not only helps the learners make better decisions on this question, but it also sets up the question to send stealth messages about what is needed for learner resilience.

Again, this question can be used to send the message that we as workplace learning-and-performance professionals—and our colleagues on the business side—can play key roles in supporting learners in being resilient.

And again, we must be cautious when asking human beings to comment on their own traits. Question 118 may simply be asking too much of learners. Indeed, two wicked-smart folks who reviewed an early version of the manuscript questioned whether learners would be good at assessing their own perseverance. I've left the question in the book to let you, the reader, decide, but also because I think it's good to emphasize again how critical it is to consider learner decision-making capability when we design our questions. One quick fix to Question 118 above is to simply ask the learners about the supports they received in the training. See Question 119.

Question 119

Question Rationale: *Used to determine the extent to which learners will persevere in the face of obstacles.*

	Sometimes people—people just like you—will face obstacles or difficulties when they attempt to apply new learning to their jobs. What preparations did the course provide to help you deal with the obstacles you might face? SELECT ALL THAT APPLY.	*Proposed Standards* *Not shown to learners*
A	The training MOTIVATED ME TO BELIEVE STRONGLY in the importance of the concepts and skills taught in this course.	Acceptable
B	The training GAVE ME PRACTICE dealing with many of the difficult situations I might face in applying the learning.	Acceptable
C	The training gave me PRACTICE IN BEING MENTALLY RESILIENT in the face of obstacles.	Acceptable
D	The training prompted me to ENLIST COWORKERS to pledge to support me in applying the learning.	Acceptable
E	The learning team helped ENLIST MY BOSS to provide guidance, support, and resources.	Acceptable
F	The training did LITTLE OR NOTHING to help me overcome the workplace challenges I may face in applying the learning.	Unacceptable

Note: Learners are NOT shown the text in the gray cells of this table.

If calculating an acceptability index, we might consider it acceptable if respondents chose two or three of the acceptable responses. As always, you should base standards of acceptability on your own circumstances, while also negotiating with your key stakeholders.

Secondary Goal #4—After-Learning Follow-Through

The final of the four pillars is After-Learning Follow-Through. Like Remembering, it is difficult to measure directly on a learner survey but will ideally be measured instead through its tertiary goals.

After-Learning Follow-Through's Tertiary Goals

- Reminding Mechanisms
- Job Aids
- Supervisor Follow-Through

It is worth noting the obvious here—in case it's not obvious. These three tertiary goals are certainly not the only things we could measure regarding after-learning follow-through. For example, we might want to measure whether learners are required to complete a work project, whether they must report their results, or whether a training application goal-monitoring system is in place. You are certainly encouraged to create your own questions if they have particular relevance to your organization or training goals.

I'm going to focus on what I consider to be the three most important factors for successful after-learning follow-through. We will look at each of these in turn but, first, I'll convey a question that attempts to cover all these considerations in one learner-survey question.

Question 120 (The Longer Version)

Question Rationale: *Used to determine the extent to which learners will get support after the learning intervention.*

	After the course, when you begin to apply your new knowledge at your worksite, which of the following supports are likely to be in place for you? **SELECT AS MANY ITEMS** as are likely to be true.	***Proposed Standards*** *Not shown to learners*
A	MY MANAGER WILL ACTIVELY SUPPORT ME with key supports like time, resources, advice, and/or encouragement.	Acceptable
B	I will have my PROGRESS MONITORED BY MY MANAGER in applying the learning.	Acceptable
C	I will use a COACH OR MENTOR to guide me in applying the learning to my work.	Acceptable
D	I will have easy access to FELLOW LEARNERS to contact for guidance and support.	Acceptable
E	I will regularly receive support from a COURSE INSTRUCTOR to help me in applying the learning to my work.	Acceptable
F	I will be ENCOURAGED BY MY COWORKERS to apply the learning to real job tasks.	Acceptable
G	I will be given JOB AIDS like checklists, search tools, or reference materials to guide me in applying the learning to my work.	Acceptable
H	Through a LEARNING APP or other means, I will be PERIODICALLY REMINDED of key concepts and skills that were taught.	Acceptable
I	I will NOT get much direct support but will rely on my own initiative.	Unacceptable

Performance-Focused Learner Surveys

There are so many answer choices in the question above that some of your respondents may get glassy eyeballs and lose their ability to focus. A shorter version might be better. Below, I have chosen the items I think are generally most important—reducing the number of choices from nine to six. Of course, you may have specific circumstances where you want to emphasize some of the support options over others. As always, we should be strategic in our answer choices, considering the stealth messages we want to send.

Question 120 (The Shorter Version)	
Question Rationale: *Used to determine the extent to which learners will get support after the learning intervention.*	
After the course, when you begin to apply your new knowledge at your worksite, which of the following supports are likely to be in place for you? **SELECT AS MANY ITEMS** as are likely to be true.	*Proposed Standards* Not shown to learners
A — MY MANAGER WILL ACTIVELY SUPPORT ME with key supports like time, resources, advice, and/or encouragement.	Acceptable
B — I will use a COACH OR MENTOR to guide me in applying the learning to my work.	Acceptable
C — I will regularly receive support from a COURSE INSTRUCTOR to help me in applying the learning to my work.	Acceptable
D — I will be given JOB AIDS like checklists, search tools, or reference materials to guide me in applying the learning to my work.	Acceptable
E — Through a LEARNING APP or other means, I will be PERIODICALLY REMINDED of key concepts and skills that were taught.	Acceptable
F — I will NOT get much direct support but will rely on my own initiative.	Unacceptable
Note: Learners are NOT shown the text in the gray cells of this table. *If calculating an acceptability index, we might consider it acceptable if respondents chose two or three of the acceptable responses. As always, you should base standards of acceptability on your own circumstances, while also negotiating with your key stakeholders.*	

While utilizing a single question here is more efficient and less taxing than using three questions to get at all three tertiary goals, it may not be as effective as more-targeted questions. Perhaps even more important, it may not engender stealth messaging as clearly

Performance-Focused Learner Surveys

and strongly as separate questions would enable. While the questions above may be perfectly acceptable, when you look at the separate questions provided below, you'll see how much more clarity can be squeezed from these interactions. Of course, you will have to weigh precision against the downside of asking three questions instead of one. Also, consider being flexible—perhaps using the shorter question normally, but drill down occasionally on one or more of the specific after-learner supports.

We'll now turn to each of the tertiary goals of After-Learning Follow-Through, starting with reminding mechanisms.

After-Learning Follow-Through—Tertiary Goal: Reminding Mechanisms

Learners benefit from reminders for three primary reasons. First, learners forget, and reminders help them remember what they've learned. Second, reminders keep learners' goals for applying the new concepts fresh in mind so they are more likely to devote metacognitive planning and effort to learning application. Third, reminders can convey social pressure in terms of expected outcomes.

The following question is designed to measure whether reminding mechanisms are in place after learning events end.

Question 121

Question Rationale: *Used to determine the extent to which learners will receive reminders after the learning intervention.*

	We humans forget stuff. We even forget important concepts and skills we've learned in training. Being reminded can help us remember. Given what you've been told by your trainers, your boss, or your other coworkers, how do you expect to be reminded after this training ends? **SELECT ALL that apply.**	*Proposed Standards* *Not shown to learners*
A	MY MANAGER will periodically remind me of the concepts and skills that were taught.	Acceptable
B	A COURSE INSTRUCTOR will regularly be in touch with me to remind me of the concepts and skills that were taught.	Acceptable
C	I will be enrolled in an EMAIL LIST from which I will receive periodic reminders of the concepts and skills that were taught.	Acceptable
D	A LEARNING APP will periodically remind me of key concepts and skills that were taught.	Acceptable
E	I will be enrolled in WORK-RELATED PROJECTS with my fellow learners, where we will use the concepts and skills that were taught.	Acceptable
F	JOB AIDS and/or SIGNS that recount key concepts and skills from the learning will be posted in my worksite where I will regularly see them.	Acceptable
G	At this time, I know of NO reminders that I will receive.	Unacceptable

Note: Learners are NOT shown the text in the gray cells of this table.

If calculating an acceptability index, we might consider it acceptable if respondents chose two or three of the acceptable responses.
As always, you should base standards of acceptability on your own circumstances, while also negotiating with your key stakeholders.

Performance-Focused Learner Surveys

The question above will be especially relevant and valuable for training courses delivered long before the new information is actually needed. The longer the time between learning and application, the more forgetting will take place—and the more critical it will be to provide learners with reminders.

On the other hand, forgetting happens almost immediately regardless of the time delay between learning and application. Here's a thought experiment that will help make this clear. Suppose you teach your learners thirty key points. How many of these will they use on their first day back on the job? Let's say they'll use five. How many in the first week? Let's say ten more. This means your learners will have to remember—and keep fresh in mind—half of what they learned longer than a week. And what of the other fifteen learning points? Certainly, some of those points won't be needed in the first month after training. Won't they be forgotten without some sort of reminder? The bottom line here is that, even when a training course is delivered just in time, much of what was learned will have to be remembered over a long period of time—and thus reminders become critical.

After-Learning Follow-Through—Tertiary Goal: Job Aids

Fortunately, most of us recognize that remembering is not the only method to spur on-the-job performance. We can prompt behavior directly through job aids, checklists, performance support tools, and other prompts.

If we take a step back for a moment and reflect on human cognition, we can see that all human behavior is engendered through working memory—and there are two general conduits to working memory: remembering and prompting.[36] We, as human beings, can activate working memory either by retrieving information from long-term memory or by being prompted by external cues in our environment.

The Learning Landscape model—my way of diagramming the practical complexity of workplace learning—has this two-source working-memory conception at the heart of its structure. In the diagram that follows, I've highlighted this two-source (remembering and prompting) notion as the Working-Memory Trigger Zone.

---

[36] Although this two-source working-memory model is a simplification of very complex cognitive phenomena, for our purposes as learning professionals it represents underlying truths that have significant practical implications.

Chapter 7—Candidate Questions

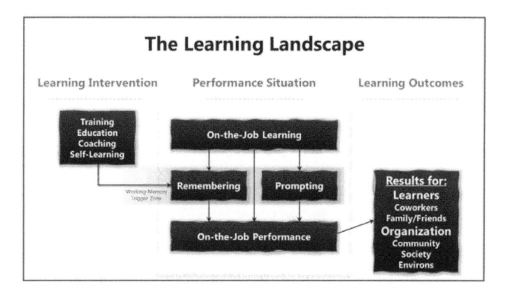

Although there are many prompts we could target on our learner surveys, I'm focusing mostly on job aids because these are the most popular—and the ones most likely to be used in conjunction with training programs.

Performance-Focused Learner Surveys

Here is a question we can use to measure the use of job aids in training.

Question 122	
Question Rationale: *Used to determine the extent to which learners will have job aids or other prompts to support themselves in applying what they learned.*	
Using job aids, checklists, or other prompts can be an effective way to ensure you properly apply skills to your job. Which of the following are true? **SELECT ALL that apply.**	***Proposed Standards*** *Not shown to learners*
A — We did NOT RECEIVE ANY WORTHWHILE job aids, checklists, or similar prompts to direct our on-the-job actions.	Alarming
B — We RECEIVED ONE OR MORE WORTHWHILE job aids, checklists, or similar prompts.	Unacceptable
C — During the course, we USED ONE OR MORE WORTHWHILE job aids, checklists, or similar prompts in REALISTIC PRACTICE EXERCISES.	Acceptable
D — Between sessions of the course, IN OUR WORKSITES, WE UTILIZED one or more WORTHWHILE job aids, checklists, or similar prompts IN A REAL-WORLD JOB TASK.	Superior
Note: Learners are NOT shown the text in the gray cells of this table. *If calculating an acceptability index, we might consider it acceptable if respondents chose two or three of the acceptable responses. As always, you should base standards of acceptability on your own circumstances, while also negotiating with your key stakeholders.*	

Note that Choice B—where our learners are just given job aids—is deemed unacceptable. This may surprise you, but the thinking is straightforward. Unless a job aid is actually used in a training course, it is not likely to be used on the job. (Nor will it engender context-based remembering, but that's another story.)

It may seem odd to ask about whether job aids are used in a training course, since we are the ones providing the training. *"Holy Dr. Bobo Doll, couldn't we just answer this question ourselves?"* That's a great query, dear reader, but the answer may be surprising. Yes, we as learning professionals can certainly answer this question ourselves. However, there are several difficulties with this tactic. What's designed into a course isn't always what is utilized with learners. For example, we may have developed a great job aid but, during our course, when we find time running short, we may only mention the job aid in passing. Also, learners may not notice the use of a job aid if we don't effectively communicate it—so it's important to gauge our learners' perceptions here. We also will want to be sure we are using job aids in the most beneficial way. Having a question on our learner survey forces us to avoid sliding into the comfort of denial. Furthermore, if we include this question, we send a stealth message to all our stakeholders about the importance of job aids and other prompting mechanisms. For every training session or every elearning program, our trainers and instructional designers will get feedback about job-aid use. In every training-effectiveness review by learning leaders, job-aid utilization will be examined. In every report to senior managers, they too will be reminded that job aids are a critical element of learning solutions. To reiterate, by including such questions on our learner surveys—even if we could answer the question ourselves with no assist from our learners—we unleash powerful ripples of guidance that remind all of us of our critical performance-focused responsibilities. Uplifting music fades . . .

After-Learning Follow-Through—Tertiary Goal: Supervisor Follow-up

Supervisors are organizational superglue. They have the power to keep organizational actors focused, to engender passionate effort and creativity, to troubleshoot problems, and to help coordinate disparate limbs of the organizational octopus.

They can also screw things up big time! We've all heard about this. "People don't quit their company; they quit their managers." "My supervisor wasn't born on planet Earth; he was born on Space Station Dilbert." Et cetera! Even these negative stories tell of the power of supervisors.

Supervisors are also powerful agents in training and development. As *Salas, Tannenbaum, Kraiger, and Smith-Jentsch said in their seminal research review:*

> [Researchers have] found that one misdirected comment by a team
> leader can wipe out the full effects of a training program. . . . What
> organizations ought to do is provide [supervisors] with information they

> *need to (a) guide trainees to the right training, (b) clarify trainees'
> expectations, (c) prepare trainees, and (d) reinforce learning.... (p. 83)*

Salas et al. further note that supervisors can increase trainees' motivation to engage in the learning process (p. 85).

> *After trainees have completed training, supervisors should be positive
> about training, remove obstacles, and ensure ample opportunity for
> trainees to apply what they have learned and receive feedback.... (p. 90)*

> *Transfer is directly related to opportunities to practice—opportunities
> provided either by the direct supervisor or the organization. (p. 90)*

The power of supervisors—or managers as they are often called—is highlighted in my recent review of the learning-transfer research.[37] In reviewing many meta-analyses and research reviews, it is clear that manager support is critical in training success.

---

[37] Thalheimer (2020).

Question 123 (The Long Version)

Question Rationale: Used to determine the extent to which learners' managers will support them in applying learning to their work.

	In what ways do you expect your supervisor will support you in applying what you learned to your job? SELECT ALL that apply.	**Proposed Standards** *Not shown to learners*
A	My supervisor will allow me to implement what I learned.	Acceptable
B	My supervisor will give me additional time if it is needed to implement what I learned.	Acceptable
C	My supervisor will give me additional resources if they are needed.	Acceptable
D	My supervisor will actively encourage me to implement what I learned.	Superior
E	My supervisor will coach me or find me a coach.	Superior
F	My supervisor will assign me with a work project where I will be expected to utilize my new knowledge and skills.	Superior
G	My supervisor will work with me to set goals for implementing what I learned.	Acceptable
H	My supervisor will monitor my progress in implementing what I learned.	Superior
I	My supervisor will ensure that I am provided with additional learning opportunities to deepen my understanding.	Acceptable
J	Unfortunately, my supervisor is not likely to provide much support to help me implement what I learned.	Unacceptable
K	Unfortunately, my supervisor is likely to make it more difficult for me to implement what I learned.	Alarming

If calculating an acceptability index, we might consider it acceptable if respondents chose at least two superior responses and two acceptable responses; also choosing neither the unacceptable nor alarming responses.

Performance-Focused Learner Surveys

Holy chocolate cannoli, Batman! Is that a freakin' great list of supervisor imperatives or what? This book may be more than just a book on learner surveys!

Seriously, though, that list is a great tool to educate supervisors about how they can maximize learning transfer application.[38] You, of course, could utilize such a list in a leadership-development course—but perhaps you don't have to, if you use this list in a learner-survey question and then feed the results back to your supervisors. Such stealth messaging will make the case for you and will make it over and over and over again—not just once as a typical leadership-development course might do. Of course, no harm in doing both!

On the other hand, the question above is an almost absurdly long question, so we might need to shorten it to make it palatable. I offer the shorter version below—essentially taking a guess at what supervisor behaviors are most important. Feel free to select your own options or rotate them periodically in and out of your question to ensure you're gauging important factors in your situation.

---

[38] "Transfer" is for training weenies like us—not for supervisors or other organizational stakeholders.

Question 123 (The Shorter Version)

Question Rationale: *Used to determine the extent to which learners' managers will support them in applying learning to their work.*

	In what ways do you expect your supervisor will support you in applying what you learned to your job? **SELECT ALL that apply.**	*Proposed Standards* *Not shown to learners*
A	My supervisor will get me whatever I need to implement what I learned (time, resources, the support of others, etc.)	Acceptable
B	My supervisor will coach me—fully supporting me in setting goals, providing guidance, and monitoring my progress.	Superior
C	My supervisor will assign me with a work project where I will be expected to utilize my new knowledge and skills.	Superior
D	My supervisor will actively encourage me to implement what I learned.	Acceptable
E	Unfortunately, my supervisor is not likely to provide much support to help me implement what I learned.	Unacceptable
F	Unfortunately, my supervisor is likely to make it more difficult for me to implement what I learned.	Alarming

Note: Learners are NOT shown the text in the gray cells of this table.

If calculating an acceptability index, we might consider it acceptable if respondents chose at least one superior response and one acceptable response, while also choosing neither the unacceptable nor the alarming responses. As always, you should base standards of acceptability on your own circumstances, while also negotiating with your key stakeholders.

Chapter Summary

Wow! So many great learner-survey questions! They make me wonder—perhaps they make you wonder, too—why we have relied on pathetic smile-sheet questions in the past. Honestly, I can't tell you. Perhaps tradition? Perhaps the easy face-validity of the old questions? I don't know but, for whatever reason, traditional smile-sheet questions were not designed with a performance focus. They were not designed with questions that enabled actionable results. They were not designed to send stealth messages.

The questions presented in this chapter may not always reach our ideals of perfection, but they're infinitely better than traditional smile-sheet questions. They're better because:

1. They are based on the learning research.
2. They help learners make better learner-survey decisions.
3. They are actionable.
4. They communicate more clearly to stakeholders.
5. They help us educate stakeholders through stealth messaging.
6. They use distinctive answer choices.

The wisdom underlying the structure of the four pillars was derived over more than a decade through in-depth research reviews and practical application. To make learning research usable and practical it must be simplified to its core elements. The four pillars—understanding, remembering, motivation to apply, and after-training follow-through—can't possibly encompass every factor relevant to the workplace learning landscape, but they encompass a huge percentage of what is practically important. By basing the questions on the four-pillar model, we will ensure that our learner surveys are focused on work performance and will produce actionable results.

Chapter 8
Special Purpose Questions

In the previous chapter, I outlined candidate questions based on the four-pillar model of training effectiveness—while simultaneously nudging us to think about our question designs more deeply. In this chapter, I offer additional candidate questions you may find relevant for particular situations or needs.

Testing the Viability of Our New Learner Survey Questions

The questions I'm recommending are powerful and effective, but they will also seem strange to many people. They are not Likert-like questions—the kinds we have experienced year after year. They utilize some odd-looking mechanisms—like capitalized words, extreme over-the-top answer choices, and standards for answer choices. Because they are new and unique, many will question them at first. That's fine! Indeed, you may be skeptical yourself!

The following question provides a compelling test. Use it when you are first rolling out your new sets of questions. I have used it with my clients many times. It just works! In my experience so far, this question demonstrates that learners like the new types of questions more than traditional learner-survey questions. In a pilot test I ran with two global organizations—one for-profit and one not-for-profit—about 80% of learners liked the new questions more than the old questions, and a full 90% liked the new questions more than or equal to the old style of questions. You may not get such overwhelming results, but I'm confident you'll find that most people like performance-focused learner-survey questions.

Performance-Focused Learner Surveys

Question 124—Question About the New Questions	
Question Rationale: *Used to assess whether learners accept a survey based on this new type of learner-survey question.*	
We're using a new type of question to get your feedback. Instead of using a scale from 1 to 5 or choices from strongly disagree to strongly agree, we're presenting questions with more specific answer choices. This question is an example. **How do you feel about these new questions?**	***Proposed Standards*** *Not shown to learners*

A	They HAVE ABOUT THE SAME LEVEL OF EFFECTIVENESS as the 1-to-5 questions or the strongly-disagree to strongly-agree questions.	Acceptable
B	They are BETTER because they GIVE ME MORE CLARITY about the choices I'm making.	Superior
C	They are WORSE because thinking through the answer choices TAKES MORE TIME.	Unacceptable
D	Their BENEFITS (BRINGING MORE CLARITY) OUTWEIGH their DOWNSIDES (TAKING MORE TIME).	Acceptable
E	Their BENEFITS (MORE CLARITY) ARE NOT WORTH the extra time required.	Unacceptable

Follow-Up Comment Question
In your own words, what do you like about these new questions? What do you dislike?
Note: Learners are NOT shown the text in the gray cells of this table.

For Webinars and Other Short Live Online Learning Programs

Webinars are useful for raising awareness. Most of the time, they are not much use for supporting skill development. The exception is when they focus on one or two small discrete skills with learners who already have some background or knowledge about the area discussed.

Let's focus here on the standard webinar. One of the biggest issues with standard webinars is that learners may not pay attention at a level that supports their comprehension. They may be multitasking, or distracted by their surroundings, or bored. Given this issue, we might want a question that gauges learner attention. I am repeating this question from earlier because it, too, is a special-purpose question—one focused on webinars.

Question 106—Question for Webinar-Like Learning *(Repeated from Earlier in the Book)*		
Question Rationale: Used after webinars or other live online learning sessions, to determine how well learner attention was maintained.		
Compared to most webinars (online meetings), how well did the session keep YOUR attention? **Select ONE choice.**		*Proposed Standards* Not shown to learners
A	I had a HARD TIME STAYING FOCUSED.	Alarming
B	My attention WANDERED AT A NORMAL LEVEL.	Unacceptable
C	My attention RARELY WANDERED.	Acceptable
D	I was very much SPELLBOUND throughout the session.	Superior/ Overconfident?
Note: Learners are NOT shown the text in the gray cells of this table.		
I use the word "spellbound" because it is over the top. The idea is to send a message to the respondents that they should choose this option only if the learning was exceedingly exceptional. Again, the meta-idea here is to encourage respondents to think deeply about their choices, not just select the "top" choices when they generally like the learning intervention. *But sometimes you or your stakeholders will balk at the over-the-top wording. In such a case, you might try to soften the exaggeration a little by using something like this for Choice D (suggested by Greg Druckman—learning professional in a large technology media company—as he and I brainstormed an alternative to "spellbound"): I was COMPLETELY FOCUSED throughout the session. Another alternative I once used: I was COMPLETELY RIVETED throughout the session. You will have to find the right balance for your learners and stakeholders—just try to keep some level of extraordinary in your "best" answer option (where you can).*		

But we might care about other things besides attention when it comes to webinars. How about a question specifically about the techniques used in the webinar?

Chapter 8—Special Purpose Questions

Question 125—Question About Webinar Techniques			
\multicolumn{3}{l}{*Question Rationale:* Used after webinars or other live online learning sessions, to determine which webinar methodologies were utilized effectively.}		
\multicolumn{3}{l}{**Which of the following methods were used effectively in the webinar you just experienced?** **SELECT ALL that were utilized EFFECTIVELY.**}		*Proposed Standards* Not shown to learners
A	POLLS were used—and used effectively.		Acceptable
B	CHAT was used effectively, enabling meaningful discussions between speaker and participants.		Acceptable
C	ANNOTATIONS were used effectively, enabling participants like me to communicate our perspectives.		Acceptable
D	BREAKOUT ROOMS were used effectively, enabling meaningful conversations between participants.		Acceptable
E	FILE DOWNLOADS were used effectively, giving us quick access to a document or media file that we viewed quickly and discussed further.		Acceptable
F	NONE OR TOO FEW of these tools were utilized, but the webinar WAS EFFECTIVE ANYWAY.		Unacceptable
G	NONE OR TOO FEW of these tools were utilized, and, as a result, the webinar WAS NOT EFFECTIVE ENOUGH.		Alarming
\multicolumn{3}{l}{Note: Learners are NOT shown the text in the gray cells of this table. If calculating an acceptability index, we might consider it acceptable if respondents chose three or four of the acceptable responses, while also NOT choosing the alarming response. As always, you should base standards of acceptability on your own circumstances, while also negotiating with your key stakeholders.}		

For Live Online Learning Programs

Online learning programs have all the same requirements as face-to-face programs, but, in addition, they come with technical requirements that affect learning. To assess these requirements, we can ask two questions—one focusing on the positive, one focusing on the negative.

Question 126—Live Online Learning (Positives)

Question Rationale: Used for online learning to assess the special requirements of the technology and the learning approach.

	SELECT UP TO THREE ITEMS—those that were most POSITIVE about the elearning experience.	*Proposed Standards* Not shown to learners
A	I found the program ESPECIALLY ENGAGING AND INTERESTING.	Acceptable
B	The program was EASY TO NAVIGATE.	Acceptable
C	The program WORKED without too many difficulties.	Acceptable
D	I liked that I could GO AT MY OWN PACE.	Acceptable
E	It was VERY VALUABLE to REVIEW CONTENT MORE THAN ONCE.	Acceptable
F	The program NICELY CHALLENGED ME WITH QUESTIONS and/or TASKS.	Acceptable
G	The elearning was AS GOOD OR BETTER THAN A CLASSROOM COURSE.	Acceptable
H	The CONTENT WAS HIGHLY CREDIBLE.	Acceptable
I	Overall, NONE OF THESE were that positive for me.	Alarming

Note: Learners are NOT shown the text in the gray cells of this table.

If calculating an acceptability index, we might consider it acceptable if respondents chose three or four of the acceptable responses, while also NOT choosing the alarming response.
As always, you should base standards of acceptability on your own circumstances, while also negotiating with your key stakeholders.

Question 127—Live Online Learning (Negatives)

Question Rationale: Used for online learning to assess the special requirements of the technology and the learning approach.

	SELECT UP TO THREE ITEMS—those that were most NEGATIVE about the elearning experience.	*Proposed Standards* Not shown to learners
A	I had SIGNIFICANT TECHNICAL PROBLEMS that made learning difficult.	Unacceptable
B	When learning online, I would much rather LEARN FROM A LIVE PERSON.	Unacceptable
C	I would much rather LEARN IN A CLASSROOM.	Unacceptable
D	The program ASKED TOO MANY QUESTIONS and/or REQUIRED TOO MANY TASKS.	Unacceptable
E	My current INEXPERIENCE WITH ELEARNING made it hard for me to use the program.	Unacceptable
F	The CONTENT WAS NOT AS CREDIBLE as I would have liked.	Unacceptable
G	I wish I were MORE ABLE TO DISCUSS things with others.	Unacceptable
H	I wish I were MORE ABLE to ASK QUESTIONS and learn from the answers.	Unacceptable
I	Overall, NONE OF THESE was a NEGATIVE for me.	Acceptable

Note: Learners are NOT shown the text in the gray cells of this table.

If calculating an acceptability index—and here, because the question focuses on negative results, it's a bit awkward—we might consider it acceptable if respondents chose UP TO two of the unacceptable responses, and/or chose the acceptable response.

As always, you should base standards of acceptability on your own circumstances, while also negotiating with your key stakeholders.

Of course, we can try to cram all these positives and negatives into one question, but we are likely to miss important considerations when we omit some of the options. Also, if we don't nudge our learners to consider all these issues—both positive and negative—they won't be able to fairly answer an open-ended question on their elearning experience either.

Question 128—Elearning Comment Question
Question Rationale: *Used to get rich feedback about the learners' elearning experience.*
In your own words, what about the elearning worked well for you, and what hurt your learning? Also, what would you recommend be done differently in the future?
Note: Learners are NOT shown the text in the gray cells of this table. *It's important on comment questions to give learners a relatively large answer block—to encourage them to write more than a few words.*

Yes! These three questions about elearning require a substantial investment by your learners! Because of this, you might choose to utilize these questions temporarily as you roll out a new elearning design—or periodically to give you occasional feedback.

Replacing the NPS (Net Promoter Score)

The Net Promoter Score or NPS is a popular marketing tool. It typically asks a question such as, "How likely are you to recommend Waldo's Wash-N-Wipes to your friends and family?" Unfortunately, many organizations are now using the NPS to evaluate training programs. This is ridiculous, of course! It's just lazy on our part as learning professionals to grab something from another field and misuse it to appease our stakeholders. Let's be professionals!

The NPS is not even universally accepted in the marketing field! You can check out the many criticisms of NPS for marketing purposes on Wikipedia.[39] But what about for learning and development? Can't we get valuable information from an NPS-like question such as, *"How likely is it that you would recommend this training course to a friend or*

---

[39] https://en.wikipedia.org/wiki/Net_Promoter

coworker?" No, we cannot! There are many problems with using an NPS-type question for learning:

- As I detailed earlier in the section on the autopsy for traditional smile sheets, learners are not always good judges of learning effectiveness. Asking them for their general recommendations leaves us with biased imperfect information.

- Learner judgments have been captured for decades in traditional smile sheets, and more than one scientific meta-analyses have found these types of judgments lacking. NPS is more of the same because it too focuses on general satisfaction.

- Because the NPS uses a fuzzy numeric scale, it exacerbates the biases already inherent in judgments of learning.

- The NPS focuses on a single dimension—the reputation of the course—when we know that learning is complex and must be measured using multiple criteria.[40]

- Finally, and most importantly, we must ask if other questions would be more useful than utilizing the NPS. The answer is clearly yes!

The NPS is clearly wrong for evaluating learning, but what happens when our stakeholders recommend it or demand it? What should we do? In a perfect world, where we could rely on the inherent power and credibility of our profession, we would tell them we don't use inadequate practices. We would tell them to buzz off—that we rate the NPS as a big fat zero on a zero to ten scale! That's maybe what we should do; but, if we're being more politic—if we are in a weaker position—we can suggest an improved NPS question like the one I recommend below. And, if we absolutely are required to use a more traditional NPS question, we should utilize it after a series of better questions and report out multiple overarching results—not just the NPS.

---

[40] Salas, Tannenbaum, Kraiger, & Smith-Jentsch (2012) cite Ford, Kraiger, and Merritt (2010) who found that *"researchers, authors, and practitioners are increasingly cognizant of the need to adopt a multidimensional perspective on learning [when designing learning measurement approaches]."*

The following NPS replacement question is better than the original because it hints at learning effectiveness and has more granularity between answer choices. And let me be clear: I don't recommend this as one of our highest priority questions; I recommend it only when circumstances call for a question about the reputation of our learning programs.

Question 129 – NPS Replacement

Question Rationale: Used as a replacement for learning-related Net-Promoter-Score questions.

	If someone asked you about the effectiveness of the learning experience, would you recommend the learning to them? CHOOSE ONE.	*Proposed Standards* *Not shown to learners*
A	The learning was INEFFECTIVE ENOUGH THAT I WOULD BE HESITANT to recommend it.	Alarming
B	The learning was NOT FULLY EFFECTIVE, BUT I would recommend it IF IMPROVEMENTS WERE MADE to the learning.	Unacceptable
C	The learning was NOT FULLY EFFECTIVE, BUT I would still recommend it EVEN IF NO CHANGES WERE MADE to the learning.	Unacceptable
D	The learning was EFFECTIVE, SO I WOULD RECOMMEND IT.	Acceptable
E	The learning was VERY EFFECTIVE, SO I WOULD HIGHLY RECOMMEND IT.	Superior

Note: Learners are NOT shown the text in the gray cells of this table.

For Conferences

Conferences are for learning. Yes, they are also for networking, career advancement, business development, and having a mental break from the day-to-day grind. But, at their center, conferences are about the learning. Many conferences use survey questions after each session. Many use surveys to assess the conference overall. Almost all use survey questions that are atrociously inadequate!

Chapter 8—Special Purpose Questions

I've helped a handful of conference organizers build more effective evaluation surveys, and I've talked with many other conference organizers. Some conference providers care greatly about whether their sessions and speakers are effective. Others don't really focus on effectiveness or don't know how to properly assess it. Indeed, many conference providers are hesitant about getting negative feedback about their conferences! I know because I've talked with them. They may believe that conference participants are not knowledgeable enough to evaluate expert speakers. They may be beholden to their speakers—people of some renown who may actively repel any feedback from the peasantry. Conference providers may not want their participants even considering that the sessions and speakers could be better. They want not even a whiff of negativity.

To me, this is all short sighted. As a learning professional, I believe that feedback—good and bad—is essential to learning and improvement. And, while it is true that human judgments are imperfect—and judgments of experts by non-experts can miss the mark—well-designed questions can ameliorate these issues. Also, let's be real. Not all conference speakers have indisputable expertise. Some have expertise but can't translate their knowledge into practical ramifications. Some are mediocre communicators. Some are arrogant, awkward, or inappropriate. Certainly, conference participants can effectively comment on these issues.

Two years ago, I cohosted my first conference, the L&D Conference 2020. Partnering with Matt Richter,[41] we wanted to create a new kind of conference in the L&D field—a conference designed specifically to support learning! It was magnificent! Beyond our expectations! It took place over six weeks with both live sessions and asynchronous online-anytime sessions—all designed to support participants in taking their new learning back into their workflows. We did it again this past summer—part of a global membership organization we formed, *The Learning Development Accelerator (known as LDA)*—so please sign up to join! The website is: https://LDAccelerator.com/.

Here's the thing. Since I was finally a conference provider myself, I could use better questions, and so we did. What was the motivation?

- Gather effectiveness data to assess our speakers' performance.

- Gather effectiveness data to benefit our speakers.

---

[41] President of the Thiagi Group.

- Gather effectiveness data to enable mid-course corrections (in a six-week conference, feedback can be used to improve the asynchronous sessions and improve the second running of our live sessions).

- Let our participants know we cared about their perspectives and their conference experience.

- Gather testimonials to market the conference in the future.

- Provide the session survey questions to speakers in advance to set expectations for what was expected of them.

- Support the brand messages we had for the conference (for example, that we cared about research and evidence-based content, that we expected asynchronous sessions to enable learning-in-the-workflow participant experiences, etc.).

We didn't meet all our goals, and some of our evaluation efforts fell short as we scrambled to create our first conference. Overall, however, these efforts did support our main goal—to help conference participants learn and utilize their learning in their work and in their lives.

I'm going to share some of the questions we used. The specific wording may not work for your conference, but the methodology will. The key is to create questions that (1) gather data you will actually use to make decisions, (2) send your stakeholders (speakers and participants) messages you need them to hear, and (3) support your brand. Remember: It's always good to get feedback on your questions from a learner-survey expert.

The two questions below were used for our live sessions. The first focuses on the session's strengths, the second on its weaknesses. It's beneficial to ask for the strengths and weaknesses separately because that sends a message to respondents that we care about both. Whereas a typical Likert-like scale pretends to give respondents an opportunity to provide negative feedback, the expectation of positivity makes honest criticism virtually impossible. If we want to hear the truth, we must explicitly ask for negative feedback.

Question 130 – Conference Session Strengths		
Question Rationale: Used to determine how well a conference session supported the attendees in gaining learning benefits they can utilize.		
STRENGTHS OF THIS SESSION. **For this session, what benefits did you get, if any?** **SELECT ALL THAT ARE TRUE FOR YOU!** **And PLEASE, do NOT just select them all unless they are all definitely true for you!**		*Proposed Standards* Not shown to learners
A	I learned NEW INFORMATION I can USE WITHIN THE NEXT MONTH.	Acceptable
B	I was exposed to ideas that significantly DEEPENED MY UNDERSTANDING of important learning and development topics.	Acceptable
C	I was provided with information that was aligned with SCIENTIFIC RESEARCH or supported with other compelling evidence.	Acceptable
D	I am confident in what I learned because the SPEAKER(S) WERE HIGHLY CREDIBLE.	Acceptable
E	UNFORTUNATELY, the information conveyed will NOT BE SUFFICIENTLY USEFUL to me.	Unacceptable
Note: Learners are NOT shown the text in the gray cells of this table. *If calculating an acceptability index, we might consider it acceptable if respondents chose two or three of the acceptable responses, while also NOT choosing the unacceptable response.* *As always, you should base standards of acceptability on your own circumstances, while also negotiating with your key stakeholders.*		

For our asynchronous sessions (those that were available 24/7 over six weeks), we added another answer option: *I have ALREADY USED WHAT I LEARNED to make at least some small, meaningful improvements in my work or in my life.* We added this question because we wanted these asynchronous sessions to encourage participants to use what they learned during the conference!

Question 131 – Conference Session Weaknesses

Question Rationale: *Used to determine whether the session avoided common pitfalls.*

		Proposed Standards *Not shown to learners*
	IMPROVEMENTS NEEDED. **To ensure our sessions are respectfully and effectively conducted, we'd like your feedback to point out areas of concern.** **PLEASE SELECT ANY THAT WERE TRUE about this session!**	
A	The session was GENERALLY WELL PRESENTED/ FACILITATED, with zero or only minor deficiencies.	Acceptable
B	The session was HARD TO FOLLOW; being boring, disorganized, or poorly communicated.	Unacceptable
C	The session too often felt like a SALES PRESENTATION rather than a discussion of ideas, tools, or practices.	Unacceptable
D	The session was TOO CONCEPTUAL, in a way that failed to inspire important insights or failed to provide practical value.	Unacceptable
E	The session shared a distracting amount of dubious information; info that is NOT SUPPORTED BY RESEARCH or EVIDENCE.	Unacceptable
F	The session was too often CONDESCENDING OR DISRESPECTFUL to participants.	Unacceptable

Note: Learners are NOT shown the text in the gray cells of this table.

If calculating an acceptability index—and here, because the question focuses on negative results, it's a bit awkward—we might consider it acceptable if respondents chose UP TO one of the unacceptable responses, and/or chose the acceptable response.

As always, you should base standards of acceptability on your own circumstances, while also negotiating with your key stakeholders.

For our online-anytime sessions, we added this answer option: *The session did not motivate me enough to TRY THINGS OUT in my work or in my life.* Again, we wanted to encourage session designs that prompted participants to try things out in their work—and we wanted to gather data on whether these learning-in-the-workflow efforts were being supported by our speakers. As you can see, you can ask different questions or highlight different ideas in your answer choices, depending on what data you want to gather and what behaviors you want to encourage.

These two conference questions gave us great data, but also helped send stealth messages about our conference expectations. They also supported the brand image we wanted to convey around (1) providing evidence-aligned information, (2) enabling and nudging attendees to use what they've learned in their work, (3) providing effective learning experiences, and (4) creating an environment that is enjoyable, inspiring, and respectful.

Let me switch gears. For online learning, or in any situation where learners are not a captive audience—where they can engage fully or hardly at all—you may want to get a sense of how much of the learning they attended or how involved they were in the learning.

Performance-Focused Learner Surveys

For our online conference-session surveys, we added the following question to gauge the level of people's engagement.

Question 132 – Amount of Engagement			
Question Rationale: Used to differentiate between participants who just sampled the session versus those who were more engaged.			
How much did you engage this session?			***Proposed Standards*** *Not shown to learners*
A	I just SKIMMED the content.		Acceptable
B	I engaged in LESS THAN HALF of the content.		Acceptable
C	I engaged in MOST of the content.		Acceptable
D	I engaged in ALL the content.		Acceptable
E	I was FULLY ENGAGED, often returning to review content, share ideas, or continue discussions.		Acceptable
Note: Learners are NOT shown the text in the gray cells of this table. *Note that all the responses are acceptable. With multiple conference sessions, it's perfectly okay that participants are sampling some sessions. The point of this question is to do further analyses based on its results.*			

We can use this question in two ways. First, we can look directly at the results of the question. This is not very useful for a conference like ours where we offered hundreds of sessions, because it can be just as valuable if someone skims the session as if they engage it fully. If they skim, they could quickly decide that they already know the content or it's not relevant to them currently. By skimming, participants could free their time to focus on other sessions that are more useful to them. A better use of this question is to use it to look at other results. You might divide session participants into "highly engaged" versus "less engaged" and see if there were differences in their responses on other questions. For example, you might hope the highly-engaged participants would utilize what they've learned in their work. If they didn't, you'd know the engagement was not as useful as it might have been. More simply, you might ignore most of the data from people who just skimmed the session—perhaps only looking at their criticisms to see what pushed them away. Finally, this type of sorting question could prove valuable to a speaker who is looking through the data individual-by-individual. For example, when they read a comment, they might have more perspective on the response by looking to see what level of engagement the person gave to the session.

We also used three comment questions for the online-anytime asynchronous sessions:

- What was great? What about the content or design was particularly helpful to you?

- What about the content or design could have been better? Your constructive feedback can be particularly helpful!

- Anything else we should have asked about? Anything else you want to tell us?

For our live sessions, to keep things short and sweet, we only asked one comment question (after three forced-choice questions):

- What was great? What was bad? What would you recommend be improved for next time?

All the questions above were designed as session feedback questions. I also created a conference evaluation survey to get people's overall impressions of their conference experience. The conference evaluation included about 20 questions and took an average of 20 minutes to complete. Because this survey was focused on the complete six-week event, the time investment of participants was rather long, and the focus of the questions was different from the session-feedback questions. We wanted to get a sense of the kinds of sessions that worked for people, their assessment of the learning, the networking, the speakers, the technology platforms in use, etc. We also wanted to get an overall sense of their satisfaction.

Here is, probably, the most important question we asked:

Question 133 – Overall Conference Quality		
Question Rationale: *Used to determine how well people liked the quality of the conference.*		
Overall, how would you rate the QUALITY OF THE LEARNING EXPERIENCES provided by the L&D Conference 2020?		*Proposed Standards* *Not shown to learners*
A	Not good enough.	Alarming
B	Mediocre. Worse than most conferences.	Alarming
C	Average.	Unacceptable
D	Good. Better than most conferences.	Acceptable
E	Outstanding. Much better than most conferences.	Superior
F	The L&D Conference 2020 was BY FAR THE BEST conference I ever attended!	Brilliant
Note: Learners are NOT shown the text in the gray cells of this table.		

We created the L&D Conference 2020 with the hope of improving on traditional in-person conferences. More than 90% of respondents rated the conference as better than most conferences. Below are the full results for that question.

Chapter 8—Special Purpose Questions

L&D Conference Results		
Overall, how would you rate the QUALITY OF THE LEARNING EXPERIENCES provided by the L&D Conference 2020?		***Actual Results***
A	Not good enough.	0%
B	Mediocre. Worse than most conferences.	1%
C	Average.	9%
D	Good. Better than most conferences.	33%
E	Outstanding. Much better than most conferences.	28%
F	The L&D Conference 2020 was BY FAR THE BEST conference I ever attended!	29%
Note: Learners are NOT shown the text in the gray cells of this table.		

Matt and I were thrilled with these results, but we also know we were given the benefit of people's generosity. This was a first-time event. We did it during the early stages of the global coronavirus pandemic. Lots of the conference participants were already fans of ours or of our speakers. Also, we received completed surveys from approximately one-third of our conference participants—better than most conferences, but still a percentage that may augur an unrepresentative sampling of the full population of participants. I tell you this story, first, to brag and to invite you to join future LDA conferences, but, just as importantly, to highlight the importance of context in determining what story the data might be telling.

Here's a question, presented below, we used to ask people which type of sessions they liked the most.

Performance-Focused Learner Surveys

Question 134 – Preference for Session Type (Positive)	
Question Rationale: *Used to determine how well people liked the quality of the conference.*	
Which kind of sessions were the most valuable to you? Pick UP TO FIVE. Yes! We know this may be difficult. Don't worry, we'll give you a comment question to help you add perspective around your answers.	***Proposed Standards*** *Not shown to learners*
A	ON-DEMAND Asynchronous Sessions	Acceptable
B	LIVE SPEAKER PRESENTATIONS	Acceptable
C	LIVE PANELS	Acceptable
D	LIVE DEBATES	Acceptable
E	LIVE ROUNDTABLES	Acceptable
F	LIVE NETWORKING Sessions	Acceptable
G	LIVE 99-SECOND PRESENTATIONS	Acceptable
H	LIVE QUIZ SHOWS	Acceptable
I	The CROWDTHINKING Project on L&D Professionalization	Acceptable
J	PRE-RECORDED VIDEOS of L&D SUPERSTARS	Acceptable
K	RECORDED SESSIONS from the conference	Acceptable
L	NONE of the sessions were valuable to me	Unacceptable
Note: Learners are NOT shown the text in the gray cells of this table.		

We followed this question immediately with one that posed the opposite—enabling our respondents to highlight types of sessions they really did not like. This was important because it's not good enough to know just what people liked. We also needed to know if there were any strong negative feelings for any of the types of sessions. Here is the negative version of the question above:

\multicolumn{3}{c}{**Question 135 – Preference for Session Type (Negative)**}
\multicolumn{3}{l}{*Question Rationale:* Used to determine how well people liked the quality of the conference.}
\multicolumn{2}{l	}{**Are there any session types that you'd recommend we get rid of if we did a conference like this again?** **Only up to five choices please!**}	**Proposed Standards** *Not shown to learners*
A	ON-DEMAND Asynchronous Sessions	Unacceptable
B	LIVE SPEAKER PRESENTATIONS	Unacceptable
C	LIVE PANELS	Unacceptable
D	LIVE DEBATES	Unacceptable
E	LIVE ROUNDTABLES	Unacceptable
F	LIVE NETWORKING Sessions	Unacceptable
G	LIVE 99-SECOND PRESENTATIONS	Unacceptable
H	LIVE QUIZ SHOWS	Unacceptable
I	The CROWDTHINKING Project on L&D Professionalization	Unacceptable
J	PRE-RECORDED VIDEOS of L&D SUPERSTARS	Unacceptable
K	RECORDED SESSIONS from the conference	Unacceptable
L	I don't want to target any of these for removal	Acceptable
\multicolumn{3}{c}{*Note: Learners are NOT shown the text in the gray cells of this table.*}

Note that, in both the positive and negative versions of the questions above, we asked respondents to select up to five items. We also set our survey tool to prevent people from selecting more than five items. I did this for a couple of reasons. First, with so many answers, allowing only five choices makes the question easier to answer—less cognitive load. Indeed, usually, for these types of questions, I recommend allowing up to three answer choices. Here, more choices were needed to avoid annoying conference participants who likely experienced many session types. Second, by limiting the number of responses, I hoped to nudge respondents to process the answer choices fully and not just select all the items. Again, we must do everything we can to ensure respondents are fully engaged when they answer our questions. When people think deeply about our questions and answer choices, we get better data.

Finally, note that we warned respondents they would get a comment question after they completed the forced-choice question *"to help you add perspective around your answers."* This was intended to make them comfortable answering the rather extensive forced-choice questions—helping them avoid any worries that the answer choices don't capture the nuances they experienced. Here is the follow-up question:

Question 136 – Preference for Session Type (Comments)
Question Rationale: *To get fuller perspectives on conference participants' views of the session types they liked and disliked.*
Want to clarify your answers from the two questions just above? Do you want to share any specific thoughts about any of the session types offered?   **Any recommendations you would make to us?**
Note: Learners are NOT shown the text in the gray cells of this table.
It's important on comment questions to give learners a relatively large answer block—to encourage them to write more than a few words.

About 40% of respondents added comments to provide a richer perspective on their answers. Many of the answers were very insightful. More than one person said the debaters were too deferential to each other. Many people said the variety was great, so why limit it. Many people told us our open presentations (where anybody could make a two-minute presentation) were too short—even if they were fun and engaging from a networking perspective. Several people told us that one of our special initiatives was unworkable. Many people said they couldn't attend so many sessions, but they were happy with the sessions they could attend. Getting these important insights would not have happened without combining forced-choice questions and comment questions!

Here's what to remember: Combining forced-choice questions with comment questions is a powerful way to push respondents to think about issues and provide perspectives that get valuable data. The two forced-choice questions above prompted conference participants to think about what they liked and what they didn't. It reminded them of the types of sessions they might have experienced. Then, it asked them for further perspective. Without the forced-choice questions, their open-ended responses to the comment questions would not have been as well informed. I have often called these "hybrid questions," implying that a forced-choice question followed by a comment question is one question working together. This is kind of misleading even though the term "hybrid question" is compelling—because, really, a hybrid question is two questions used in combination, working together to produce better data.

Wow! That was a long section on conference learner-survey questions. Let me quickly summarize. First, performance-focused learner-survey questions can be used for conferences to get much better data. They can support conference organizers in nudging their speakers to create more effective sessions. They can bring value to speakers to help them improve their performance. They can support a conference's brand by sending messages about the values and mission of the conference.

For Mentoring, Coaching, Managing, and Tutoring Relationships

One-on-one relationships are a driving force in human behavior—and especially in human learning and development. Yes, we are social animals, but our most important social connections are made between us and one other person. Think marriage, friendships, and (go ahead) think about lovemaking too! Yes, we can do all these things in groups—it's good fun to imagine—but mostly we do these things person to person. It's the same when we try to develop ourselves. We find a coach, or a mentor, or a tutor. Or, we have a boss or a coworker who takes us under his or her wing and lifts us up.

These nurturing relationships can be great, but let's get real. A lot of us aren't as good at coaching, mentoring, managing, or tutoring as we could be. We may not be trained or trained adequately. Some of our instincts might be wrong. Those we intend to serve may be so grateful or shy or kind that they avoid giving us the feedback we need to get better.

Performance-Focused Learner Surveys

Probably the best thing we could do to improve is to ask for feedback from those we try to coach, mentor, manage, or tutor. But it's painful or anxiety-producing and we tend to avoid asserting ourselves to get honest feedback. Ideally, we build trusting relationships—more of a two-way communication than a soliloquy of wisdom. We can do this for ourselves and get the feedback we need to improve; but, to support others who are having these nurturing relationships, we can use a short set of survey questions. I'm going to use a mentoring program as an example.

Question 137			
Question Rationale: Used to assess where a mentoring relationship stands on a timeline from not yet started through to an after-mentoring relationship.			
How far has your mentoring relationship progressed to date? Select ONE ITEM ONLY.			*Proposed Standards** Not shown to learners
A	It never really got started.		Alarming
B	We set expectations.		Unacceptable
C	We built rapport.		Unacceptable
D	We focused on my work and development.		Acceptable
E	We transitioned to an after-mentoring relationship.		Acceptable
Note: Learners are NOT shown the text in the gray cells of this table.			
* The standards here would have to be adjusted based on the amount of time the mentors and mentees have had to develop their relationship. The standards above assume a substantial amount of time has passed from the beginning of the mentoring initiative.			

This question would not be used alone but is designed to give an indication of how well the mentoring relationship has progressed at a particular time. Indeed, this is the type of question that could be used at multiple times to track the progress of a mentoring initiative.

Chapter 8—Special Purpose Questions

Question 138		
Question Rationale: Used to get an idea from the mentor's perspective on the types of activities that have been utilized in the mentoring relationship.		
Which of the following have you and/or your mentee done? We'd like to understand what's worked and what did not, and particularly on how we might improve our instructions and recommendations. SELECT ALL THAT ARE TRUE!		*Proposed Standards* Not shown to learners
A	We created a mentoring contract.	Acceptable
B	We planned our mentoring work around the mentee's priorities and goals.	Acceptable
C	We have had mentoring meetings on a regular basis.	Acceptable
D	We have had mentoring meetings not regularly, but periodically.	Unacceptable
E	We discussed the mentee's results on the Self-Assessment Questionnaire (the one indexed on our "Expectations of Managers" page).	Acceptable
F	We developed a trusting relationship.	Acceptable
G	We did NOT do any of these things.	Alarming
Note: Respondents are NOT shown the text in the gray cells of this table.		
If calculating an acceptability index, we might consider it acceptable if respondents chose at least three of the acceptable responses and neither the unacceptable nor alarming responses. Or you could also consider it acceptable if respondents who chose the unacceptable item, also choose at least four of the acceptable items while avoiding the alarming item.		
As always, you should base standards of acceptability on your own circumstances, while also negotiating with your key stakeholders.		

Performance-Focused Learner Surveys

Note that the question stem says, *"We'd like to understand what's worked and what did not, and particularly how we might improve our instructions and recommendations."* This sends a signal to respondents that we are not judging them as much as we are judging our performance as learning professionals. Because people tend to want to look good in the eyes of others, we as question writers need to do what we can—even if it may not be enough—to lower the temperature and emphasize that we are focused on our own improvements. This is not needed in every question but is beneficial in questions that ask people to judge their own behaviors.

Note also that this question asks the mentors what they thought. We can also ask the mentees a corresponding question.

	Question 139	
\multicolumn{3}{	l	}{*Question Rationale:* Used to get an idea from the mentee's perspective on the types of activities that have been utilized in the mentoring relationship.}
\multicolumn{2}{|l|}{**Which of the following have you and/or your mentor done? We'd like to understand what's worked and what did not, and particularly on how we might improve our instructions and recommendations. SELECT ALL THAT ARE TRUE!**}	*Proposed Standards* Not shown to learners
A	We created a mentoring contract.	Acceptable
B	We planned our mentoring work around my priorities and goals.	Acceptable
C	We have had mentoring meetings on a regular basis.	Acceptable
D	We have had mentoring meetings not regularly, but periodically.	Unacceptable
E	We discussed my results on the Self-Assessment Questionnaire (the one indexed on our "Expectations of Managers" page).	Acceptable
F	We developed a trusting relationship.	Acceptable
G	We did NOT do any of these things.	Alarming

Note: Respondents are NOT shown the text in the gray cells of this table.

If calculating an acceptability index, we might consider it acceptable if respondents chose at least three of the acceptable responses and neither the unacceptable nor alarming responses. Or you could also consider it acceptable if respondents who chose the unacceptable item, also choose at least four of the acceptable items while avoiding the alarming item.

As always, you should base standards of acceptability on your own circumstances, while also negotiating with your key stakeholders.

Performance-Focused Learner Surveys

By getting responses from both mentors and mentees, we can reality-check the data and ensure it paints an accurate picture.

What if we create a handbook to help mentors be more effective? Wouldn't it make sense to find out how useful it is? Also, whether it is used at all?

Question 140			
Question Rationale: Used to determine how much the Handbook for Mentors was used by the mentors.			
How closely did you use the document, *Handbook for Mentors*? Choose ONE.			*Proposed Standards* Not shown to learners
A	I did NOT use it much.		Alarming
B	I read it once or twice.		Unacceptable
C	I referred to it regularly.		Acceptable
D	I used it quite often to guide my mentoring efforts.		Superior
Note: Learners are NOT shown the text in the gray cells of this table.			

It might be tempting to measure both usage and value in the same question, but a cleaner way is to use two questions. This first question above focuses on how much the *Handbook* was used. The second question below focuses on whether the mentors found it valuable.

Question 141	
Question Rationale: Used to determine mentors' perspectives on the value of the Handbook for Mentors.	

How valuable was *Handbook for Mentors* for you? Choose ONE.			*Proposed Standards* *Not shown to learners*
	A	Extremely valuable.	Acceptable
	B	Very valuable.	Acceptable
	C	Somewhat valuable.	Unacceptable
	D	Not at all valuable.	Alarming

Follow-up Comment Questions
HOW EFFECTIVE. Please describe how the Handbook was effective for you.
HOW INEFFECTIVE. Describe how the Handbook was not as effective as it could have been. We need to hear from you so we can make any needed improvements.
Note: Learners are NOT shown the text in the gray cells of this table.

"OMG. Dr. Will! You used Likert-like answer choices." Yes! I did! Very observant of you—even if I put the words in your mouth. Maybe I could have come up with a question that highlighted the many ways a handbook could be effective and ineffective. Maybe my mind's little hobgoblins were foolishly playing havoc; but neither I nor my client could come up with better. Sometimes, to be self-reliant, we must be pragmatic. In the question as written, the dangers of Likert-like fuzziness are lessened by using words that are more concrete than "strongly agree," etc. We ask about the value of the *Handbook*—how valuable it was. More importantly, the two follow-up comment questions enable us to learn what we need to learn, eliciting details and specifics to help us discern the good and bad of the *Handbook for Mentors*.

Performance-Focused Learner Surveys

We also might want to get a sense of how much effort the mentors made. Here's a question that asks them to gauge their own level of effort.

Question 142	
Question Rationale: *Used to determine mentors' level of effort.*	
How would you rate your effort as a mentor?	***Proposed Standards*** *Not shown to learners*
A I wish I had put more into it.	Unacceptable
B I did enough to create some value for my mentee.	Unacceptable
C I worked hard to create some value for my mentee.	Acceptable
D I was well-organized and worked hard to create maximum value for my mentee.	Superior
Note: Learners are NOT shown the text in the gray cells of this table.	

Finally, because mentoring programs are often sold to potential mentors as providing value to them as well as their mentees, we might want to get a reality check on the benefits they perceived.

Question 143

Question Rationale: Used to find out if the mentors felt they got benefits from being an mentor, and what types of benefits.

	What benefits, if any, did the mentoring experience provide to you? **SELECT ALL THAT ARE TRUE. PLEASE don't just choose all the positive responses unless they are truly true!**	*Proposed Standards* *Not shown to learners*
A	Considering everything, it was NOT worth the time and effort required.	Unacceptable
B	It helped me reflect on my own skills and competencies.	Acceptable
C	It helped me understand how other people experience the organization.	Acceptable
D	I found it rewarding to help my mentee.	Acceptable
E	It helped me feel more connected.	Acceptable
F	The benefits I gained were worth the time and effort.	Acceptable

Note: Learners are NOT shown the text in the gray cells of this table.

If calculating an acceptability index, we might consider it acceptable if respondents chose three or more of the acceptable responses while not choosing the unacceptable response.

As always, you should base standards of acceptability on your own circumstances, while also negotiating with your key stakeholders.

To summarize, in this section, I used the example of a mentoring program to show how learner-survey questions can be used to provide insight and feedback. These types of questions could be used to help managers and direct reports improve the effectiveness of their one-on-ones. They could be used to help tutors or coaches perform better. As always, try to find a measurement expert—one who knows how to write good performance-focused survey questions—to give you a reality check on the questions you develop or to work with you from the beginning to develop your question sets.

For Examining Values in Action

When values are demonstrated through a person's actions, they convey meaning, they educate, they induce learning. Yes, like all learning events, they can do this imperfectly or weakly, but, still, values demonstrated in action are learning events—and, as such, they can be examined through survey questions. In the earlier section on sending stealth messages, I shared a question that directly asks learners about the values exemplified in the learning.

Question 144		
Question Rationale: Used to determine the extent to which the organization's values were exemplified in the learning intervention.		
We at Good-For-All strive to be a values-driven organization in all that we do—and this is important in our learning activities as well. **How did this workshop exemplify or fail to exemplify Good-For-All's values? Choose one answer.**		*Proposed Standards* Not shown to learners
A	Significant aspects of the workshop WERE DIRECTLY CONTRARY to Good-For-All's values.	Alarming
B	The workshop WAS NEUTRAL in regard to Good-For-All's values—it neither encouraged nor discouraged such values.	Unacceptable
C	Significant aspects of the workshop DIRECTLY EXEMPLIFED Good-For-All's values.	Acceptable
D	The workshop WAS EXCEPTIONAL IN EXEMPLIFYING Good-For-All's values.	Superior
Note: Learners are NOT shown the text in the gray cells of this table.		

Of course, there may be specific values we want to target. In the next question, we look at belongingness—an important goal in our work around diversity, equity, and inclusion.

Question 145

Question Rationale: Used to determine how well the learning intervention helped people feel a sense of belonging to the whole group.

How much did you feel a part of the sales team during the workshop? Choose AS MANY ANSWERS as are true for you.		*Proposed Standards* *Not shown to learners*
A	In terms of feeling part of the sales team, I DID NOT FEEL MOVED one way or the other during the workshop.	Unacceptable
B	At times I felt a SENSE OF DISTANCE from other members of the sales team.	Alarming
C	Overall, I felt a strong sense of being a VALUED MEMBER of the sales team.	Acceptable
D	At times I felt SINGLED OUT as someone who was different from others on the sales team.	Alarming
E	Overall, I felt a SENSE OF SOLIDARITY with my fellow members of the sales team.	Acceptable

Follow-up Comment Question:

In your own words, how would you assess the workshop design and how it was conducted in making you feel a part of the group?

What was done well to make you feel valued and respected?

What could have been done better?

Note: Learners are NOT shown the text in the gray cells of this table.

If calculating an acceptability index, we might consider it acceptable if respondents chose at least one of the two acceptable responses while not choosing the unacceptable or alarming responses.

As always, you should base standards of acceptability on your own circumstances, while also negotiating with your key stakeholders.

Performance-Focused Learner Surveys

Note that I added a follow-up comment question above to enable learners to give a fuller accounting of how the workshop supported them in feeling a sense of belonging. This seems important here for two reasons—first, because we're dealing with subtle human emotions; second, because the follow-up question can assess the factors in the workshop that made a difference.

For Determining Topic Relevance

Here's a question that can help us get a sense of what topics our learners found most relevant. It also has the added advantage of nudging learners to take action when they get back to work. Below, I use examples from the content of my *Presentation Science Boot Camp*[42], an online workshop that teaches train-the-trainer presentation skills.

---

[42] The Presentation Science Boot Camp website: https://www.presentationscience.net/.

Chapter 8—Special Purpose Questions

Question 146		
Question Rationale: *Used to determine the topics learners felt were most immediately relevant for them.*		
Which of the following Presentation Science slide-redesign techniques will you WORK HARDEST ON over the next month, if any? CHOOSE THE THREE ITEMS that will be most important for you in your next few presentations?		*Proposed Standards* *Not shown to learners*
A	[Example] Turning my bullet points into objects.	Acceptable
B	[Example] Avoiding the use of a logo on every slide.	Acceptable
C	[Example] Maximizing slide geography.	Acceptable
D	[Example] Showing slide objects one at a time.	Acceptable
E	[Example] Utilizing white space to make my slide elements pop out.	Acceptable
F	It is UNLIKELY that I will be able use any of these methods over the next month.	Unacceptable
Note: Learners are NOT shown the text in the gray cells of this table. *If calculating an acceptability index, we might consider it acceptable if respondents chose any of the acceptable responses while also avoiding the unacceptable response.* *As always, you should base standards of acceptability on your own circumstances, while also negotiating with your key stakeholders.*		

For Determining Why Learners Chose to Enroll

Here's a question—modified somewhat here and presented below—that I've used to determine why my learners chose to attend one of my workshops.

Performance-Focused Learner Surveys

Question 147		
Question Rationale: Used to determine the reasons that compelled learners to enroll in the learning event.		
What were you hoping to accomplish by taking this workshop? SELECT ALL THAT ARE TRUE for you.		*Proposed Standards* Not shown to learners
A	I just wanted to LEARN SOMETHING NEW.	Acceptable
B	I wanted to LEARN FROM Will Thalheimer.	Acceptable
C	I wanted to be able to CREATE MORE EFFECTIVE LEARNER SURVEYS.	Acceptable
D	I wanted to REALITY-CHECK our current learner-survey practices.	Acceptable
E	I was ENCOURAGED TO ATTEND by one or more people.	Acceptable
F	I was told I HAD TO ATTEND.	Acceptable
G	I DID NOT WANT to attend but was PLEASANTLY SURPRISED by the value I got out of it.	Acceptable
H	I DID NOT WANT to attend and overall I DID NOT get enough value from the time spent.	Unacceptable
Note: Learners are NOT shown the text in the gray cells of this table. If calculating an acceptability index, we might consider it acceptable if respondents chose any of the acceptable responses, and avoided choosing the unacceptable response. As always, you should base standards of acceptability on your own circumstances, while also negotiating with your key stakeholders.		

Here's a question for you. Is the question above worth having? Seriously, think about it. The data can be valuable for me as I think about how to market the workshop, but the general principle is the following: If we don't use the data, we shouldn't be asking the question.

It's easy to see that we could do an in-depth data analysis where we look at people's responses to *other* questions in light of their responses to this question. For example, we might look at responses by comparing the Thalheimer groupies to professionals who still haven't swallowed the magic elixir.[43] We might compare results for people who wanted to attend versus those who were required to attend or those who just wanted to learn something new. The truth is, I rarely go back and do these analyses. To me, so far, the cost benefits haven't been worth it. You may have stakeholders who would find value in these breakdowns, but most organizations don't do these second-order calculations.

Note the two choices at the end of the question. Workshop participants choosing one of these would be telling us they did not originally want to attend. Those choosing the first of these options would be telling us they were pleasantly surprised and found value in the workshop. For the other choice, there would be no surprises—no happy endings. If lots of people were forced to attend, these answer choices could be very diagnostic. They could also be useful in marketing the workshop. *"Of your colleagues who said they didn't want to attend the workshop, even 92% of them said they were PLEASANTLY SURPRISED in the value they got out of it."* On the other hand, if nobody was ever forced to attend the workshop, these answer choices would be completely superfluous—and should be removed.

The point I'm making here is: Be very careful what questions you ask and what answer choices you utilize. Why waste time and effort on a question that produces no usable insights? Also, let me add that it's okay—and even a best practice—to look at your data over time and modify your use of questions and answer choices based on what you're discovering.

For Nudging Learners Toward Goal-Directed Behavior

Another way to assess the likely outcomes of learning interventions is to ask learners what goals they have for implementing their learning. This is not a foolproof method because learners may invent goals they don't have, or they may have intentions—even strong intentions—that later they don't follow through on. Still, goal setting has scientific backing in showing benefits—marking goal setters as more likely to reach goals—so asking learners to write down their goals may be beneficial, at least to get learners some of the benefits of goal setting.

---

[43] The Kool-Aid.

And let me be clear here. Just because learners say they have created a Goal X, doesn't mean they will reach Goal X. Don't use goal setting alone as evidence for learning success! On the other hand, nudging a learner to set Goal X will likely increase the likelihood that he/she will accomplish the tasks embodied in Goal X.

Here's a question we might use to move learners to set goals:

Question 148
Question Rationale: *Used to push learners to set goals.*
Of all the things you might have learned in this session, WHAT TWO OR THREE THINGS ARE YOU HOPING TO USE RIGHT AWAY IN YOUR CURRENT WORK or in YOUR LIFE?
1 — Type Goal 1 Here
2 — Type Goal 2 Here
3 — Type Goal 3 Here (Optional)
Note: Learners are NOT shown the text in the gray cells of this table. *It's important on comment questions to give learners a relatively large answer block—to encourage them to write more than a few words.*

Note that we're not asking people to set ten goals. Usually, having too many goals is counterproductive because we humans can't focus on a zillion things at once.

So, let me ask you to focus on this intriguing finding from the research: Goal setting is good, but goal setting alone is not nearly as good as goal setting with triggered action planning. I mentioned triggered action planning earlier, even offering a question (Question 113) to help us determine if triggered action planning was utilized during learning. As a reminder, when we do triggered action planning, we help people set a situational trigger for themselves—a trigger that will nudge them to remember what they learned. We help people connect situations with actions. The following question will help learners set triggers to enable spontaneous remembering.

Question 149
Question Rationale: Used to create situation-action plans to support learners in spontaneous remembering.
For the first goal you mentioned above, when will you get started working toward that goal? The more specific you are, the more likely you'll follow through with your intentions! For example: Situation: My next staff meeting. Timing: Next Tuesday at the end of the meeting. Action: I will ask for feedback about the quality of the meeting.

1	Type Situation Here
2	Type Timing Here
3	Type Action Here

Note: Learners are NOT shown the text in the gray cells of this table.

It's important on comment questions to give learners a relatively large answer block—to encourage them to write more than a few words.

How to Start and End Your Learner Survey

While we can present our learners with questions alone, it's generally more effective to offer some sort of introduction to the questions and some sort of thank-you after the questions.

Introducing our questions can make it more likely that people complete our survey and answer our questions with full attention and honesty. Providing a thank-you can make it more likely that people engage subsequent learner surveys.

Performance-Focused Learner Surveys

I used the following introduction for a conference-session survey at the Learning Development Conference:

Introductory Text (Used for Conference Session)

Please complete the following six-question survey about the session provided by [NAME OF FEATURED SPEAKER].

Our goal at the L&D Conference 2020 is to provide you with a series of highly effective learning experiences. By providing these questions to our speakers in advance and by getting your feedback, we seek to ensure that you are getting information you can trust and insights and practices that you can utilize in your work or in your life.

Thank you for contributing to this goal and for giving speakers feedback they can use to maintain and enhance the great stuff they are doing and improve the content and methods where improvements might be made.

We have kept these surveys short, but you are welcome to provide detailed feedback in the open-ended questions.

I used the following introduction for my Presentation Science Boot Camp workshop:

Introductory Text (Used for Online Workshop)

I Need Your Considered Feedback

Thank you for participating in this workshop! I've endeavored to make it as effective as possible. But, of course, there are certainly improvements I can make. I need your help in that regard.

The feedback you provide is really important to me. It helps me get better. It helps my audience members – people just like you – get an improved learning experience. And, because the content of this workshop helps everybody create better presentations, your feedback indirectly helps people and organizations throughout the world.

The data you provide is private and confidential. Only I will see the details. I may aggregate the data in the future to share important insights, but no identifying information will be revealed.

Thank you!

This set of questions should take you about ten minutes to complete, more or less depending on how much you write.

Performance-Focused Learner Surveys

Here is an introduction used by one of my clients for a mentoring program. This survey was for the mentor, not for the learner.

Introductory Text (Used for Mentoring Program)

Thank you!

Thank you for taking the time to give us anonymous feedback about the impact of your mentoring experience.

We want to hear about your experience in working with a mentee and your thoughts on the guide and process. We will use your feedback to make improvements.

We are grateful for your energy and effort in answering this brief set of questions.

From the Learning Team

Here are key components of an introduction:

- Is short and concise.

- Shows appreciation.

- Manages time expectations.

- Motivates completion, attention, honesty.

- Truthfully describes how data will be used, and by whom.

- Truthfully describes confidentiality protections.

- Is clear about who is asking for the survey to be completed.

It's difficult to meet all these requirements—especially because the first requirement is that the survey introduction be short and concise. You will need to figure out what is most important for your situation. And, if you have the resources and the need, you might want to A-B test different introductions to find out what works best.

Ending Your Survey

Ending your survey is easier. Usually, a simple thank-you will do. On the other hand, we can add other components. Here are key components of an ending:

- Is short and concise.

- Thanks learners for completing the survey.

- Describes again how data will be used.

- Tells learners when they will be notified of survey findings.

> ### Ending Text (For Use in Training Program)
>
> **Thank you!**
>
> Thank you for taking the time to share your perspective on the Leadership for Supervisors workshop.
>
> We will compile the data over the next two weeks, and we'll share with you our general findings by November 15th so you can see how the feedback we received (from you and other front-line supervisors) is helping to maintain and improve the quality of our learning programs.
>
> We are grateful for your energy and effort in providing your insights!
>
> **From the Learning Team**

Summary: Special-Purpose Questions

In this chapter I shared about two dozen special-purpose questions. I could have shared a hundred more. The distinctive questioning technique is relevant to many types of surveys. I tell you this so you will feel free to create your own questions for your own special purposes. Don't forget to have a survey expert give your questions a second set of eyes—or at least find someone who is sensitive to wording and empathetic to your target audience. Also, don't forget to pilot test and improve!

Chapter 9
Comment Questions

There are essentially two types of survey questions: choice questions and comment questions. Choice questions, sometimes known as forced-choice questions, require survey respondents to make choices from a list of options. There are several variations of choice questions, including choose-one multiple choice, choose-many multiple choice, choose-from-two options, sliders, and star ratings. Most of the questions I've shared so far in this book are choice questions, which are great for capturing data from a wide range of respondents and for creating clarity and urgency in the data we present. When we see that only 23% of learners feel they understand key concepts, we are jarred into a clear picture of failure.

Comment questions, on the other hand, ask respondents to write, type, or voice their responses. Comment questions for surveys basically involve short-answer responses or comment boxes. Short-answer responses, as the name suggests, ask respondents to provide one or a few words. Comment boxes encourage respondents to write a sentence or two or more. Whereas choice questions create clarity and urgency, comment questions provide data that has richness and depth—enabling us to gain a fuller appreciation of respondent perspectives. Also, comment questions can provide a gold mine for powerful quotes—the kind of quotes that can move stakeholders to take matters seriously.

In the first edition of the book, I completely forgot to write about comment questions, probably under the assumption that most of our learner-survey mistakes were getting made with choice questions. This was an oversight on my part. Comment questions can be extremely beneficial, but there are subtleties that should be taken into consideration.

Ending Our Surveys with Comment Questions

The most common use of comment questions is to have a few at the end of our surveys. This is a great idea because it gives learners a chance to fill in any gaps our choice questions might have missed. Also, if we first ask good choice questions—questions that get learners thinking about important learning considerations—our learners will respond with more prescient ideas in our comment boxes. For example, often our learner won't be thinking about the after-learning support they might need or about the importance of realistic practice during training. If we ask a choice question that raise these issues, then, later—in the comment questions—learners will be more likely to focus on these mission-critical issues than on less important things like the temperature in the room, the quality of the food, or the enjoyment of the experience.

Here are three questions I often recommend for ending a survey—starting with a question focused on the learners' perceptions of what was good.

Question 150 – Positive Feedback Comment Question
Question Rationale: *Used to get open-ended positive feedback about the learning experience.*
What aspects of the training made it MOST EFFECTIVE FOR YOU? What should WE DEFINITELY KEEP as part of the training?
Note: Learners are NOT shown the text in the gray cells of this table. *It's important on comment questions to give learners a relatively large answer block—to encourage them to write more than a few words.*

Note the messaging here. The first sentence asks about effectiveness from the respondent's point of view. It doesn't talk about satisfaction; it talks about effectiveness. It doesn't talk in generalities; it asks about the effectiveness for the person answering the question. The second sentence focuses specifically on what should be kept in the training. This shares the expectation that some parts of the training are good and should be kept. This messaging is important to set high expectations, but it's also valuable in maintaining trainer buy-in. The bottom line is that, if the survey doesn't seem fair, trainers will discount the data.

To be balanced, if we ask about the positive, we must ask about the negative.

Question 151 – Constructive Feedback Question
Question Rationale: Used to get open-ended constructive feedback about the learning experience.
What aspects of the training COULD BE IMPROVED? **Remember, your feedback is critical, especially in providing us with constructive ideas for improvement.**
Note: Learners are NOT shown the text in the gray cells of this table. *It's important on comment questions to give learners a relatively large answer block—to encourage them to write more than a few words.*

Note that, when we ask for constructive feedback, we may need to provide permission for people to share their negatives. Yes, many people will share their gripes easily, but some need an extra nudge. And here's something very important: Our survey respondents are listening—sometimes consciously and sometimes subconsciously—to the signals our words are sending. If we ask only for positives or negatives, people will hear that and be less engaged and less interested in our survey—and less likely to provide us with unbiased feedback.

Here is my secret-weapon end-of-survey question.

Question 152 – The Anything-Else Question
Question Rationale: Used to get additional feedback and to honor the perspectives of our learners.
Is there anything else we should have asked about? Is there anything you want to tell us?
Note: Learners are NOT shown the text in the gray cells of this table. *It's important on comment questions to give learners a relatively large answer block—to encourage them to write more than a few words.*

This question sends a message that we, the survey writers, are open to whatever feedback our learners want to provide. Note the first sentence: *"Is there anything else we should have asked about?"* This may seem like a throw-away, but it adds a human element. It tells the respondents they are not just answering questions; they are having a conversation with other people—people who are open and authentic and who care. Not everyone will answer this question—sometimes only a few will answer it—but, in my experience, some of the most prescient comments are added here. Even if a person doesn't answer it, he or she is left with the impression that the survey was more than an exercise in question answering—it was part of an important conversation to maintain and improve learning effectiveness.

Using Comment Questions to Augment Choice Questions

Comment questions don't have to be used only at the end of our surveys. They can play other functions as well. One of their best uses is to augment choice questions—enabling respondents to do the following:

- Clarify their choice-question response.

- Provide more detail about their choice-question responses.

- Disambiguate their responses.

- Share stories related to their answers.

The question below is a good case in point. It asks about the value of work-related learning projects in the choice question and follows up with a clarifying comment question. Both are portrayed in the table below.

Question 153

Question Rationale: *Used to determine how well the learning projects supported learners' ability to take what they learned back to their work.*

	In this workshop, you were asked to complete five "missions," using what you learned by applying it to your work. How useful were these missions in helping you prepare to take what you learned back to the job? SELECT AS MANY AS ARE TRUE FOR YOU.	*Proposed Standards* *Not shown to learners*
A	Too many of the missions were NOT RELEVANT to the real work I will be doing.	Unacceptable
B	Too many of the missions seemed more like BUSY WORK than useful practice.	Unacceptable
C	Too many of the missions were NOT WELL CONSTRUCTED to be fully useful.	Unacceptable
D	In general, the missions provided USEFUL PRACTICE that helped me get better at the skills I learned.	Acceptable
E	In general, the missions helped me DIAGNOSE areas I still needed to work on.	Acceptable
F	In general, the missions helped me UNDERSTAND the content of the workshop in even more depth.	Acceptable

Follow-Up Comment Question:

In your own words, how valuable were the missions in supporting you in providing realistic practice and feedback?

What was effective about them, if anything?

What could have been better?

Note: Learners are NOT shown the text in the gray cells of this table.

If calculating an acceptability index, we might consider it acceptable if respondents chose at least one of the three acceptable responses while not choosing any of the unacceptable responses. As always, you should base standards of acceptability on your own circumstances, while also negotiating with your key stakeholders.

I'm not going to belabor the point that comment questions and choice questions can be used in tandem to capture better data. Previous chapters provide several examples of these tandem questions, so you may already be a convert. Let me provide one warning: While these pairings can be very powerful, I wouldn't recommend using a comment question after every choice question—except, perhaps, in some rare circumstance. Not every choice question requires further clarification or enrichment, and every question we ask takes time away from another question that might be asked.

Summary: Comment Questions

Comment questions should be added to almost all our learner surveys. They provide rich, detailed data from which we can draw insights. They enable learners to comment on issues we hadn't mentioned. They work powerfully when paired with choice questions. They enable us to capture quotes that tell powerful stories about our findings.

Chapter 10
Tailoring Your Questions

Almost all the questions I've shared in this book are generic—written to be broadly applicable for a wide range of organizations and learning experiences. I purposely wrote them this way to be relevant to the vast array of readers I expect may read this book. But I plead with you: Don't be so inflexible to insist on the generic wording!

I want you to think about it. Stop and reflect. Does it make sense to provide our learners with generic questions? Are you thinking? Or just reading at a surface level?

I know, because I've talked with thousands of you—with many learning professionals over the years—and I know your gut instinct says you need to ask all your learners the exact same questions regardless of whether you're teaching how to complete a charity pledge form or how to counteract a terrorist attack.

Let's start with the basics. When we provide learners with a question, we hope we'll get their full attention, they will answer forthrightly, and they will answer the question we intended to ask with high levels of clarity. When we write our surveys, we need to create questions that are (1) undeniably clear in supporting learner decision making, (2) motivating enough to prompt learners to engage attentively, and (3) relevant enough to spur learners to go beyond routine responses and instead give higher levels of inquiry and thoughtfulness. Yes! This is what distinctive questions do by getting rid of fuzzy answer choices. But, for maximum effectiveness, we can go even further! We can tailor our questions and our answer choices.

Let me show you some examples. Let's start with Question 101. First, I'll share the generic version from earlier in the book. Read through it.

	Question 101—The Generic Version	
	Question Rationale: Used to determine how prepared learners feel in being able to take what they've learned and use it in their work.	
	HOW ABLE ARE YOU to put what you've learned into practice in your work? CHOOSE THE ONE OPTION that best describes your current readiness.	
A	My CURRENT ROLE DOES NOT ENABLE me to use what I learned.	
B	I AM STILL UNCLEAR about what to do, and/or why to do it.	
C	I NEED MORE GUIDANCE before I know how to use what I learned.	
D	I NEED MORE EXPERIENCE to be good at using what I learned.	
E	I CAN BE SUCCESSFUL NOW in using what I learned (even without more guidance or experience).	
F	I CAN PERFORM NOW AT AN EXPERT LEVEL in using what I learned.	
	Note: Learners are NOT shown the text in the gray cells of this table.	

Now, let's look at two tailored versions. The first is for a workshop on how to utilize Microsoft Excel to help learners use charts and graphs in their sales presentations.

	Question 101 – Tailored for Excel Workshop
	Question Rationale: *Used to determine how prepared learners feel in being able to use Excel to create charts and graphs for presentations.*
	HOW ABLE ARE YOU to use Microsoft Excel to create charts and graphs that you can use in presentations with prospective clients? CHOOSE THE ONE OPTION that best describes your current ability.
A	My CURRENT ROLE DOES NOT ENABLE me to make presentations or use charts and graphics in presentations.
B	I AM STILL UNCLEAR about how to use Excel to make charts and graphs for my presentations.
C	I NEED MORE GUIDANCE before I know how to use Excel to make charts and graphs for my presentations.
D	I NEED MORE EXPERIENCE to be good at using Excel to make charts and graphs for my presentations.
E	I CAN BE SUCCESSFUL NOW in using Excel to make charts and graphs for my presentations. (even without more guidance or experience).
F	I CAN PERFORM NOW AT AN EXPERT LEVEL in using Excel to make charts and graphs for my presentations.
	Note: Learners are NOT shown the text in the gray cells of this table.

Here is another version of the same question. This one follows the original generic version even less. It is a question I used in my Presentation Science Boot Camp workshop.

Question 101 – Tailored for Presentation Science Workshop	
Question Rationale: Used to determine how prepared learners feel in being able to make presentations that enable their audiences to engage, learn, remember, and act.	
How READY are you to MAKE A HIGHLY EFFECTIVE presentation in terms of engagement, learning, remembering, and action? Check all that apply!!!	
A	I'm still NOT SURE WHERE TO BEGIN.
B	I KNOW ENOUGH TO GET STARTED.
C	I can now tell when GOOD AND BAD presentation approaches are used.
D	I can now ENGAGE my audience in meaningful presentation and activities.
E	I can now help my audience to LEARN AND COMPREHEND the concepts and skills that I teach.
F	I can now support my audience in REMEMBERING what they've learned.
G	I can now prepare and support my audience to ACT on what they've learned.
H	I can now successfully PREPARE MYSELF TO DELIVER an upcoming presentation.
Note: Learners are NOT shown the text in the gray cells of this table.	

Note how I really went off script from the original. I was able to do this because I know the goals of the workshop, and, more importantly, the learners know the goals too. The organization of the workshop is very clear—the aim is to support audience members to

Chapter 10—Tailoring Your Questions

Engage, Learn, Remember, and Act. With this clarity, I can ask a question that gets at each of these goals.

But let me share a warning here. I'm not 100% confident in my redesign of the question because of the results I've been getting. About half the people who've answered the question simply select all the options from D to H. This could mean my Presentation Science Boot Camp is extraordinary, but I worry that people who are generally pleased with the workshop are experiencing kind of a halo effect—just judging everything with a positive bias. So, what can we do if we have these kinds of worries? Two things. First, we can look at the results from this question in conjunction with results of other questions. In the case of the Boot Camp, many people also report that the workshop was transformational for them in the way they create presentations. More importantly, I can look at another question that asks them which of the key concepts from the workshop they found most valuable. If these were all in the Engage part of the workshop—not in the Learn, Remember, and Act sections—then the overall glowing reports should be discounted.

Another alternative is to have separate questions for each of the main areas of the workshop. Many of my clients have decided to use this technique even though it lengthens their surveys. So, for example, I might have instead created a separate question for each of the main topic areas—engagement, learning, remembering, and action. Here's how a question on remembering might look:

Question 101 – Tailored for Remembering Section of the Presentation Science Boot Camp	
Question Rationale: Used to determine how prepared learners feel in being able to make presentations that enable their audience to remember what they've learned.	
HOW ABLE ARE YOU to make a presentation that supports your audience in remembering what they've learned? CHOOSE THE ONE OPTION that best describes your current ability.	
A	My CURRENT ROLE DOES NOT ENABLE me to make presentations that support learners in remembering what they've learned.
B	I AM STILL UNCLEAR about how to craft a presentation that will support my learners in remembering.
C	I NEED MORE GUIDANCE before I know how to craft a presentation that will support my learners in remembering.
D	I NEED MORE EXPERIENCE to be good at crafting a presentation that will support my learners in remembering.
E	I CAN BE SUCCESSFUL NOW in at crafting a presentation that will support my learners in remembering. (even without more guidance or experience).
F	I CAN PERFORM NOW AT AN EXPERT LEVEL in crafting a presentation that will support my learners in remembering.
Note: Learners are NOT shown the text in the gray cells of this table.	

So, what do these tailored questions do? First, they have greater face validity and thus more power to communicate with clarity and urgency. If we teach a course on Microsoft Excel and then ask if people feel they are competent in using Microsoft Excel, then the resulting data is just more powerful compared to a question that asks more generically if people feel competent to use what they learned.

Imagine if the data comes back and shows that 60% of learners say, *"I NEED MORE GUIDANCE before I know how to use Excel to make charts and graphs for my presentations."* This is damning information that clearly shows our training was not effective enough. The alternative would be the following. Imagine 60% of learners saying, *"I NEED MORE GUIDANCE before I know how to use what I learned."* That is certainly not great, but it is simply not as clear—nor does it create the urgency the data demands.

Tailored questions have greater face validity, which helps create more clarity and urgency. But tailored questions are also more motivating to learners, more relevant, more believed in. Tailored questions, then, not only motivate attention and forthrightness on the current survey, but they also inspire learners—and our other organizational stakeholders too—to see more value in learner surveys. These long-term systemic effects are important too! They lend credibility to us on the learning team and they create a positive spiral where learner surveys are taken more seriously, we get better and better data, we make more and more improvements, the learning becomes more and more effective, and the results become a true competitive advantage.

Summary: Tailoring Your Questions

Tailoring questions takes more time, but the benefits are well worth it. Tailoring questions motivates learners to engage more fully and forthrightly in answering our questions, helps learners make clearer decisions, creates better data, and builds the credibility of the learner surveying we do. While there are benefits to tailoring every question, we don't have to invest to that extent to see some benefits. We could decide to tailor half our questions or some subset.

And let's be real: Once we have a core set of generic questions, it doesn't take that long to tailor our learner surveys. I've become very fluent in doing this. For an average twelve-question survey, I could probably tailor it in less than an hour if the content wasn't too foreign to me. You may take a little bit longer—and there are always conversations and tweaking needed after a first draft—but, really, the investment in tailoring is totally worth it! Even if you must limit tailoring to your most important or most visible programs, find a way to tailor your questions.

Chapter 11
Follow-Up Learner Surveys

At several points earlier in this book, I mentioned follow-up learner surveys. In this chapter, I will focus on them in more detail—because they deserve to be observed from an elevated vista above the haze of other considerations.

Follow-up learner surveys tell us things that end-of-training learner surveys cannot. They give learners an entirely different perspective from which to make their learner-survey decisions. In particular, follow-up learner surveys:

1. Help learners overcome the top-of-mind problem that occurs with end-of-training learner surveys. Specifically, they enable learners to evaluate how well they've remembered what they learned.

2. Help learners see on-the-job practical outcomes they cannot see within training.

3. Help learners rethink the value of the training in light of how well their learning-implementation efforts have gone.

4. Enable learners to report on their actual successes and failures in attempting to implement the learning.

5. Enable learners to report on the specific obstacles they've faced and the success factors that enabled them to reach their learning-implementation goals.

These insights are huge! Especially given that our whole goal with performance-focused learner surveys is to produce on-the-job performance improvement. Follow-up learner surveys give us more of a window into the job situation than an end-of-training learner surveys could ever give us.

Performance-Focused Learner Surveys

Benefits of Follow-Up Learner Survey

The five-item list above outlines the different perspectives learners gain from follow-up learner surveys. These perspectives lead to a variety of benefits, which we'll now discuss.

When learning is measured at the end of training, memory retrieval is artificially enhanced. When learners' perspectives on their own learning are measured at the end of training—as they are on end-of-training learner surveys—learners suffer from a top-of-mind bias that makes them think the learning is more effective than it actually is. The best way to reduce these biases is to also provide learners with delayed measures of learning—and follow-up learner surveys. Follow-up learner surveys ensure that learning is not top of mind for the learners, but is more representative of their on-the-job cognitions. Because of this, learners will have greater insight about the potency of the training to support their remembering and their ability to apply what they have learned on the job.

When learners are back on their jobs and are asked to evaluate a previous training program, they know whether they've attempted to apply the new concepts or not. They know whether they've encountered situations that are relevant to the training topics covered previously. If they did make extra efforts to apply what they've learned, they know how successful they've been. These perspectives enable the learners to reflect with clear eyes on the relevance and value of the training.

Follow-up learner surveys also give learners an opportunity to report on their successes and failures. Both can help other learners be more successful in implementing their own learning. Success stories can be gathered to motivate and guide others in their own efforts. Failures can be explored for lessons learned, enabling others to navigate difficulties. If desired, capturing successes and failures and their organizational implications—for example, using Brinkerhoff's Case Method or Phillips's ROI data-gathering protocols—can provide feedback to the organization on the cost-benefit implications of training-inspired actions.

Finally, and very powerfully, follow-up learner surveys can capture information about the obstacles and success factors learners have faced in applying what they've learned. This is particularly useful because the information gathered about obstacles and success factors can (1) help instructional designers address weaknesses in the training and maintain its strengths, (2) help work-learning professionals improve training deployment and after-training support strategies, and (3) inform business-line managers and learners' supervisors about improvements they can make to support learning implementation.

Chapter 11—Follow-Up Learner Surveys

Special Logistics for Follow-Up Learner Surveys

I recommend delivering follow-up learner surveys between two and four weeks after training ends. These time boundaries are not definitive—they could be a little bit shorter or a little bit longer—but they are designed to balance the need to give learners time to apply what they've learned and the need to ensure that training wasn't delivered so long ago that the learning process has become completely irrelevant to the learners.

In this day of easy online survey software, follow-up learner surveys will almost always be delivered electronically. While some organizations require that these instruments be delivered behind a firewall, I'm not sure I fully understand the need for such high security. The questions you use are likely to be similar to the questions other companies will use—and the data you gather on your learner surveys are highly unlikely to contain any critical intellectual property. There's no reason not to use survey software like SurveyMonkey—at least in terms of security. On the other hand, you may want to connect your findings to your Learning Management System, especially if it's running Experience API (xAPI, a software module that enables extensive data-collection possibilities).

Follow-up learner surveys can often use some of the same questions a standard performance-focused learner survey uses—although sometimes slight changes of wording will be required to make the questions make sense.

For example, on our end-of-learning learner survey we would ask:
- In what ways do you expect your supervisor will support you in applying what you learned to your job?

On our follow-up learner survey, we would modify it to say:
- In what ways did your supervisor support you in applying what you learned to your job?

Indeed, this consanguinity can be useful in comparing learners' expectations to actual outcomes. For example, look at the two question options above. It might be very interesting to compare what learners expect from their supervisors and what supervisors actually deliver. The implications of sharing this kind of data with organizational actors are massive. And, I'm not just talking about this example. I'm talking about all the comparisons we might conjure between the results of end-of-training learner surveys and the follow-up learner surveys.

Performance-Focused Learner Surveys

One pushback I sometimes get when I advocate for follow-up learner surveys is that learners don't have time to complete another survey. This is a fundamental issue—one not to be dismissed lightly. We're talking about two critical things here: the potential for actual productivity loss and the reputation of us learning professionals as time vacuums. There are several considerations worth reflecting on.

First, how much actual time does it take folks to complete a follow-up learner survey? If we figure an average of sixty seconds per question, we're talking about ten minutes, depending on the length of the follow-up learner surveys. The question then becomes, what value is there in that time investment? For traditional smile sheets there was zero value in the results—because nothing ever changed and no valuable information was uncovered. But, with better questions, we will be able to provide real value. It might, however, take us some time and change-management effort to demonstrate that value. We'll talk more about how we should do that in a coming chapter.

Second, we may have to compromise and deliver follow-up learner surveys only for high-importance training programs or only for a few pilot programs at first until we can prove their value. We may have to prioritize our questions and cut some to use less time. Finally, perhaps we need to think in terms of a cultural change in the way we deliver training and the value we create. Certainly, we need to educate our stakeholders in the value of these types of performance-focused interventions. But follow-up learner surveys could become part of a larger strategic learning renaissance within your organization. At minimum, we will have to convince our learners—the folks who will decide whether to give their time to our follow-up learner surveys—that their additional investment is worth it.

One final thought for this section on the logistics of follow-up learner surveys. Many organizations do this funny thing in trying to follow the Kirkpatrick Model. Specifically, in wanting to go beyond Level 1, learner reactions, and Level 2, tests of learning—to get to Level 3, on-the-job behavior—they essentially send out follow-up learner surveys and declare the results as Level 3 results. They ask learners about whether they've been able to apply the learning successfully and they inappropriately transmogrify these responses into an index of actual on-the-job performance. If you've gotten this far in the book—and if you have read about the problems with self-report data—you'll readily see how this *behaviorization*[44] of learner-survey data is an entirely dubious enterprise. Let me put this simply: Follow-up learner surveys are not good measures of on-the-job behavior. They

---

[44] I'm using the made-up word "behaviorization" to represent the practice of turning data from learners' opinions into behavioral data at Level 3 of the Kirkpatrick taxonomy.

don't align with Kirkpatrick's Level 3 (nor to LTEM Tier 7). I have written that this practice—of labeling learner perceptions of likely Level 3 and Level 4 results (LTEM Tier 7 and 8)—*"one of the biggest lies in learning evaluation."*[45] To measure on-the-job behavior accurately, we must do more than ask learners to evaluate their own learning application.

Additional Question Opportunities

In addition to standard performance-focused learner-survey questions, follow-up learner surveys should offer an additional set of questions, starting with the *pivot question*:[46,47]

Question 154 – Pivot Question

Question Rationale: Used to determine the reasons that compelled learners to enroll in the learning event.

	Have you used what you learned in the training to make a significant improvement in your work?	Proposed Standards Not shown to learners
A	NO, and I DOUBT THAT I WILL USE what I learned.	Alarming
B	NO, BUT I PROBABLY WILL USE what I learned.	Unacceptable
C	NO, BUT I HAVE A SPECIFIC PLAN TO USE what I learned.	Unacceptable
D	YES, I HAVE ALREADY USED what I learned.	Acceptable

Note: Learners are NOT shown the text in the gray cells of this table.

Pivot questions like this enable us to branch to one of two follow-up questions. If learners answer "no"—if they select one of the first three answer choices above—we give

---

[45] Thalheimer (2018).

[46] Another variant of this question is a five-item question with two affirmative responses, as follows: D. Yes, I HAVE ALREADY USED what I learned (ONCE OR TWICE). E. Yes, I HAVE REPEATEDLY USED what I learned.

[47] I call this a "pivot question" because it enables us to pivot toward two or more follow-up questions, based on the answer given by the respondent.

Performance-Focused Learner Surveys

them a question that asks them what is holding them back from being successful. If they answer "yes," we give them a question that asks them what success factors enabled them to be successful. The logic of the branching is shown in the diagram that follows:

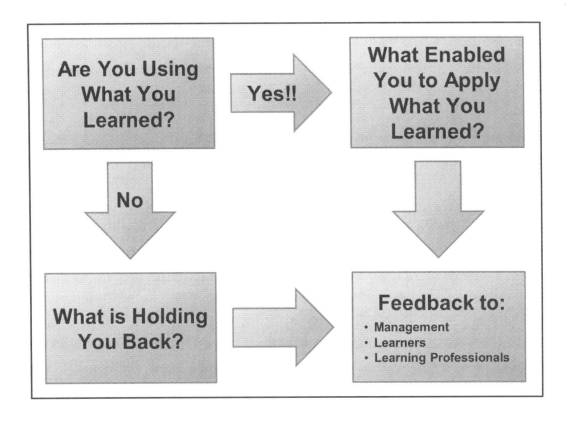

Let's examine the two post-pivot questions. First, we'll look at a follow-up question when learners say they have been successful.

	Question 155—The Pivot "Yes" Follow-Up	
	Question Rationale: Used to determine the factors learners believe are most important in enabling their successful learning application.	
	What factors have enabled you to put the training's learning points into practice to make beneficial on-the-job improvements? Select the top THREE or FOUR factors.	
A	My management has made this a high priority.	
B	I have decided to lead a change effort to make this happen.	
C	I believe strongly in the workshop's learning points.	
D	I will be sanctioned or punished if I do NOT do this.	
E	My management is fully supportive of my efforts.	
F	I have the authority to make necessary changes.	
G	My coworkers are fully supportive of my efforts.	
H	I will be acknowledged or rewarded if I do this.	
I	I remember (or can look up) the workshop's learning points.	
J	My team (or our whole unit) is working together on this.	
K	I have the time to put this into practice.	
L	I have the resources to put this into practice.	
M	Other (please specify) _____	
	Note: Learners are NOT shown the text in the gray cells of this table.	

The answer choices—because they do not have an inherent order—can be randomized (except for the last choice, the "Other" choice). And note that the "Other" choice is very

Performance-Focused Learner Surveys

important because you might find—for this topic or group of learners—that there are unique success factors that are critical. If you capture what people write for the "Other" response, you'll be able to hardwire it into a later version of the survey. And, please, let me know if you found another critical success factor—so I can let the world know. Thanks!

The following question can be used when learners state they have not yet put their learning into practice.

	Question 156—The Pivot "No" Follow-Up
	Question Rationale: Used to determine the factors learners believe are most important in enabling their successful learning application.
	What is holding you back from using what you have learned to make changes in your work? Select the top THREE or FOUR factors.
A	The learning content is not relevant to my current job.
B	I don't think the learning content is valid.
C	I don't see how making the changes will benefit me.
D	I don't know how to make the case for change.
E	I don't have the authority to make changes.
F	I'm not comfortable leading such a change effort.
G	I can't remember the learning content well enough.
H	I'm not sure I know enough to take the next steps.
I	I haven't had the time.
J	I have had higher priorities.
K	I have not had the resources.
L	The risk of making these changes is too high.
M	I'm still working to persuade management.
N	I'm still working to persuade my teammates.
O	I have been blocked by management.
P	Others around me don't support the changes.
Q	Other (please specify) _____
	Note: Learners are NOT shown the text in the gray cells of this table.

Performance-Focused Learner Surveys

Hmm. Funny that I found more obstacles than success factors, isn't it? Note that the same options apply in this question as in the previous one—you can randomize the answer choices, and the "Other" choice is critical to gather additional obstacles that folks may be encountering in your organization.

Also, if you want to use this question for people who have stated they have begun to apply their training—just to make sure you capture all the obstacles—you can change the wording of the question to, "What obstacles, if any, have made it challenging to apply your learning?"

Feedback to Key Stakeholders

The pivot question and the two post-pivot questions can provide critical—and sometimes urgent—feedback to key stakeholder groups. I've experienced this in conducting my own workshops. For example, I found in one company that the learners who had already begun implementing the learning were motivated by a management-driven initiative. I learned this based on the learners' responses to the questions. I was then able to feed that insight back to the training manager at the company and tell her that she needed to continue to actively lead the initiative—because otherwise her folks might not continue in applying what they had learned.

This feedback can be valuable not just to learning executives, instructional designers, and trainers, but also to line leaders, learners' supervisors, and the learners themselves. Imagine the power in sending messages like these:

To learners:
- "Sixty-eight percent of you have already successfully applied what you learned."
- "The two most important success factors that have propelled those who have been successful are _____."
- "The biggest obstacle your cohort has faced is _____. What advice do you have for your colleagues who are hung up on this obstacle?"

To learners' managers:
- From the CEO: "Along with Chief Learning Officer Holting, I've reviewed the recent feedback on the Excelsior Training Class. While this may not reflect on you as an individual supervisor, many direct reports

from the Excelsior Training indicate that supervisors are one of the biggest obstacles they are facing in applying what they've learned. Specifically, they don't feel they have the authority to make changes. Here's my recommendation: Work with your direct reports to set training-implementation goals, grant them the authority to implement what they've learned, see what help they need, and follow up with them in two weeks to ensure they're making progress. As you know, Excelsior is one of the keys to our continued strategic success. I'm counting on you as supervisors to make this program successful."

- From the course instructors: "Good news! Your direct reports—the ones who took my February class—tell me that most of you are doing a great job supporting them in applying their new learning on the job. Keep up the good work, and, if you feel you're having difficulty, please let me know, as I want to ensure that everyone is successful."

To instructional designers and/or trainers:

- "Houston, we have a problem. More than 50% of the learners don't value the content in Course 392. We're going to have to take a deeper look."

- "On Course 582, about 40% of the class seems stuck because they don't have enough time to apply what they've learned. Let's get together with the head of Marketing and see if there's anything we can do on our end. Perhaps we could provide a booster session after they get through their big crunch. Or maybe Marketing management will want to make changes at their end to enable the learners who need it to have a little more learning-application time."

Asking learners about whether they've been successful in applying what they've learned is the most critical pivot question, but it's not the only pivot question that is useful. For example, I've used a second pivot question sometimes—"Have you taught others what you've learned?"—and found the results illuminating. Certainly, one goal for some training classes is that the learners share what they've learned with others. By using the "have-you-taught" pivot question, we can both assess how successful we've been in encouraging such sharing and also send stealth messages that sharing is part of what's expected.

Performance-Focused Learner Surveys

In addition to the two pivot questions I've mentioned, you might ask other critical questions. Be sure to let me know if you come up with another valuable pivot question.

Summary: The Benefits of Follow-Up Learner Surveys

Follow-up learner surveys make sense, they're not hard to implement, and they provide real and undeniable value. We may have to spend a little political capital to get them implemented at first, but the rewards to our organizations will likely be large and self-reinforcing.

By using follow-up learner surveys, we send several key messages to our organization, including the following:

1. Training isn't successful until learning is applied to the job.

2. Learners often need support and encouragement to apply what they've learned.

3. Learners must take responsibility for after-training efforts.

4. Learners' managers can provide critical after-training support.

5. Learners may face obstacles in implementing what they've learned—obstacles that should be targeted to be overcome.

6. Success factors for implementing new concepts should be catalogued and parlayed into additional successes.

Follow-up learner surveys provide a more realistic view of the worth of training—a view tempered by real-world after-training experience. They overcome some of the biases inherent in top-of-mind responding during training. They give workplace professionals, learners, and learners' managers feedback on how learning application is going—enabling midcourse corrections that can significantly improve the outcomes of learning.

Chapter 12
Motivating Learners to Respond

If you create the best learner survey ever, but nobody answers your questions, you've got nothing! That's obvious. But what if you get 20% or 50% or 80% of people responding? Are these percentages good enough? This is an extremely difficult question, so it's important to examine this issue in more depth.

Ideally, we'd get everybody to respond. And, let's not forget, we want them not just to respond but to respond to every question with full attention and candor. In some sense, we don't want to maximize the number of people who answer our questions. We want to maximize the number of people who answer our questions with genuine thoughtfulness.

In the research world, survey experts are worried about "*nonresponse bias*," the situation where people who don't respond to a survey are different in some way from those who do respond. Let me illustrate the problem with a trivial example. Imagine surveying people about their hair color. The people who respond generate the following results:

- 66% — Dark Black/Brown
- 18% — Brown
- 7% — Blonde
- 5% — Red
- 3% — Gray
- 1% — Bald

If we had surveyed 99% of the whole population, we could be very confident in our overall results. Even if *all* the non-respondents had been bald, it wouldn't change our results very much, except for the bald category, which we would have undercounted by half. But what if the numbers above were from only 50% of everyone we surveyed? What if the other 50%—the non-respondents—had all been bald? Our survey results would have been way off. Where our survey had found 1% of people with bald heads, the actual number would be about 50%. Where our survey found Dark Black/Brown hair at 66% the actual number would be near 33%.

But what if we got a 50% response rate and the non-respondents had the exact same percentages as those who did respond? All would be good because our conclusions from our survey results would not change with the addition of the non-responding 50%.

Note what I did there. I used the extremes to illustrate a very critical point. If our non-respondents are like our respondents, the response rate doesn't matter. But, if our non-respondents are different from our respondents, we are likely to have a problem.

So back to our example. What if we surveyed people about hair color but only people under 45 years of age answered our survey? Obviously, we would undercount gray hair and bald heads. Look through the table to see how far off we might have been.

	Respondents (under age 45)	Non-Respondents (over age 45)	Actual
Dark Black/Brown	66%	32%	49%
Brown	18%	8%	13%
Blonde	7%	3%	5%
Red	5%	3%	4%
Gray	3%	45%	24%
Bald	1%	9%	5%

Are low response rates always a problem? No! They are not! Indeed, in political polling, response rates on telephone surveys in the United States have dropped from 35% in 1997 to 6% or less today[48]—and yet polling has become more and more accurate over time.[49] But let's be careful here! Political pollsters have the resources and expertise to make statistical adjustments that help correct for survey biases. We do not have the same capability—nor is it likely we will ever have access to resources that would enable us to do the same sort of analyses. More importantly, there is no reason to think we need to invest in advanced statistical techniques to get the data we need. More about this later.

A 6% response rate is very low. At the higher end, let's use the U.S. Bureau of Labor Statistics as an example. Most of their surveys range from 50% to 90% response rates.[50] Here are some examples. The American Time Use Survey (ATUS) averaged about 50% response rates from 2010 to 2012, but now it averages closer to 40%. The Current Employment Statistics Survey (CES) has averaged about 60% response rates since 2010.

---

[48] Kennedy and Hartig (2019).
[49] Deane, Kennedy, & Keeter (2019).
[50] See BLS response rates webpage: https://www.bls.gov/osmr/response-rates/

Chapter 12—Motivating Learners To Respond

The Consumer Price Index on Housing (CPI-Housing) usually falls between 60% and 70%.

"But, Dr. Thalheimer, none of this is even remotely related to learning and development!" Yes! You are right, dear reader! What are our numbers? The truth is that we just don't have good enough data to say. I've talked with training-evaluation vendors who claim to get at least 70%, on average, and I've talked with hundreds of practitioners who complain because they rarely get above 20%. The best current research on learner-survey response rates comes from university course evaluations—where a lot of research is done—but even this research is unlikely to be directly relevant for us, and it is not comprehensive, either. One recent review of university student evaluations found response rates ranged from 17% to 83%, looking at both online and paper surveys.[51]

Before I get to my recommendations, we should first look more skeptically at the importance of response rates. There is evidence from survey researchers that response rates do not sufficiently influence nonresponse bias. Indeed, in their review of the literature, Hendra and Hill (2019) found *"little relationship between response rate and nonresponse bias"* and they concluded there was no optimal response rate to target—that is, no minimum threshold response rate. But, again, we should be careful in interpreting these results for our purposes. The surveys they reviewed were focused on employee retention and advancement—not learning and development—and they were focused on surveys that purported to aim for an 80% response rate. Still, their conclusions should open our minds to the possibility that a low response rate for us may not be the end of the world.

Let's consider also other complications regarding response rates. How do we count a completed survey? Is a survey complete only if a person answers every question or every required question? What if people answer 75% of the questions or 50% or 25%? Response rates can differ between online surveys and paper surveys. The U.S. Census—done every ten years to count the number of people in the United States—offers a response rate for mailed census forms (about 60-70%) and then an overall response rate of 99.9% after people have been tracked down through phone calls and door-to-door canvassing.[52] Finally, response rates of surveys in general seem to be falling over the past few decades as people are less willing to engage surveys and as they disperse their attention over multiple communication channels—making it harder for survey providers to reach them with survey requests.

---

[51] Ahmad (2018).
[52] Available as of November 2020: https://www.2020census.gov/en/response-rates/nrfu.html

How to Think About Response Rates

"Please, Will Thalheimer! Tell us what all this means for learner surveys!" Dear reader, let me say that my head is exploding too! There is simply not—at this time—definitive research about response rates for learner surveys. Still, there is enough wisdom from research and practice to make recommendations. Here goes.

First, there is no magic threshold for response rates. This point has been emphasized by researchers focused on survey methodology in general,[53] and by researchers focused on university teaching evaluations.[54] Researchers focused on university teaching evaluations generally recommend that more be done to increase response rates, yet very few have offered clear recommendations for a minimum response rate. Some have made recommendations, but their recommendations are inconsistent, varying from about 45% to 80%[55]—and these thresholds, as designed for university teaching, may not relate directly to our work in learning and development.

Second, we ought to do what we can to improve our response rates. Even if our data is subject to zero nonresponse bias, it doesn't look great if we only get 10% of people completing our surveys. Low response rates are a failure on our part! Below I offer a whole host of things we can do to increase our response rates.

Third, we should look at our results even when we get a low response rate. Almost always we can find some nugget of interest—something to investigate further. Written responses are especially valuable in situations where there are low response rates. Where results from a forced-choice question might be skewed due to the bias of our sample, several comments highlighting a problem or a success factor are usually illuminating taken as a whole. Also, there is some evidence from university teaching that lower-rated courses get lower response rates.[56] So, it could be that a low response rate is indicative—in and of itself—of a problem in the learning design or facilitation. We can't assume this causal directionality, but it may be useful to investigate low-response courses for signs of problems.

Fourth, we should be open to using online surveys. While it's true that online surveys have historically gotten lower response rates than paper surveys, online surveys have several advantages, and we can increase their response rates even if they start out being low. In a

---

[53] Hendra & Hill (2019).
[54] Berk (2012).
[55] Luo (2020); Nulty (2008).
[56] Luo (2020).

recent university study, online survey response rates averaged about 64%.[57] Online surveys prompt learners to provide longer written responses.[58] Learners, at least university students, often prefer online surveys and feel they convey more confidentiality.[59]

There are also logistical advantages to online surveys, especially in data collection. On the other hand, when we have our learners in a training room and we tell them to fill out the evaluations, it's very unlikely that they will avoid responding. They are a captive audience. They may not pay full attention. They may not respond with sincere thoughtfulness, but they are responding. This response-rate advantage fades somewhat when we teach online, but there are ways to increase rates of responding.

Paper surveys' response-rate advantage is not because people prefer pencils to keyboards, but because paper surveys are delivered to a captive audience. Some trainers have figured this out and ask their learners to complete their online surveys while still in the classroom or online meeting. Researcher and university educator Loran Nordgren increased his evaluation response rates from below 75% to closer to his goal of 100% by carving out time in class for his students to complete the evaluation survey.[60] His experience aligns with his research-inspired belief that lowering friction is more important than highlighting the benefits of completing the evaluation.[61] Recently, I used Nordgren's technique and also got a very high response rate. My one warning is for classroom situations where learners are not using devices with keyboards—that is, where they are using their phones. I worry that the advantage provided by online surveys—in getting longer and more thoughtful responses to open-ended questions—will vanish when learners are using their phones.

Fifth, we must consider the purposes our survey data will be used for. If we are using our learner surveys for improvement—to improve our training program or improve an instructor's performance—then a robust response rate is important but not critical. On the other hand, if we are evaluating an instructor or a learning architect who designed the training—and we use the results to impact their employability—then a much higher response rate is warranted, and perhaps legally required. It is simply unacceptable to use invalid or unreliable data for job reviews, employment status, promotions, pay grades, or career trajectories. For any of these personnel decisions a much higher response rate is required.

---

[57] Luo (2020).
[58] Ahmad (2018).
[59] Khorsandi, Kobra, Ghobadzadeh, Kalantari, & Seifei (2012).
[60] Norgren (2021).
[61] Nordren & Schonthal (2021).

"*Damn you, Thalheimer! Just give us a number! Please, dear goodness! Make a recommendation!*" But, reader, I am worried! The research is not definitive and so I'm not fully confident! Also, pushing up response rates may lead to funkier data as people comply but do so with less attention and less forthrightness. I honestly don't know what the right balance is. Also, I am unqualified to render legal advice. "*Dr. Thalheimer, we don't care. We want a number!*" I know. I know, but should I give you a number or will that cause more damage than help? Sigh!

Okay, I'm going to conjecture some recommendations based on faint whiffs of intuition—from reading many studies reporting response rates for learner surveys, from years collecting my own data and working with clients who collect data from their learners, from the work of expert survey masters like those who work at the U.S. Bureau of Labor Statistics, from Hendra and Hill's (2019) article on nonresponse bias, and from Nulty's (2008) thoughtful if imperfect conjectures.[62] I am providing these recommendations not because I think they are indisputable but rather because I think they will motivate us to aspire to raise our expectations. I guess, ultimately, I feel that leaving you without recommendations is a worse sin than leaving you with feeble recommendations. These are tentative until more research is available. Have I been clear and honest enough that these are based on my weak and flimsy intuitions?

	Minimum Learner-Survey Response Rates While Surveying for Learning Improvement				
	< 15 learners	16-30 learners	31-60 learners	61-100 learners	101 plus learners
Lower Minimum	50%	40%	35%	30%	25%
Ideal Minimum	70%	60%	55%	45%	35%
When surveying for personnel decisions	85%	75%	70%	65%	60%

---

[62] Nulty's conjectures in his 2008 article are thoughtful and intriguing, but I don't buy into them fully because (1) they are based on statistical musings the author admits are not warranted and (2) they represent only a subset of the full range of considerations that impact the integrity, validity, and reliability of the data we are collecting.

Let me add some more clarifications. The recommendations above—even flimsy as they are—assume we are attempting to survey 100% of our learners, not a subset of our learners. If we tried to sample from the full population of our learners to get a subset, we would introduce more noise into our data—and we would then likely need even higher response rates. Fortunately, for most of us in learning and development, we are interested in surveying all our learners.

Let me be clear about something else. If learners drop out, we should survey them too! If we can't survey them, we should count them as part of our learner population and calculate our response rate with those dropouts included. Here's an example. Assume 100 learners start our MOOC workshop and 20 drop out along the way and disappear and can't be contacted. We survey the 80 remaining learners and 50 of them complete our survey. 30 don't complete the survey. What's our response rate? Our response rate is then 50%. We lost 20% to dropping out and 30% to survey nonresponse.

Worse yet, our dropouts are probably different in some way from our non-dropouts—adding bias to our data. Ideally, we'd figure out a way to survey them. If we can't, we should expect that our survey data is suffering from nonresponse bias. We can't be sure of the direction of that bias. A likely hypothesis is that the dropouts would have rated the workshop more harshly. A competing hypothesis—one we'd like to believe—is that dropouts were perfectly happy and got what they needed from the learning.[63] Here's the point: When we can't survey our learners, we can't know for sure what they thought—so we ought to do what we can to increase our survey response rate.

There is also evidence that learners may be most likely to opt out of responding when the learning experience is seen as average or within the normal range of expectations. In other words, they may be most likely to respond if they've had a great experience or a bad one. This has been found in at least one research study, which asked learners why they didn't respond.[64] It is also a common refrain from learning and development professionals. I have heard this from hundreds of learning professionals over the years, though I can't verify whether it's actually true. Why might we believe that it's mostly the happy and

---

[63] Of course, if we remember that learners are not always good judges of learning, we might worry that their assessments of the value of learning might be inaccurate. For example, given that learners are often overconfident in their ability to remember, they tend to avoid the repetitions and practice they need to reinforce memory. Dropouts may think they've gotten what they need but leave without strong enough memories for what they learned.

[64] Guder & Malliaras (2013). Note, of course, that learners' reasoning could be post hoc and inaccurate. They could say they didn't respond because the learning was not exceptionally bad or good, but that might not be the primary causal impetus for their nonresponse.

unhappy learners who respond? Probably because we remember the most salient comments from our open-ended questions—comments that praise and comments that criticize. Here's the difficulty. Even if this is true, it's hard to know whether it's a problem or not. We can make the case that it's most important to hear from the extremes, but, at the same time, we can make the case that it's the folks who felt the learning met expectations that we should hear from. My conclusion? We should do what we can to raise our response rates—so we can worry less about these issues.

Let me add one other complication. All this response rate complexity assumes that learners have the flexibility to decide for themselves whether they want to complete the learner surveys they are asked to complete. Some organizations get almost full compliance by requiring learners to complete their learner surveys. Of course, completions and full survey engagement may be two different things. It's possible that forcing people to complete a learner survey creates other problems. Forcing compliance has two major risks. First, learners may act with haste, inattentiveness, or outright sabotage—answering questions willy-nilly and creating aberrant data.

Second, learners may come to see their learner-survey efforts as compelled rather than freely given. We may thus be training them to see learner surveys not as a constructive practice that supports improved learning for everyone, but as a useless drudgery to be tolerated or avoided. On the other hand, perhaps if we require our learners to complete learner surveys, they will be more likely to identify themselves as people who virtuously give feedback to help maintain and improve their organizations' learning interventions. While I know of no direct research on this relating to learner surveys, my guess—based on Ryan and Deci's seminal research on motivation[65]—is that enticing people rather than requiring compliance will produce better results. Learner surveys freely engaged will engender more people to see learner surveys as valuable and worthy of their attention—and thus create long-term benefits.

How to Get Better Responses and Higher Response Rates

1. Use well-designed questions—distinctive questions learners can answer with confidence, that ask about important information, and that provide clear and meaningful answer choices (not Likert-like or numeric scales). Also avoid obviously biased questions as these may alienate your learners.

---

[65] Ryan & Deci (2017, 2019).

Chapter 12—Motivating Learners To Respond

2. Give learners time during learning to complete the survey. Do whatever you can to lower the friction learners may experience in starting and in working through your surveys.

3. Where possible, have a trusted person make a personal request to the learners to complete the survey (ideally an instructor the learners have come to trust and respect). Just below this list is a separate list including some useful talking points.

4. Write a brief introduction to the survey using a conversational tone. Avoid formal, impersonal language.

5. Early in the training (and more than once) mention that the learner survey is coming—so learners know it is an integral part of the learning, not just an add-on.

6. Tell learners that the data will be confidential, that the data is aggregated so an individual's responses are never shared.

7. Tell learners how feedback from previous learners has improved the current learning program—or previous learning programs if this is the first run of the program.

8. Tell learners how and when you'll let them know the results of their feedback.

9. After data is compiled and analyzed, share with learners the results of everyone's feedback, telling them the themes in the data and what improvements you and the learning team are considering making.

10. Don't have demographic questions at the beginning of a survey. This has two negative impacts. First, it can scare people away from answering the survey. Second it may prompt people to be less forthright as they answer.

11. Ensure that survey distribution and collection are independent and free from tampering or review by interested parties like instructors. Learners may hesitate to be forthright if they think their responses can be linked directly to themselves.

12. Monitor instructor response rates—perhaps even acknowledging or rewarding instructors who hit the response-rate goal, and/or punishing or sanctioning those who are below the goal.

13. Design online course flows that include the learner surveys as a regular learning task rather than as an add-on. Don't put the survey as the very last item on the learning agenda.

14. Ask questions that encourage constructive criticism. Ask for both praise and criticism directly. Provide both positive and negative answer choices. Avoid using question stems that assume positive answers.

15. Let learners make some decisions about what questions to answer. You can do this simply by making some questions optional or by having learners choose which of several questions to answer.

16. Keep the learner survey relatively brief and aligned with the length or importance of the learning. For example, for a five-day leadership-development intensive, a twenty-minute survey may be acceptable, whereas, for a one-hour short awareness training, probably five minutes is a maximum.

17. If you've got a long learning program, consider breaking your learner survey into shorter interim surveys.

Options for Making a Personal Appeal to Learners

Some learning programs have an instructor, facilitator, or coach. Other programs are self-study programs—for example, some elearning programs are unfacilitated or simply provide a reading list, a video list, and a recommended set of exercises, reflections, or tasks to complete. When there is an instructor, facilitator, coach, or manager, a personal appeal to learners can be very helpful. Below are talking points that may be useful.

1. As the survey is being introduced and delivered, make a modestly impassioned request to the learners to complete the survey.

2. Tell learners what you and the organization will do with the data—for example, say the data will be used to improve the weakest parts and maintain the strongest parts of the learning.

3. Tell learners how personally valuable the feedback is to you, your future performance, and your continual improvement, as well as to others on the learning team.

4. Acknowledge the effort that they—your learners—will be making, maybe even commiserating with them that you know how hard it can be to give their full attention when it's the end of the day or when they are back at work.

5. Put the time devoted to the survey in perspective—for example, "We spent seven hours today in learning—that's four hundred twenty minutes—and now we're asking you for ten more minutes."

6. Tell learners that their feedback will be part of a whole cycle of feedback and improvement that began as the course was being developed.

7. Remind learners that providing feedback to create improvement is part of the organizational culture—"It's what we do here; it's who we are."

8. Note that, while each of these talking points may be potent, it's probably not smart to go on too long. Don't use all of them. Instead, prioritize and select messaging that will be most persuasive with your audience.

Special Instructions for Online Surveys

1. Ensure the survey technology is stable, easy to access, and easy to use.

2. Give your learners time to complete the learner survey during the learning event. If this is not feasible, send your survey request immediately after the learning event or before it ends. Don't wait more than an hour after the learning to send the survey.

3. Write a short survey introduction that motivates learners to fully engage the survey. Include the value of their feedback, a promise of confidentiality, and an appreciation for their efforts. Keep it short!

4. To maximize the benefits of comment questions, push the use of computers with keyboards rather than phones or tablets. This assumes phones and tablets will discourage comments—an assumption that may be worth testing if you think your audience is especially comfortable using their devices to write comments.

5. Let your learners know the percentage of people like them who typically complete the survey (caveat: if it's relatively high).

Performance-Focused Learner Surveys

6. On the survey itself, use a progress bar or similar mechanism to discourage learners from dropping out as they complete the survey.

7. Where necessary, give learners a preview of the survey technology—making them comfortable with access, navigation, answering.

8. Send personalized follow-up reminders. If possible, send these only to folks who have not yet completed the survey. You may need two or more reminders.

9. When sending reminders, share with your learners a sense of the number of their fellow learners who have already completed the survey. "Already, 46% of your fellow learners have completed the survey, with some intriguing tentative results. Please add your perspective so we have a full picture." In addition, consider sharing the job titles of some of the people who have already completed the survey. Or, if you can do it, share with your learners the percentage of people from his/her unit who have responded already or share a comparison across units.

Special Instructions for Follow-Up Learner Surveys

Sometimes, we'll want to survey our learners well after a learning event—for example, two to four weeks later. Follow-up learner surveys are perfectly positioned to find out how the learning is relevant to the actual work or to our learners' post-learning application efforts. Unfortunately, prompting action—that is, getting learners to engage our follow-up learner surveys—can be particularly difficult when asking for this favor well after learning. Still, there are some things we can do—in addition to the list above—that can make a difference.

1. During the learning, tell the learners that a follow-up survey is coming to gauge how useful the learning is to their work, that questions will be asked that are different from those on the regular learner survey, and that their feedback is especially valuable because it's about the ultimate goal of the learning—whether the learning helps them back on the job.

2. Send out the follow-up surveys two to four weeks after the learning ends and expect that people will respond within a week or so. This ensures a nice balance between too little and too much time. We want enough time to have elapsed that learners have had a chance to start using what they've learned. On the other hand, we want the time delay to be short enough that learners will still be motivated to fulfill obligations to the learning event or instructor.

3. Tell learners what you learned from the end-of-learning learner survey they previously completed.

4. Where applicable, ask instructors—or others who bonded with the learners—to send the request (instead of an unknown person from the learning unit).

5. Send multiple requests, preferably using a mechanism that only sends these requests to those who still need to complete the survey.

6. Select an official end date for the learning experience at a time AFTER the follow-up learner survey is completed, even if that is largely just a perception. Note that multiple-event learning experiences lend themselves to this approach, whereas single-event learning experiences do not.

What About INCENTIVES?

When I ask audiences for their ideas for improving responses and increasing response rates, they often mention some sort of incentive, usually based on some sort of lottery or raffle. "If you complete the survey, your name will be submitted to have chance to win the latest tech gadget, a book, time off, lunch with an executive, etc."

I'm a skeptic. I'm open to being wrong, but I'm still skeptical about the cost/benefit calculation. Certainly, for some audiences, an incentive will increase rates of completion. Also, for some audiences, the harms that come with incentives may be worth it.

What harms, you might ask? When we provide an external incentive, we might be sending a message to learners that we know the task has no redeeming value or is tedious or difficult. People who see their own motivation as caused by external incentives are potentially less likely to seriously engage our questions—producing bad data. We're also not just influencing the current learner survey. When we incentivize people today, they may be less willing next time to engage in answering our questions. They may also be pushed into believing that learner surveys are difficult, worthless, or worse.

Ideally, we'd like our learners to want to provide us with data, to see answering our questions as a worthy and helpful exercise—one that is valuable to them, to us, and to our organization. Incentives push against this vision.

Summary: How to Motivate Learners to Respond

Our main goal in surveying learners is to get data we can use to evaluate and improve our learning interventions. If the data is biased, our decision making will be flawed. If our response rates are low, we are at a greater risk of surveying an unrepresentative sample of our learners. For this reason, we should endeavor to increase our response rates using better questions, positive appeals to our learners, and behavioral prompts that promote survey engagement. At the same time, we should avoid punitive measures, forced compliance, extrinsic incentives, and other mechanisms that may skew results or color our learner surveys as unimportant drudge work.

In this chapter, I've provided over thirty concrete steps you and your organization can take to improve your learner-survey response rates. Of course, as always, you must use your own wisdom about which steps will work best in your organization, with different types of learning interventions, with different learners. Don't follow a recipe! Instead, take a learning approach. First use what's written here and take your best guess as to which methods will increase your response rates. Then, do a whole series of A-B tests to determine what will work best for you. Be careful about short- and long-term effects. You don't want to increase response rates for your current course at the expense of the next five courses. Take a long-term approach—experimenting, tweaking, improving.

Feedback is at the heart of every improvement effort. We should take pride in our learner surveys and work to imbue learners with that same sense of pride and accomplishment.

Chapter 13
Presenting Learner-Survey Results

Up till this point, we have focused on gathering data. But, of course, we also have to present data—to both our stakeholders and ourselves. This chapter illustrates how to do this effectively.

Where traditional smile-sheet data are often transformed into meaningless numbers, performance-focused learner surveys can present results that inform, elucidate, and engender urgency and action. It's really not difficult. Mostly, we should just present the results as they are. This, of course, provides an advantage because, with minimal transformation, there is less loss of meaning than with traditional smile sheets.

Here is the job-aid question we looked at earlier.

Question 122 – Copied from Earlier			
Question Rationale: Used to determine the extent to which learners will have job aids or other prompts to support themselves in applying what they learned.			
Using job aids, checklists, or other prompts can be an effective way to ensure you properly apply skills to your job. Which of the following are true? **SELECT ALL that apply.**			*Proposed Standards* Not shown to learners
A	We did NOT RECEIVE ANY WORTHWHILE job aids, checklists, or similar prompts to direct our on-the-job actions.		Alarming
B	We RECEIVED ONE OR MORE WORTHWHILE job aids, checklists, or similar prompts.		Unacceptable
C	During the course, we USED ONE OR MORE WORTHWHILE job aids, checklists, or similar prompts in REALISTIC PRACTICE EXERCISES.		Acceptable
D	Between sessions of the course, IN OUR WORKSITES, WE UTILIZED one or more WORTHWHILE job aids, checklists, or similar prompts IN A REAL-WORLD JOB TASK.		Superior
Note: Learners are NOT shown the text in the gray cells of this table. *If calculating an acceptability index, we might consider it acceptable if respondents chose two or three of the acceptable responses.* *As always, you should base standards of acceptability on your own circumstances, while also negotiating with your key stakeholders.*			

And here's a graph displaying results for this question:

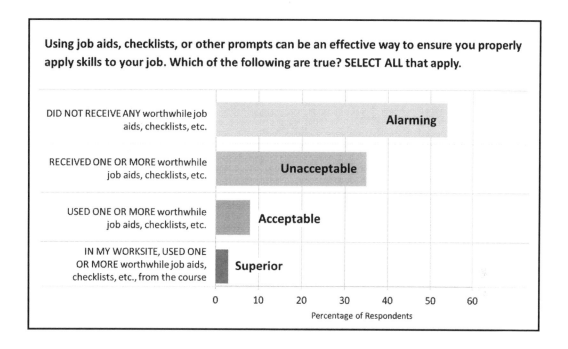

The power in such a graphic is self-evident. Note the answer choices first. They clearly distinguish between different realities. Learners either received a worthwhile job aid or they did not. They either used a job aid during learning or they did not. There are no squishy comparisons between "agree" and "strongly agree" to numb us into inaction.

Here, in this book, I show the graph in grayscale; but, when I make a presentation, I usually use color to send a clearer message. I use green as a signal of good results and red as a signal of poor results. You, of course, will want to conform to the meaning of colors as perceived by your audience. For example, in some regions of the world, red connotes positive meaning, not negative. Also, you should probably do more than I have to consider accessibility standards and color-blindness.

There are several things to note about how to make such a graph. First, I was able to easily use the chart function in PowerPoint® to create this graph. I had to adjust the chart outputs a bit to improve the chart's appearance, but it did not take too long. Moreover, once you get the settings right, you can just make duplicates by copying your original chart and then changing the data.

Second, the answer choices as displayed on the chart were shortened to enable quick readability. Care must be taken in doing this so you don't lose or distort the meaning or

Performance-Focused Learner Surveys

significance of the answer choices. Indeed, it may be useful to offer your audience the full question on a separate slide or document if you decide to shorten the answer choices.

Third, the adjectives on each data point—the standards of acceptability—help make the data more meaningful, but care must be taken in choosing these words. The key is to figure out *first*—before you even deploy your learner survey—what labels you'll use for your standards. If you create labels after you have the data, you're opening up the process to bias and political pressure. As I said earlier, negotiating standards with your stakeholders is a golden opportunity for building understanding and trust, and laying the foundation for improving your learning programs and the supports that enable their success.

You'll note that the chart does not use a legend. Legends are a poor design choice because they force viewers to look back and forth between the data and the label—overwhelming working memory. Where possible, put the label on or near the actual data.

Finally, note that, for select-as-many-as-you-like questions, labels like the "Unacceptable" choice in the graph—"Received one or more worthwhile job aids"—will need an explanation. In this instance, it's not unacceptable if learners get a worthwhile job aid; it's unacceptable if that's all they get. Learners should also be asked to use the job aid in the training program to ensure they know how to use it—to motivate their future use of it and to increase the likelihood that they will remember to use it.

Chapter 13—Presenting Learner-Survey Results

Comparing Current Findings to Previous Findings

While these questions can stand alone, you may also want to compare the current results to previous results to uncover trends. You can do that within the same kind of chart, as shown here.

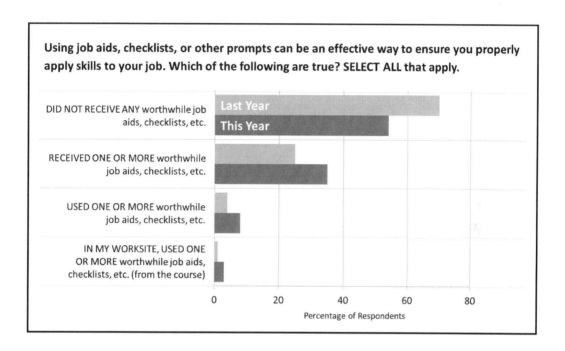

Note that it's probably not good to show this comparison chart first. By showing the noncomparison visual first, and then showing this comparison view, you will help your viewers focus initially on the current findings and then compare those findings to the previous year's findings. This tactic is helpful because it gets your viewers to look deeply at the current situation rather than focusing on the year-to-year differences.

Providing Summary Data Using a Single Question

Looking at the findings for individual questions is great to get folks to focus on critical issues, but you may want to provide some overall summation of the findings as well. There are two ways to do this. First, you can designate one question (or maybe two or three) as the one that best provides an overall sense of the success of your training program.

We might use this question, depicted here with example results.

Performance-Focused Learner Surveys

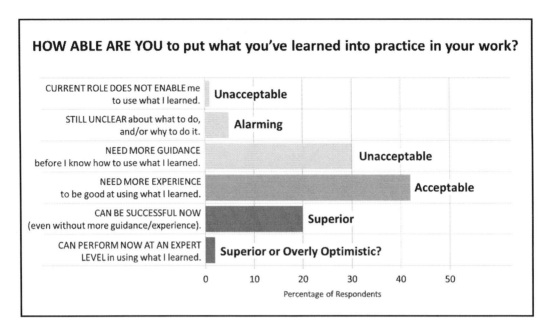

Using one question as indicative of the success of a learning program has benefits and dangers. The benefit is that it provides clear data that can be easily understood. The danger is threefold:

1. By providing one question, we ignore other relevant information.

2. By oversimplifying, we fail to educate our stakeholders about the complexity of our work.

3. By using one question from our learner survey to stand in for all the realities of our learning program, we exacerbate the glorification of our learner-survey results.

By elevating learner perceptions, we are pushing out of mind other learning metrics we are failing to use. We highlight learner perceptions but fail to show whether the learning created knowledge, decision-making competence, and task competence. We fail to show whether the learning was applied on the job and whether it produced beneficial results. To reiterate, when we use learner survey results as our sole benchmark, we glorify learner perceptions beyond their actual worth—as we also ignore their dangers.

Providing Summary Data Using Acceptability Indexing

Instead of using one question, you could create an index using multiple questions—all indexed to the four pillars discussed earlier: (1) understanding, (2) remembering, (3) motivation to apply, and (4) after-training follow-through. To create an index for these, you would first decide which question—or which questions—would be used to calculate a score for each of the four pillars.

Then, for each question, you would calculate the percentage of responses that met the minimum standard for acceptability. Finally, if you were using more than one question to calculate a score for one of the four pillars, you would average the percentage of acceptable-or-better responses.

Let's look at an example.

We'll begin with the first pillar, Understanding. Suppose we were going to use the following question as our sole index of Understanding. Look at the third column, which shows the percentage of responses for each answer choice.

Performance-Focused Learner Surveys

Question 104 – Copied from Earlier		
Question Rationale: Used to determine how well the training helped learners comprehend the concepts taught.		
Now that you've completed the learning experience, how well do you feel you understand the concepts taught? CHOOSE ONE.	*Proposed Standards* Not shown to learners	*Percent of Responses* Not shown to learners
A — I am still at least SOMEWHAT CONFUSED about the concepts.	Alarming	5%
B — I am now SOMEWHAT FAMILIAR WITH the concepts.	Unacceptable	20%
C — I have a SOLID UNDERSTANDING of the concepts.	Acceptable	60%
D — I AM FULLY READY TO USE the concepts in my work.	Superior	14%
E — I have an EXPERT-LEVEL ABILITY to use the concepts.	Superior/ Overconfident?	1%
Calculated Acceptability Index *Percentage of Acceptable Responses*		75%
Note: Learners are NOT shown the text in the gray cells of this table.		

Calculating an acceptability index is easy. All we have to do is add up all the responses that are acceptable or better. In this case, answers C, D, and E are included. C is acceptable. D is superior. E is Superior/Overconfident. We include responses that may be overconfident because we assume that respondents' real level of competence—even if their responses are deemed "Superior/Overconfident?"—are at least "Acceptable." By adding up these percentages, we find the acceptability index for Understanding is 75%.

For the second pillar, Remembering, let's suppose we wanted to use three of the tertiary questions recommended earlier. We would calculate the acceptability index for each question and then take an average. For example:

1. Realistic Retrieval Practice   Acceptability Index: 67%
2. Spaced Repetitions   Acceptability Index: 54%
3. Situation-Action Triggering   Acceptability Index: 23%

Our calculated acceptability index for Remembering would then be 48%: 67 plus 54 plus 23—divided by three. Thus, for the first pillar of training effectiveness (Understanding), our acceptability index would be 75%. For the second pillar (Remembering), our acceptability index would be 48%.

You could, of course, get fancier and utilize weighted averaging—but simple is often better because simple is easier to explain.

Suppose you continued further and calculated acceptability indices for all four pillars and for the overall ability question (Question 101). You could then display your results, for example, on a PowerPoint® slide, as shown here.

Targets	Acceptability Indices GOALS for THIS YEAR	Acceptability Indices ACHIEVED THIS YEAR
The Overall Question	50%	64%
Understanding	60%	75%
Remembering	35%	48%
Motivation to Apply	70%	57%
After-Learning Follow-Through	45%	24%

You'll notice in the chart that goals were created for the acceptability results so the actual results could be compared to the goals. As we all know, goals facilitate motivation, effectiveness, and goal-relevant performance.

Performance-Focused Learner Surveys

Note that, while the chart above is in grayscale, we could colorize or shade the chart to indicate our level of success. For example, goals that were met could be displayed in a deep lush green, while goals nearly met could be orange and goals not met could be red. One piece of advice: If you don't have a talent for creating aesthetically appealing visuals—or you don't know the visual-accessibility standards—you might want to find a graphic designer to help you plan the colors or shades you use.

Complications in Calculating Acceptability Indices

The questions above from which we calculated acceptability indices have required relatively straightforward calculations. Unfortunately, not all questions will be so easy. Take the case of the question we looked at earlier related to "applying learning to the job."

Question 120 – Repeated from Earlier		
Question Rationale: Used to determine the extent to which learners will get support after the learning intervention.		
After the course, when you begin to apply your new knowledge at your worksite, which of the following supports are likely to be in place for you? **SELECT AS MANY ITEMS as are likely to be true.**		*Proposed Standards* *Not shown to learners*
A	MY MANAGER WILL ACTIVELY SUPPORT ME with key supports like time, resources, advice, and/or encouragement.	Acceptable
B	I will use a COACH OR MENTOR to guide me in applying the learning to my work.	Acceptable
C	I will regularly receive support from a COURSE INSTRUCTOR to help me in applying the learning to my work.	Acceptable
D	I will be given JOB AIDS like checklists, search tools, or reference materials to guide me in applying the learning to my work.	Acceptable
E	Through a LEARNING APP or other means, I will be PERIODICALLY REMINDED of key concepts and skills that were taught.	Acceptable
F	I will NOT get much direct support but will rely on my own initiative.	Unacceptable
Note: Learners are NOT shown the text in the gray cells of this table. *If calculating an acceptability index, we might consider it acceptable if respondents chose two or three of the acceptable responses. As always, you should base standards of acceptability on your own circumstances, while also negotiating with your key stakeholders.*		

The tricky part is that, if a learner chooses only one of the acceptable answer choices, we might not deem that as acceptable; we might want learners to have the benefit of at least two or three of these after-training supports, for example. Unfortunately, if we want the

Performance-Focused Learner Surveys

learners to select more than one choice for their response to merit overall acceptability, then we will experience some mathematical complications. In particular, we won't be able to simply add up the percentage responses received by each answer choice.

Here's the problem: Let's say we have ten learners and they all choose only A and B. Take a look above to see what I'm talking about. Using the simple method discussed above, Answer A would have 100% acceptability. So would Answer B. Answer C, D, E, would have 0% acceptability because nobody chose them. If we then added up and averaged our acceptability, we would have 33.3% acceptability (essentially here, two of the six answers)—which doesn't make any sense at all. Simply put, when we give learners the option of choosing multiple answers, we have to find another way to calculate acceptability.

The way that makes the most sense—that is easiest to understand—is that we simply decide in advance what is acceptable. You'll notice I've done this work for you for each of these types of questions. Look at the bottommost gray cells of each question. There I have recommended an acceptability calculation (only for the choose-as-many-as-you-like questions). Of course, if you tailor the questions, you'll have to determine your own acceptability rules for each question.

To reiterate, look in the bottommost cell of the table. I say, *"If calculating an acceptability index, we might consider it acceptable if respondents chose two or three of the acceptable responses."* I'm giving you a choice between two or three as your threshold. I hope it's obvious that, if a respondent selects four or five of the acceptable options, that's great too!

Remember: We're not seeking perfection, but validity with workability.

Chapter 13—Presenting Learner-Survey Results

Summary: Sharing Learner-Survey Results

In this chapter, I attempted to give you some ideas and guidelines about how to report the learner-survey data. As I hope I made clear, this is not a throwaway task but an extremely critical one.

I have identified nine keys to reporting the data:

1. Share all the data gathered or you'll introduce bias into the process. The corollary to this is that you should not gather data you're not going to share.

2. Before presenting the data, share the four-pillar model to ensure your audience knows why you're tracking what you're tracking.

3. Also, share the standards for acceptability to guide and support your audience's interpretation of the data.

4. When sharing the results, first examine each of the learner-survey questions separately—because each has been designed to get at a specific critical aspect of training design, deployment, and follow-through. Wait to share any summary data.

5. Use good visual design principles in sharing the data—especially putting labels near the data, keeping the visual as uncluttered as possible, and seeking to send clear messages through the visual design elements.

6. Integrate the concept of acceptability into your visuals, letting your audience know where the data show good results and where the data show poor results. In other words, don't just share the data without framing its meaning.

7. Consider setting goals for your acceptability indices and comparing current results to those goals.

8. Consider comparing current results to previous results to see if outcomes are trending in the right direction.

9. Consider sharing the LTEM framework and showing how your learner surveys are represented at Tier 3—Learner Perceptions. This will also highlight to your audience how learner surveys are capturing only some of the data you could be measuring—perhaps enticing some stakeholders to support additional evaluation efforts.

Chapter 14
Making It Happen

The ideas in this book are freakin' revolutionary. That's both good news and bad news. It's good news because the old way of doing learner surveys just wasn't working. It's bad news because, now that you've read this book, you too are out on the bleeding edge of the revolution—unless you're reading this somewhere ages and ages hence, and then this warning won't make all that much difference.

Revolutions are difficult. Mere change efforts are difficult. This is no time for an extended dissertation on how to lead a change effort. Instead, I'm going to keep this short and sweet and target this for those of you who want to bring performance-focused learner surveys to your organization.

Arguments to Make Your Case

Providing rational arguments is worth a try—even if they don't always work that well. This book, in some sense, is a rational argument; so, if you want to craft your own argument, you might want to borrow heavily from the arguments in this book. Here are some shortcuts:

You: "Our current smile sheets have the following flaws: (1) they are not designed based on research-based best practices and are not aligned with how workplace learning actually works to support on-the-job performance; (2) they use poorly constructed questions, often with fuzzy answer choices; and (3) they don't support our learners in actually answering the questions—so our learner surveys suffer from the garbage-in, garbage-out problem. Indeed, scientists who have studied learner surveys like ours have found them almost completely uncorrelated with learning! Fortunately, this gorgeous man-hunk of a learning consultant, Dr. Will Thalheimer—who's also a brilliant, humble humanitarian—has developed a new research-based design for learner surveys: the performance-focused learner survey."

Performance-Focused Learner Surveys

You: "What is our primary goal in workplace learning? If we had to choose between creating highly rated training or creating actual on-the-job performance improvement, wouldn't we choose performance improvement? But what do our current learner surveys focus on? They focus on training; they focus on the classroom; they focus on online learning. It's time we updated our learner surveys to be more performance focused. Fortunately..."

Them: "But learner surveys really aren't that important. Why are we spending any time on them?"

You: "As business leaders have so wisely observed, 'what gets measured, gets managed.' Now it's true that most learner surveys aren't used to actually manage anything, but that's a function of the quality of the data they've been producing. There's a new method for creating learner surveys that will actually help us gather meaningful data—data we can use to make our training more effective and more efficient."

Them: "But won't better learner surveys take more time and resources?"

You: "No, not really. They'll actually help save time and money by giving us the feedback we need to make our training programs significantly better, wildly better, orders of magnitude better! How many trainings have you been to where you forgot most of what you learned after a couple of weeks? Or, how many trainings do we have in this organization that get people all pumped up but then send them back to work where they're overwhelmed, where they get no support to implement what they learned in training, where the momentum from the training basically fades away? Well, these new learner surveys will actually track critical factors in training that support long-term performance.

You: "Specifically, these performance-focused learner surveys—that's what they're called—index data under four key factors that link training to performance outcomes: (1) Do the learners actually understand what they're learning well enough to make job-relevant decisions and successfully apply job-relevant skills? (2) Do the learners actually remember what they've learned? Because, if they don't remember it, we've wasted a ton of money! (3) Are the learners invested in what they've learned; are they motivated to take what they've learned and use it in their jobs? (4) Are after-training supports in place to remind learners of what they learned, guide them to appropriate actions even when they can't remember everything, keep them motivated to follow through, and provide them with guidance, support, and oversight to propel their success? These four key success factors—understanding, remembering, motivation to apply, and after-training follow-through—are used to design the questions used on the learner survey. So now, if we use the new learner survey design, we'll actually get learner-survey data that means something. Finally, these performance-focused learner surveys were inspired by the scientific research on learning—which is more than we can say for our current smile sheets."

Them: "But won't these performance-focused learner surveys make some of our trainers and instructional designers uncomfortable?"

You: "Yes, they will. Damn right! Two things about that. First, they'll make our weakest trainers and instructional designers nervous because they'll finally be held accountable for performance. Because our current learner surveys are uncorrelated with learning results, nobody can be held accountable. Not even me. For our best and brightest, however, these new learner surveys will be a breath of fresh air. For years, our best folks have been pushing for better learning designs, but the organization hasn't been responsive because the data leaves all of us in the dark about costs and benefits. We've even lost some of our best people when they've seen we weren't going to implement proven learning designs. With the new learner surveys—and the better feedback loops they enable—our best and brightest will be able to innovate to actually drive improved on-the-job performance. Not only that, but the insights from the new data will help our best and brightest learn more quickly in their work—creating a more responsive improvement cycle. Our best and brightest will love the cultural change engendered by the new learner surveys! And, we'll gradually get a reputation as a great place to do good work, with all of the recruiting benefits that implies. "Second, change is hard. This change may be resisted at first. We'll all be a touch uncomfortable, but we'll get through it—to a much better place."

Them: "What's the business case for using these new learner surveys?"

You: "The bottom line is that the new learner surveys are going to make our training much, much more effective. That, in turn, will help our folks perform better, be more innovative, waste less time doing the wrong things, waste less time in training that has little impact, and enable our organization to succeed. That's the standard business case argument, but here's another way to look at this. Performance-focused learner surveys create a competitive advantage. If our competition starts using these before we do, they'll accelerate their learning-based job improvement before we do—and this is likely to be subject to reciprocal causality—a snowball effect. Improvements will get magnified with every iteration. If our competition gets started first in improving their learning results, we may not be able to catch up for years!"

Suggestions for Getting Started

Your great persuasion skills notwithstanding, arguments will only get you so far. One of the best ways to get traction in any change initiative is to try stuff out, experiment a little, pilot something to learn how it works and how to make it work better. Fly under the radar until you have some data to show that the new way of doing things is having an impact in your organization. Find one or two trainers and/or instructional designers who want to try this out—people who are really hungry to learn and are open to honest (and maybe even harsh) feedback as long as it's informative. Roll it out for their courses. Praise their initiative. Let them talk to you and to their colleagues about what they learned. Make improvements based on their insights. Gather their testimonials.

Another way to think about this is to frame the performance-focused learner surveys as part of a larger strategic initiative to look for ways to improve your training-and-development results. You know what you need to do here! First, gather information. Use the performance-focused learner surveys as one of several data-gathering techniques to capture baseline data and look for blind spots. Second, begin to reeducate your workplace learning-and-performance team to be more focused on performance improvement. With your full team, build a new strategic vision. As you begin implementing the new strategic vision for workplace learning, continue to use performance-focused learner surveys to gauge your progress.

Caveats and Warnings

Traditional smile sheets are a clear and present danger to our field. A much better option—as this book demonstrates—are performance-focused learner surveys using distinctive questioning. But, my dear reader, let me remind you of a key idea that I have already emphasized with rough language and insightful argumentation. Learner surveys *are not* and *cannot* provide us with all the feedback we need as workplace professionals. Neither can they provide full information to our organizations, to our clients, or to our learners. Nor can we rely on the Kirkpatrick-Katzell Four-Level Model or the Phillips five-level ROI model or Roger Kaufman's societal-impact model, or any of the Kirkpatrick-

Katzell variants. In my forthcoming book (circa 2022-2023), *The CEO's Guide to Training, eLearning & Work: Reshaping Learning into a Competitive Advantage*, I will more fully discuss my emerging LEADS framework, but for now let me just list some of the key aspects we can also measure as learning professionals:

- On-the-job behavior targeted for performance improvement.
- On-the-job behavior not specifically targeted for performance improvement.
- Factors that support and enable on-the-job behavior.
- Factors that hinder on-the-job behavior.
- Learner understanding.
- Learner remembering.
- Realistic decision-making performance.
- Validity, deployment, use, and effectiveness of prompting mechanisms.
- On-the-job learning support for remembering.
- On-the-job learning support for just-in-time learning.
- On-the-job learning support for prompting.
- Learner benefits.
- Organizational results.

So, I beg of you, please do *not* end your learning-measurement efforts with learner surveys. Have I been clear enough about this?

Creating A Learner Survey—Recommended Process

In this book, I have provided a ton of recommendations, but I'm betting you still want to know what process I recommend for creating your own learner surveys. Here it is. Please modify to fit your organizational culture and needs. Most importantly, fit this process into a larger learning-evaluation process where you are considering more than just learner perceptions!

1. *Audit Past Learner Surveys*

    Gather your previous learner surveys and analyze their strengths and weaknesses. Utilize a learner-survey expert, where budget and resourcing allows.

2. *Create Advisory Team*

    Gather a learner-survey advisory team—including your key stakeholders, if possible—and especially where you don't have full authority to create, deploy, report, and draw conclusions from any learner surveys you create. Add a learner-survey expert to your team, where budget and resourcing allows.

3. *Determine Purpose*

    Determine the purpose of creating a learner survey. Who will see the data? How might they use it? What decisions will it enable them to make?

4. *Determine Target Messaging*

    What messages do you want to send with your learner survey questions? Who will benefit from these messages? What brand or reputation do you want to convey with your learner survey?

5. *Rough Draft*

    Create a first draft of your learner survey—utilizing performance-focused learner-survey questions as inspiration. Alternatively, ask a learner-survey expert to craft the first draft based on input from the purpose and messaging phases listed above.

6. *Review Rough Draft*

    Get review from a learner-survey expert; or, if your expert created the first draft, you should review draft.

7. *Craft First Draft*

    Based on review, craft the first draft—that is, the first draft available for public review, with your advisory team and other key stakeholders.

8. *Get Stakeholder Feedback*

    Get review from your advisory team and other key stakeholders.

9. *Craft Pilot Version*

    Craft the pilot version of your learner survey—asking your learner-survey expert or crafting it yourself.

10. *Deploy Pilot Survey*

    Utilize the pilot version of your survey for one or more learning programs.

11. *Review Pilot Data*

    Review the pilot data with two purposes in mind. First, look at what the data tells you about the learning programs you've targeted with your learner survey. Second, see if the questions on the survey are working as intended and whether question improvements are warranted. Where possible, utilize a learner-survey expert to do this work.

12. *Utilize Pilot Survey Findings*

    Utilize the pilot survey findings as you would normally. For example, if you would share the results with instructors to determine course improvements, do that! Take note of how this all works out to utilize later for survey improvements.

13. *Build Final Survey*

    Based on everything you've learned—and after getting feedback from your advisory team and other key stakeholders—craft your final survey, while also keeping track of your lessons learned.

14. *Do Periodic Reviews*

    Periodically review the survey data to determine whether improvements are needed. Also, periodically consider whether you want to rotate new questions into your surveys and/or rotate questions out.

My Best Wishes—And My Offer of Help

Thank you! Thank you for reading this far, for listening to my ideas, and for occasionally laughing at my jokes (I hope!). My goal in writing this book is to get us to improve our learning-and-performance results—and to get us to reinvent our learner surveys, taking them more seriously as the change lever they can be.

I hope you'll put some or all of this into practice. Please feel free to let me know how I can help—and, just as importantly, let me know how it's going! I would love to hear your success stories, your lessons learned, and your improvements. I've spent years thinking about this, but what I've learned along the way is that I'm always able to make things better. Please help me in that.

Good luck, and may you gather good folks to work with you on this. Pushing for change is much more pleasant and more likely to succeed when we find a cadre of friends and supporters to help us push for improvement together.

Finally, if you'd like me to help your organization, feel free to set up a free thirty-minute conversation by going to: WorkLearning.com/Contact/. Also, you may contact me at TiER1 Performance.

Chapter 15
Measuring Learner Perceptions in Other Ways

Learner surveys are not the only way to gather learner perceptions. There are alternatives—some worthy, some dangerous, and some both. This chapter will be short, but it's important that we consider these options.

Just Ask the Learners

Some trainers avoid learner surveys and simply ask the learners what they think of the learning. *"Okay, it's important that I get feedback on this workshop; but, rather than having you fill in one of those smile sheets, I'd rather hear directly from you. Let's take fifteen minutes to give me feedback on what was good and what could be better."* Red flags, anyone? There are several problems with this design. Most importantly, there is a strong bias against ripping people in public or criticizing them to their face—especially if they've made a good effort. I know, some of you will say that people give you both good and bad feedback, but how do you know they're telling you what you really need to hear? They are probably not!

Also, what about you? Are you really listening? Are you really open to criticism? Or are you hearing what you really want to hear? And do you have a record of their responses or are you remembering their responses clearly or just remembering what you want to remember? The bottom line is that there are two sources of bias when you ask learners to give you feedback: their bias and your bias. Together, this is bad enough, but it is not the only problem.

Let's remember that learners don't always focus on key drivers of learning. By asking them general questions—which most of us are inclined to do when we query our learners in this way—we are not nudging our learners to think of the most relevant learning factors, like whether they got enough challenging practice, whether they will get after-learning supports, whether they are really motivated to put what they learned into practice.

Performance-Focused Learner Surveys

Another problem with this ask-the-learners design is that people may be swayed by what other people say. The first person who speaks may completely bias the rest of the responses—corrupting all the subsequent data.

Let's take a minute. If we were designing these feedback discussions, what would we do to make them as productive as possible? Here's a brief list.

- We would have the instructor leave the room and have another person ask the questions and compile the answers.
- We would ask individuals to write their responses down without first being influenced by others. Maybe we'd give them a learner survey first. LOL.
- We would have a set of questions that nudged learners to think about the most critical learning factors.
- We would have a way to capture the feedback fully so we could review that feedback later without doing it from memory.

In short, we would do the opposite of what many trainers do when they simply ask their learners for feedback! We would realize that asking learners for their feedback is a fool's game.

Okay, let me step off my horse here. Let me admit that I have gained valuable insights by asking my learners for feedback. When it's worked for me, I've been engaged with my learners for a dozen hours or more—where we've built trust. I ask them for feedback because I honestly want to know—they could tell if I was just going through the motions. Still, I don't recommend asking your learners for feedback as an everyday best practice. If you're going to do it, have them first complete a well-designed learner survey, one that highlights critical learning factors. Ask with a real desire to listen. Write down each item of feedback so you can review it later without ignoring the criticisms. Welcome positive and negative feedback alike. Avoid being defensive and avoid blaming circumstances. Be grateful for their forthrightness.

Focus Groups

Focus groups—bringing people together in a small group and asking them questions—is a method that some learning teams have utilized. Commonly used in marketing to get feedback from customers or potential customers, focus groups can provide valuable information, but they suffer from dangers too. First, they take time and resources to accomplish. Second, they take a skilled focus-group facilitator and a list of well-designed questions. Also, they suffer from the same groupthink biasing that can occur when we just ask learners what they think. On the other hand, they can help us explore lines of inquiry to see if there is agreement among participants. A skilled focus-group facilitator can drill down to investigate areas of importance. Unfortunately, it is difficult to find a person who is both skilled in focus-group facilitation and in learning design—to ensure the focus-group conversations are relevant.

Structured Interviews

Structured interviews are interviews that are structured around a set of questions that all interviewees are asked. In some sense, structured interviews are like surveys except that the interviewer can ask follow-up questions to get clarification and to explore a particular aspect of an issue being discussed. The keys to successful structured interviews are finding a good interviewer, creating a good set of questions, finding a representative sample of participants, and having a good way to capture the data so it is valid and can be meaningfully analyzed and presented.

Online Whiteboarding

Online whiteboarding—for example, through tools like Miro, Mural, and Jamboard—can be used to gather learner feedback. We can set up the whiteboarding tools to give learners confidential or semi-confidential responding options: for example, by typing on a virtual sticky note. One advantage is that it may feel more natural to have people do this task during the learning, perhaps increasing response rates—compared to giving them an online survey. Most people will probably focus on their own responding, but some are certainly likely to look at what others type, introducing bias and groupthink into the process. Another downside is that the data will be difficult to report out. And, because all the data is comment data, it is likely to lack clarity and urgency compared to having learners respond to choice questions. In general, I would NOT recommend the use of online whiteboarding for our formal evaluation efforts. On the other hand, I do think online whiteboarding may have value where trust has been built and where learners are engaged in a relatively long learning journey—and the whiteboarding is used almost as formative evaluation to respect your learners and enable mid-course corrections.

Combining Methods

Of course, we don't have to use only one method. We can use a combination. Some companies use a standard learner survey and then sample a small subset for structured interviews or focus groups. Most famously, Rob Brinkerhoff's Case Method utilizes a two-stage process, with a survey followed by structured interviews. Brinkerhoff recommends analyzing the survey data to find people at different levels of learning-application success—learners who created likely successes, those who produced non-successes, and those who experienced middling successes.[66] By first surveying the whole population of learners and then interviewing people represented across the three samples, Brinkerhoff combines surveys and interviews into a purposeful funnel.

Other People's Perceptions

Although this chapter is focused on measuring learner perceptions, I should note that we can measure other people's perceptions as well. We could, for example, ask learners' managers for their perceptions about the progress their direct report is making in utilizing what was learned. As in all evaluation efforts, we would have to be sure that those asked about their perceptions could reliably make the judgments they are asked to make. To ask managers about their perceptions of their direct reports' progress, we would have to have confidence that the managers had access to clear evidence of performance.

In leadership training, there's often a special opportunity to get feedback from others—besides from the manager who is being trained. Let's do a quick thought experiment. If we train a manager to run better team meetings, who will know best how well those team meetings are being run? Will it be the manager running those meetings, the manager's manager, or the manager's direct reports? The manager may be biased and in denial. The manager's manager likely doesn't see these team meetings. The direct reports—those who sit in the team meetings—are likely to provide the best data. If we can figure out the logistics, we may be able to get valuable data from them.

Finally, let me add an idea for you to reflect on. Often experts' perceptions are more accurate than others' perceptions. If we trained sixteen-year-old basketball players to run the pick-and-roll, we would be better off having an expert basketball coach share his or her perceptions than we would getting the perceptions of the players who were trained. It's the same for the team meeting example I shared just above. Although I argued that the best data might come from the learners' direct reports, an expert on meetings would almost

---

[66] Brinkerhoff (2006); Thalheimer (2018).

certainly have more prescient perceptions. I offer this point of reflection even though we typically don't have access to experts. We rely on surveys of learners and their coworkers because expert observers are unavailable or too expensive. Still, when we think about gathering perception data, we ought to see the big picture.

Triangulating from Multiple Sources

It's easier and cheaper to get data from only one source—for example, asking for learners' perceptions on a single survey and that is all. Of course, this is not our only option. By getting data from multiple sources, we may be able to get a clearer picture of what really happened. So, instead of asking only learners for their perceptions, we might ask learners and their coworkers to complete surveys. We might ask learners and their managers. We've already discussed the benefits of getting data from learners at multiple time points—from end-of-learning surveys and follow-up surveys. But let's be a bit careful here. Perception data has the drawback of being subjective, and we humans tend to be poor judges of what works best to spur learning. Even if we get multiple sets of perceptions, we may still be led astray by data that tells a faulty story.

It's much better to pair perception data with more objective forms of data. We can also measure learners' knowledge, their decision-making competence, their ability to use their new skills in realistic, challenging tasks. Obviously, we need to be cognizant of the costs and benefits, but we ought to keep in mind that triangulating from multiple sources—particularly when they demonstrate meaningful learning outcomes—is likely to reveal truer insights. In the next chapter, I will introduce LTEM, a new learning-evaluation model, that consolidates this wisdom by having separate categories for learner perceptions, knowledge, decision-making competence, and task competence.

Chapter 16
LTEM: The Big Picture of Learning Evaluation

Learner surveys may be in the foreground of our learning-evaluation thinking, but they are not (and should not) be the only focal element. Indeed, as I have argued many times in this book, we rely on learner surveys too much while neglecting the full canvas of learning evaluation. In this chapter, I will introduce you to LTEM, pronounced "L-tem" (The Learning-Transfer Evaluation Model), a revolutionary model in learning evaluation—one meant to replace the moribund Kirkpatrick-Katzell Four-Level Model.

The Four-Level Model has strengths and weaknesses. I've outlined these in detail in the LTEM report,[67] but here I will highlight just a few key things. First, the Kirkpatrick-Katzell Model rightly highlights the importance of looking at work performance and ultimate outcomes. It does this simply by having Level 3 Behavior and Level 4 Results placed at a higher priority in its taxonomy. Recall the four levels:

- Level 1—Reactions
- Level 2—Learning
- Level 3—Behavior
- Level 4—Results

It's my belief that the Four-Level Model was one of several major forces in moving the learning-and-development field from a focus on learning to a focus on performance. The Four-Level Model also nicely highlights the low priority we should give to learner surveys—it places them at Level 1.

Unfortunately, the Four-Level Model has more problems than benefits. Ideally, we want our models to push us toward good practices and away from bad practices. The Kirkpatrick-Katzell Four-Level Model fails fundamentally in guiding us. First, it fails to

---

[67] Thalheimer (2018).

warn us about inadequate evaluation approaches. It is silent on our tendency to measure attendance and completion rates as important outcomes. These are insufficient because people can attend a learning event but not learn. The Four-Level Model is silent in warning us about measuring learner activities as an outcome measure. It is insufficient to measure learner attention, interest, or participation—because learners may do all these things but still not learn sufficiently.

The Kirkpatrick-Katzell Model is also insufficient in reminding us that "Results" can go beyond business results. Certainly, there are other results and other stakeholders to consider! What about the impact on learners themselves—on their compensation, their job security, their promotions, their career trajectories, their health, and well-being? What about coworkers? What about looking at impacts to the community, or society, or the environs—as the legendary Roger Kaufman encouraged us to do?[68] As more organizations and business leaders look beyond shareholder value as the only result to target, shouldn't we in learning and development define results more broadly too? Even the Business Roundtable, an organization of United States CEOs, has declared that corporations should promote "an economy that serves all"—that specifically serves multiple stakeholders, including the community beyond the business organization.[69] It's not uncommon to see the Kirkpatrick-Katzell Model's Level 4 being labeled "Business Results" rather than the more expansive "Results" from Donald Kirkpatrick's original writings. This is myopic and inexcusable. I can't help but wonder if it is simply unethical to focus only on organizational results when we do learning evaluation.

The biggest weakness of the Kirkpatrick-Katzell Four-Level Model is its paltry focus on learning. We are *learning* professionals. We are talking about *learning* evaluation. Our evaluation models should illuminate *learning* results, not diminish them. The Four-Level Model puts learning all in one bucket at Level 2—even though learning is at the heart of what we do in learning and development. Here are just some of the learning results that fit into the Level 2 bucket:

- Regurgitation of trivial information
- Recognition of low-importance knowledge
- Recall of low-importance knowledge
- Short-term recognition of high-importance knowledge

---

[68] Roger Kaufman died recently in 2020. You can learn of Roger's work at: https://megaplanning.com/
[69] Business Rountable (2019); Gelles, D., & Yaffe-Bellany (2019).

- Short-term recall of high-importance knowledge
- Long-term recognition of high-importance knowledge
- Long-term recall of high-importance knowledge
- Short-term competence in realistic decision-making
- Long-term competence in realistic decision-making
- Short-term competence in realistic task performance
- Long-term competence in realistic task performance
- Improved creative-ideation based on what was learned
- Et cetera

Obviously, a simple evaluation model can't cover each learning result specifically, but the Kirkpatrick-Katzell Model does serious damage by having no differentiation at all. In practice, the Four-Level Model pushes us toward simple knowledge assessments and poor instructional designs! When our learning teams consider measuring Level 2, we almost always default to simple knowledge checks. This is catastrophic—both from a learning evaluation perspective and a learning design perspective. When we evaluate learning only by assessing knowledge, we become blind to our success in enabling decision-making competence and task competence—results that are much more important than knowledge-creation alone. Secondly, when our evaluations focus only on knowledge, our learning designs follow. What gets measured gets managed. What gets measured gets designed! When we evaluate for knowledge, we design for knowledge! The Kirkpatrick-Katzell Four-Level Model pushes us away from good learning designs by pushing us toward the measurement of knowledge in lieu of measuring deeper levels of learning like decision-making competence and task competence.[70] In short, the Four-Level Model lacks learning intelligence—and, since we are in the learning business, the model is insufficient even if we consider this weakness alone.

---

[70] Another learning result that is worth contemplating is the ability of a person to use what they've learned to spark useful creative insights. I have not added this to the LTEM framework because measuring creative ideation is not as straightforward as measuring knowledge, decision-making competence, or task competence.

How LTEM is Better

LTEM was designed specifically to support us as learning professionals—specifically to nudge us away from inadequate learning evaluations and toward more useful evaluation approaches. Although in this book I can only touch on LTEM briefly, I will describe and comment on each of the eight tiers of the model.

LTEM is pronounced "L-tem." I keep emphasizing this so we can communicate clearly—so we can all sing in unison. LTEM stands for the Learning-Transfer Evaluation Model. It is designed to help us gauge our success in moving learners to use what they've learned in their work. The word "transfer," at least in learning-and-development parlance, means learners take what they've learned and use it in their jobs or in their lives. If we teach managers to coach better, we will see transfer when they use their new skills to coach their direct reports. If they use their new coaching skills outside of the workplace—for example, to organize a team to help build a shelter for the homeless—we would still consider transfer to have occurred, though we may or may not register this as a success, depending on our goals.

Okay, so here is LTEM, one tier at a time.

- *Tier 1—Attendance.* There is value in measuring attendance and completion rates—to give us basic insights about how people are engaging in learning—but, because people can attend but not learn, measuring attendance is insufficient to validate learning results.

- *Tier 2—Activity.* There is value in measuring attention, interest, and participation—to give us insights into how our learning activities are being engaged—but, because learners may do all these things but still not learn sufficiently, measuring activity is not sufficient to validate learning.

- *Tier 3—Learner.* Perceptions. There is value in measuring learner perceptions—because the reputation of our learning events can affect future engagement and our ability to gain resources and autonomy— but measuring learner perceptions is tricky for many several reasons, as already noted in this book. Learners are not always good judges of learning. Our learner surveys are not always well designed. Bias can creep in where precautions are not taken.

   Tier 3 is divided into two levels. Level A is focused on learning effectiveness and Level B is focused on learner satisfaction and the reputation of the learning. Performance-focused learner surveys aim for Level A. Traditional smile sheets are represented at Level B. Neither A nor B is sufficient to validate learning results but, by focusing on learning effectiveness at Level A, we can provide hints of important learning outcomes.

- *Tier 4—Knowledge.* There is value in measuring knowledge, but usually knowledge alone is insufficient to enable performance. For this reason, measuring knowledge is usually inadequate to validate learning. Starting at Tier 4, LTEM highlights short-term effects versus long-term effects. Almost always we want our learning interventions to support relatively long-term retrieval of what was learned—at least over several days or more. Momentary improvements are not usually sufficient to create behavior-change benefits.

- *Tier 5—Decision-Making Competence.* This tier represents the first level that is adequate to certify the kind of competence required to lead to learning transfer. We want our learners to use what they've learned to be able to make realistic relevant decisions. Here again, as in Tier 4, it is remembered competence that is the higher goal. If learners only show decision-making competence in the learning event, but can't show it three or more days afterward, we can't really certify full success.

- *Tier 6—Task Competence.* This tier is fulfilled when learners can perform relevant realistic actions and make decisions that go along with them. Again, it is remembered task competence that is the goal. It is not enough to show competence during learning, but learners must be able to demonstrate competence after a delay of several days or more.

- *Tier 7 – Transfer.* This tier is the first that focuses on work performance rather than performance in learning. To go back to our coaching example, if a person trained in coaching uses their skills competently with their direct reports, then they have transferred their learning and achieved Tier 7 results.

- *Tier 8—Effects of Transfer.* This tier measures our ultimate outcomes. We hope managers who coach better don't just coach better. We hope that those they coach will produce better results—for example, creating higher quality outputs, helping raise revenues, reducing costs, improving safety, producing more innovative work products, and the like. LTEM here specifically highlights the effects of transfer on a variety of stakeholders, *"including (a) learners, (b) coworkers/ family/friends, (c) organization, (d) community, (e) society, and (f) the environs."*

LTEM is no panacea, but it is extremely helpful in many regards. Even though it is relatively new, already it is being studied by academic researchers. Elham Arabi at the University of Nevada Las Vegas did her doctoral dissertation on LTEM and found that introducing LTEM to a learning team spurred the learning team to aspire to higher levels of learning evaluation and better learning designs. I encourage you to learn more about LTEM: Look at the one-page framework and the 34-page report—both of which I have made available for free on the Work-Learning Research website.[71]

I introduced LTEM here—not only because I think it will provide value to you and your organization—but also to make it clear that even well-designed performance-focused learner surveys are still not everything we should be measuring. More bluntly, as the LTEM model says about learner surveys, *"such measures can hint at outcomes but should be augmented with objective outcome measures."* The bottom line is this: You can radically improve your learner surveys—and you should do that—but you should go beyond LTEM Tier 3 (learner perceptions) and consider measuring Tier 4 (knowledge), Tier 5 (decision-making competence), Tier 6 (task competence), Tier 7 (transfer), and Tier 8 (effects of transfer). We don't need to measure all eight tiers for every learning program—that would be too expensive and too often redundant—but we should examine our evaluation approaches and look for opportunities to gather better data so we can make better decisions, so we can make improvements, so we can be more effective.

---

[71] LTEM Framework and Report are available at: WorkLearning.com/LTEM

Epilogue
Where Do We Go from Here?

This book has ended, but I'd like to leave you with a bigger message. Performance-focused learner surveys are a powerful improvement over past evaluation practices, but they are only a starting point in a cycle of improvement. I've worked in the workplace learning-and-performance field for over thirty years, and I—along with many people in our field with whom I communicate—have concluded that our field is accelerating toward greater and greater professionalization.

Within the span of my career, research psychologists have been able to confirm and illuminate key factors that are critical to the effectiveness of learning interventions. Similarly, research on training has demonstrated where and how additional supports are crucial in creating success. We now know a great deal about what needs to be done—but, unfortunately, there are still pockets where ineffective learning interventions are the norm. Poor learner-survey design is a potent factor, one that can easily be fixed—but learning evaluation is just one point of leverage for us.

We Need to Work Together!

The truth is that we have, in our field, a dedicated cadre of brilliant, passionate, and tireless champions of good learning-and-performance approaches. Let us join together in moving the field forward. Let us seek out and gather around people who are doing great work. Let us learn from them. Let us learn from each other.

Since I wrote the first edition of this book in 2015, I have been thrilled with the increasing visibility of research-to-practice learning-and-development consultants such as Julie Dirksen, Patti Shank, Clark Quinn, Karl Kapp, Mirjam Neelen, and Jane Bozarth (among others), and the continuing reach of Ruth Clark even after her retirement. These are my heroes and should be your heroes as well. They put blood, sweat, and tears (believe me when I say this!) into compiling and curating research and making it available to the L&D field. They have pushed to make their work available to you as a learning professional, but sometimes their work (and mine, if I'm honest) has gotten sidelined in a sea of vendor marketing and underemphasis from some of our professional organizations.

Performance-Focused Learner Surveys

For my small part, I will continue encouraging and supporting people like you who are doing good work. I am writing a new book, *CEO's Guide to Training, eLearning & Work: Reshaping Learning into a Competitive Advantage,* which will educate senior leaders about learning and development, while simultaneously encouraging us as learning professionals to develop a more productive partnership with our organizational sponsors.

The key to transformation in the L&D field is to simultaneously undermine the structures that weaken our work while celebrating and sharing the good work that we are doing and the ideas that enable our continued effectiveness!

I'd like to give you an invitation to a very special organization that I founded a year ago with Matt Richter, the Learning Development Accelerator (LDA). We founded LDA to provide a place dedicated to professionals in the learning-and-development field.

In the first year of COVID, in 2020 before we'd even thought to start LDA, Matt and I created the L&D Conference to provide a place for people in our field to meet when all the face-to-face conferences were being cancelled. We took the opportunity to rethink what a conference might be. In short, we wanted a conference that was designed to support learning—to help attendees take their learning back to their work. The L&D Conference 2020 was a place where validated ideas were surfaced, attendees were encouraged to embrace more practically rigorous methods, and thought leaders and sponsors were celebrated for taking evidence-based approaches. The conference was a six-week online experience—the first of its kind—yet it was a resounding success, with 90% of attendees saying it was better than other L&D conferences they had attended, and almost 30% saying it was "BY FAR THE BEST conference" they had ever attended—whether face-to-face or online!

This is all good news—and I'm clearly bragging—but I'm sharing all this as an example of the kind of community-building effort that we should continue in the learning-and-development field.

In the big picture, research-aligned practices are being utilized more and more. The most popular book sold by the Association for Talent Development is Clark Quinn's *Learning Science for Instructional Designers*. Julie Dirksen's *Design for How People Learn* is one of the bestselling books of all time in the L&D field. Patti Shank continues to publish research-inspired books like her instant classic on how to *Write Better Multiple-Choice Questions*. Mirjam Neelen recently authored—with researcher Paul Kirschner—*Evidence-Informed Learning Design: Creating Training to Improve Performance*. Jane Bozarth continues to publish research-inspired reports like, *The Truth About Teaching to Learning Styles, and What to Do Instead*. Karl Kapp brings research wisdom to the areas of gaming, gamification, and microlearning. Guy Wallace shares information on myths to avoid and compiles critical historical insights on his *HPT Treasures* website. Paul Kirschner continues his seminal work related to both education and training with his many books and co-authors. And, of course, there is the legendary Ruth Clark who continues to write and update her many classic books—keeping them current and formidable in their practicality.

We need to continue this accelerating trend, to promote research-aligned practices, to build on our diverse and global community of learning professionals, to work together to build professionalization into the DNA of our field, to build partnerships of members helping members learn, connect, and support each other in development.

I encourage you to join professional organizations that provide their members with unbiased research-aligned content and speakers, like LDA (https://ldaccelerator.com/), like ISPI (https://ispi.org/), and the Learning Guild's research work by Jane Bozarth.

I have another invitation for you. After 22 years at my one-person consulting practice—Work-Learning Research, Inc.—I joined TiER1 Performance last year as a principal. TiER1 is an amazing organization, with a mission to help people do their best work, to make the world of work better for everyone, to help organizations activate their business and operational strategies—including learning strategies—through the performance of their people. As part of a team of nearly 300 people, I can now do more good work. Please join me, sign up on our list (https://tier1performance.com/), and stay tuned as we stand up learning opportunities through our Performance Institute, through our articles and research, and through our consulting work (https://tier1performance.com/performance-institute/).

And, finally, I invite you to stay in touch with me by signing up for my newsletter at WorkLearning.com/sign-up/. Yes! I'm still keeping my Work-Learning website up and running—the research reports will remain there and I'll add periodic updates on my blog with links to new research, new articles, new books, new workshops, new special moments.

Performance-Focused Learner Surveys

How You Can Help Spread the Word

If you liked this book, pass it along to your colleagues, blog about it, tweet about it, write an honest review of it, or rate it on Amazon.com. Better yet, buy several copies and gift them to friends and colleagues. Consider hiring me and the world-class team at TiER1 Performance to help your organization.

Thank you for supporting my work! Thank you for creating great learning! Thank you for helping the learning field! Thank you for helping make the world a little bit better through learning!

= Will Thalheimer

References... Research Inspiration

Ahmad, T. (2018). Teaching evaluation and student response rate. *PSU Research Review, 3*, 206-211.

Alliger, G. M., Tannenbaum, S. I., Bennett, W., Jr., Traver, H., & Shotland, A. (1997). A meta-analysis of the relations among training criteria. *Personnel Psychology, 50*, 341–358.

Bahrick, H. P., & Hall, L. K. (2005). The importance of retrieval failures to long-term retention: A metacognitive explanation of the spacing effect. *Journal of Memory and Language, 52*, 566–577.

Berk, R.A. (2012). Top 20 strategies to increase the online response rates of student rating scales. *International Journal of Technology in Teaching and Learning, 8*, 98-107.

Bjork, R. A., & Richardson-Klavehn, A. (1989). On the puzzling relationship between environmental context and human memory. In C. Izawa (Ed.) *Current Issues in Cognitive Processes: The Tulane Flowerree Symposium on Cognition,* pp. 313–344. Hillsdale, NJ: Erlbaum.

Boehle, S. (2006). Are you too nice to train? *Training Magazine*, August.

Bransford, J. D., Franks, J. J., Morris, C. D., & Stein, B. S. (1979). Some general constraints on learning and memory research. In L. S. Cermak & F. I. M. Craik (Eds.), *Levels of Processing in Human Memory*, pp. 331–354. Hillsdale, NJ: Erlbaum.

Brinkerhoff, R. O. (2006). *Telling training's story: Evaluation made simple, credible, and effective.* Berrett-Koehler.

Brown, P. C., Roediger, H. L., III, & McDaniel, M. A. (2014). *Make It Stick: The Science of Successful Learning*. Cambridge, MA: Belknap Press of Harvard University Press.

Business Roundtable (2019). *Business Roundtable redefines the purpose of a corporation to promote 'An economy that serves all Americans.'* Available at: https://www.businessroundtable.org/business-roundtable-redefines-the-purpose-of-a-corporation-to-promote-an-economy-that-serves-all-americans.

Cain, L. F., & Willey, R. (1939). The effect of spaced learning on the curve of retention. *Journal of Experimental Psychology, 25*, 209–214.

Carpenter, S. K., Cepeda, N. J., Rohrer, D., Kang, S. H. K., & Pashler, H. (2012). Using spacing to enhance diverse forms of learning: Review of recent research and implications for instruction. *Educational Psychology Review, 24* (3), 369–378.

Crowder, R. G. (1976). *Principles of Learning and Memory*. Hillsdale, NJ: Erlbaum.

Davies, G. (1986). Context effects in episodic memory: A review. *Cahiers de Psychologie Cognitive, 6*, 157–174.

Deane, C., Kennedy, C., Keeter, S. (2019). *A field guide to polling: Election 2020 edition*. Pew Research Center. Available at: https://www.pewresearch.org/methods/2019/11/19/a-field-guide-to-polling-election-2020-edition/.

Delaney, P. F., Verkoeijen, P. P. J. L., & Spirgel, A. (2010). Spacing and testing effects: A deeply critical, lengthy, and at times discursive review of the literature. In B. H. Ross (Ed.), *The Psychology of Learning and Motivation. Vol. 53, Advances in Research and Theory,* pp. 63–147. San Diego: Elsevier Academic Press.

Dempster, F. N. (1988). The spacing effect: A case study in the failure to apply the results of psychological research. *American Psychologist, 43*, 627–634.

Dempster, F. N. (1989). Spacing effects and their implications for theory and practice. *Educational Psychology Review, 1*, 309–330.

Dempster, F. N. (1996). Distributing and managing the conditions of encoding and practice. In E. L. Bjork & R. A. Bjork (Eds.), *Memory,* pp. 317–344. San Diego: Academic Press.

Donovan, J. J., & Radosevich, D. J. (1999). A meta-analytic review of the distribution of practice effect: Now you see it, now you don't. *Journal of Applied Psychology, 84*, 795–805.

Eich, J. E. (1980). The cue-dependent nature of state-dependent retrieval. *Memory and Cognition, 8*, 157–173.

Fiske, S. T., Cuddy, A. J. C., & Glick, P. (2007). Universal dimensions of social cognition: Warmth and competence. *Trends in Cognitive Sciences, 11*(2), 77–83.

Ford, J. K., Kraiger, K., & Merritt, S. (2010). The multidimensionality of learning outcomes revisited. In S. W. J. Kozlowski & E. Salas (Eds.), *Learning, training, and development in organizations* (pp. 135–165). Mahwah, NJ: LEA.

Friedman, S., & Ronen, S. (2015). The effect of implementation intentions on transfer of training. *European Journal of Social Psychology, 45*(4), 409-416.

Gelles, D., & Yaffe-Bellany (2019). Shareholder value is no longer everything, top CEOs Say. *New York Times*. Available at:

https://www.nytimes.com/2019/08/19/business/business-roundtable-ceos-corporations.html

Glenberg, A. M. (1979). Component-levels theory of the effects of spacing and repetitions on recall and recognition. *Memory & Cognition, 7*, 95–112.

Gollwitzer, P. M., & Sheeran, P. (2006). Implementation intentions and goal achievement: A meta-analysis of effects and processes. *Advances in Experimental Social Psychology, 38*, 69–119.

Gude, F., & Malliaris, M. (2013). Online course evaluations response rates. *American Journal of Business Education, 6*, 333-338.

Hendra, R., & Hill, A. (2018). Rethinking response rates: New evidence of little relationship between survey response rates and nonresponse bias. *Evaluation Review, 43*, 307-330.

Hintzman, D. L. (1974). Theoretical implications of the spacing effect. In R. L. Solso (Ed.), *Theories in Cognitive Psychology: The Loyola Symposium,* pp. 77–99. Potomac, MD: Erlbaum.

Hughes, A. M., Gregory, M. E., Joseph, D. L., Sonesh, S. C., Marlow, S. L., Lacerenza, C. N., Benishek, L. E., King, H. B., Salas, E. (2016). Saving lives: A meta-analysis of team training in healthcare. *Journal of Applied Psychology, 101*(9), 1266-1304.

Kennedy, C., & Hartig, H. (2019). *Response rates in telephone surveys have resumed their decline*. Pew Research Center. Available at: https://www.pewresearch.org/fact-tank/2019/02/27/response-rates-in-telephone-surveys-have-resumed-their-decline/.

Khorsandi, M., Kobra, A., Ghobadzadeh, M., Kalantari, M., & Seifei, M. (2012). Online vs. traditional teaching evaluation: A cross-sectional study. *Procedia—Social and Behavioral Sciences, 46*, 481-483.

Kirschner, P. A., & van Merriënboer, J. J. G. (2013). Do learners really know best? Urban legends in education. *Educational Psychologist, 48*(3), 169–183.

Lee, T. D., & Genovese, E. D. (1988). Distribution of practice in motor skill acquisition: Different effects for discrete and continuous tasks. *Research Quarterly for Exercise and Sport, 60*, 59–65.

Luo, M. N. (2020). Student response rate and its impact on quantitative evaluation of faculty teaching. The Advocate (Kansas Association of Teacher Educators), 25, 1-9.

Melton, A. W. (1970). The situation with respect to the spacing of repetitions and memory. *Journal of Verbal Learning and Verbal Behavior, 9*, 596–606.

Nordgren, L. (2021). Personal story told on the podcast *Hidden Brain*. Available at: https://hiddenbrain.org/podcast/work-2-0-the-obstacles-you-dont-see/.

Nordgren, L. & Schonthal, D. (2021). *The Human Element: Overcoming the Resistance that Awaits New Ideas*. Wiley.

Nulty, D. D. (2008). The adequacy of response rates to online and paper surveys: What can be done? *Assessment & Evaluation in Higher Education, 3*, 301-314.

Rea, C. P., & Modigliani, V. (1988). Educational implications of the spacing effect. In M. M. Gruneberg, P. E. Morris, & R. N. Sykes (Eds.) *Practical Aspects of Memory: Current Research and Issues*. Vol. 1, *Memory in Everyday Life,* pp. 402–406. New York: John Wiley & Sons.

Roediger, H. L., III, & Guynn, M. J. (1996). Retrieval processes. In E. L. Bjork & R. A. Bjork (Eds.), *Memory,* pp. 197–236. San Diego: Academic Press.

Ruch, T. C. (1928). Factors influencing the relative economy of massed and distributed practice in learning. *Psychological Review, 35*, 19–45.

Ryan, R. M., Deci, E. L. (2017) *Self-determination theory: Basic psychological needs in motivation, development, and wellness.* New York: Guilford Publishing.

Ryan, R. M., Deci, E. L. (2019) Brick by brick: The origins, development, and future of self-determination theory. *Advances in Motivation Science, 6*, 111-156.

Salas, E., Tannenbaum, S. I., Kraiger, K., & Smith-Jentsch, K. A. (2012). The science of training and development in organizations: What matters in practice. *Psychological Science in the Public Interest, 13*(2), 74–101.

Shrock, S. A., & Coscarelli, W. C. (2007). *Criterion-Referenced Test Development: Technical and Legal Guidelines for Corporate Training, 3rd ed.* San Francisco: Wiley.

Sitzmann, T., Brown, K. G., Casper, W. J., Ely, K., & Zimmerman, R. D. (2008). A review and meta-analysis of the nomological network of trainee reactions. *Journal of Applied Psychology, 93*(2), 280–295.

Smith, S. M. (1988). Environmental context-dependent memory. In G. M. Davies & D. M. Thomson (Eds.), *Memory in Context: Context in Memory,* pp. 13–34. Chichester, UK: Wiley.

Smith, S. M., & Vela, E. (2001). Environmental context-dependent memory: A review and meta-analysis. *Psychonomic Bulletin & Review, 8*, 203–220.

Thalheimer, W. (2007). *Measuring learning results: Creating fair and valid assessments by considering findings from fundamental learning research.* Available at: https://www.worklearning.com/2007/05/08/measuring_learn/.

Thalheimer, W. (2018). *One of the biggest lies in learning evaluation—Asking learners about Level 3 and 4 (LTEM Tiers 7 and 8).* Available at: https://www.worklearning.com/2018/01/18/one-of-the-biggest-lies-in-learning-evaluation-asking-learners-about-level-3-and-4/.

Thalheimer, W. (2018). *Brinkerhoff Case Method—A better name for a great learning-evaluation innovation.* Available at: https://www.worklearning.com/2018/06/27/brinkerhoff-case-method-a-better-name-for-a-great-learning-evaluation-innovation/.

Thalheimer, W. (2018). *Donald Kirkpatrick was NOT the Originator of the Four-Level Model of Learning Evaluation.* Available at: https://www.worklearning.com/2018/01/30/donald-kirkpatrick-was-not-the-originator-of-the-four-level-model-of-learning-evaluation/.

Thalheimer, W. (2018). *The Learning-Transfer Evaluation Model: Sending Messages to Enable Learning Effectiveness.* Available at: https://www.worklearning.com/ltem/.

Thalheimer, W. (2020). *Factors that Support Training Transfer: A Brief Synopsis of the Transfer Research.* Available at: https://www.worklearning.com/2020/01/06/major-research-review-on-learning-transfer/.

Tulving, E., & Thompson, D. M. (1973). Encoding specificity and retrieval processes in episodic memory. *Psychological Review, 80,* 352–373.

Uttl, B., White, C. A., Gonzalez (2017). Meta-analysis of faculty's teaching effectiveness: Student evaluation of teaching ratings and student learning are not related. *Studies in Educational Evaluation, 54,* 22-42.

About the Author...
Will Thalheimer, PhD, MBA

Will Thalheimer is a learning expert, researcher, instructional designer, speaker, and writer. He holds an MBA from Drexel University and a PhD in Educational Psychology: Human Learning and Cognition from Columbia University. He has worked in the learning-and-performance field since 1985—playing a diverse set of roles, including leadership trainer, instructional designer, simulation architect, project manager, business product line manager, researcher, speaker, author, and consultant.

Beginning in 1998, Dr. Thalheimer dedicated his career to bridging the gap between research and practice in the workplace learning field, founding Work-Learning Research as his research and consulting practice. His clients have included giant multinationals, elearning companies, government agencies, trade associations, and universities.

In 2007, Dr. Thalheimer published a seminal research-to-practice report titled *Measuring Learning Results: Creating Fair and Valid Assessments by Considering Findings from Fundamental Learning Research*. Since then, he has been the learning-and-development field's most innovative expert in learning evaluation—publishing the first edition of this book in 2016, revolutionizing learner surveys; creating LTEM (Learning-Transfer Evaluation Model) in 2018, a replacement for the Four-Level Model; and devising a brand-new approach to learning evaluation, LEADS (Learning Evaluation As Decision Support), in the works to be published in 2023 in the book, *The CEO's Guide to Training, eLearning & Work: Reshaping Learning into a Competitive Advantage*.

Dr. Thalheimer is regularly asked to lead learning-audit workshops, write articles, do research, and give keynotes on the topic of learning measurement, presentation science, and the practice of using science-of-learning insights. Will co-created the innovative L&D Conference, the first learning-in-the-workflow conference. Will also co-founded the professional membership organization LDA (The Learning Development Accelerator)—where research-aligned practices are encouraged.

In 2021 Will Thalheimer joined TiER1 Performance as Principal. He has continued to publish important contributions and work with clients—and is currently crafting a new L&D framework, the Performance Activation Model, with support from Jerry Hamburg and other members of the TiER1 team.

Index

Acceptability Indexing, 52, 221, 222, 223, 224, 226, 227

Actionable results, 30, 45, 52, 79, 130

Adam Neaman, x, xv

After-learning supports, 40, 42, 43, 52, 53, 57, 58, 73, 225, 230, 237

Albert Einstein, xi

Allison Rossett, xv

Association for Talent Development, 250

Awareness training, 32, 33, 34, 36, 43, 110, 210

Bias, 8, 9, 10, 15, 16, 17, 19, 20, 22, 26, 27, 46, 47, 50, 53, 67, 69, 85, 92, 94, 97, 110, 139, 177, 185, 190, 200, 202, 204, 207, 208, 214, 218, 227, 237, 238, 239, 240, 251

Bill Coscarelli, xv, 10, 18

Business results, 244, *See Organizational results*

Case method, 240

Chad Udell, xv

Charles Dickens, 15

Clark Quinn, vi, xv, xvi, 249, 250

Comparisons, 18, 24, 25, 52, 167, 191, 217, 219

Confidence, 19, 20, 51, 110

Context alignment, 22, 36, 38

Contextual cues, 16, 18, 22

Correlation, xviii, 3, 11, 12, 13, 24, 29, 75

Creating a learner survey, 234

Decisive Dozen, 36, 37, 38, 39, 40, 41

Distinctive questioning, x, 48, 174, 181, 208, 232

Donald Kirkpatrick, ix, 5, 244, 257

Feedback, v, vii, xi, viii, x, xv, xvii, xviii, 4, 6, 7, 8, 21, 31, 33, 34, 36, 37, 40, 41, 62, 63, 65, 67, 68, 69, 71, 73, 75, 77, 79, 82, 89, 125, 126, 138, 141, 142, 147, 153, 154, 161, 177, 178, 190, 198, 200, 208, 209, 210, 211, 212, 214, 230, 231, 232, 235, 237, 238, 239, 240

Focus groups, 238

Follow-up learner surveys, 48, 53, 82, 96, 189, 190, 191, 192, 193, 200

Forgetting, 9, 20, 122

Four pillars of training effectiveness, 39, 43, 52, 53, 71, 73, 80, 86

Fred Estes, 13
Guy Wallace, xvi, 250
Incentives, 213, 214
Instructional designers, vii, xiii, 46, 56, 125, 190, 198, 199, 231, 232
Instructional-design process, 8
ISPI, 251
Jack Phillips, xv
Jane Bozarth, xi, xvi, 4, 249, 250, 251
Julie Dirksen, v, xv, xvi, 249, 250
Karl Kapp, xvi, 249, 250
Kirkpatrick-Katzell Four-Level Model, ix, 3, 5, 13, 14, 29, 192, 232, 243, 244, 245, 257, 259
Leadership training, 240
LEADS, ix, 233, 259
Learner attention, 37, 38, 46, 81, 89, 133, 244
Learner engagement, 33, 37, 38, 40, 41, 47, 53, 63, 75, 89, 90, 92, 126, 145, 146, 147, 169, 177, 181, 185, 186, 187, 208, 211, 212, 214, 239, 246
Learner perceptions, 193, 220, 227, 234, 237, 240, 241, 246, 248
Learner satisfaction, 6, 7, 29, 31, 40, 75, 246
Learners remember, 20, 41
Learners understand, 40, 41, 86
Learning and forgetting curves, 9
Learning Development Accelerator, xvi, 141, 250, 251, 259
Learning effectiveness, x, 6, 7, 30, 52, 53, 75, 139, 140, 178, 246, 247, 257
Learning evaluation, x, ix, 5, 7, 193, 243, 244, 245, 248, 249, 256, 257, 259
Learning genome, 36, 48
Learning Guild, xi, 4, 19, 251
Learning Landscape model, 122, 123
Learning Maximizers, 35, 36, 39, 40, 43
Likert-like scales, 17, 18, 19, 23, 25, 26, 27, 46, 63, 67, 75, 92, 131, 142
LTEM, ix, x, 5, 193, 227, 241, 243, 245, 246, 247, 248, 256, 259
Marc J. Rosenberg, vi
Matt Richter, xvi, 141, 250
Measuring effectiveness, 29
Meta-analysis, 11, 12, 13, 24, 29, 126, 139, 253, 255, 256, 257
Mirjam Neelen, xi, xvi, 249, 250
Motivate learners, 214
Motivated to apply, 21, 40, 41, 42, 71, 105
Motivating learners, 201

Neil Rackham, 12
Net Promoter Score, 19, 77, 138, 139, 140
Nonresponse bias, 201, 203, 204, 206, 207, 255
Numeric scales, 18, 19, 26, 46, 63, 208
Objective measures, 5, 14, 241, 248
Online whiteboarding, 239
On-the-job performance, 2, 3, 22, 25, 32, 34, 39, 40, 43, 45, 73, 77, 82, 83, 110, 122, 189, 192, 229, 230, 231
Organizational results, xiii, 5, 31, 233, 244
Patti Shank, viii, xvi, 249, 250
Paul Kirschner, 250, 251
Performance assistance, 32, 33, 34, 43
Performance training, 32, 33, 34, 35, 36, 43, 51, 84, 99
Pilot testing, x, 91, 131, 174, 192, 232, 235
Prior knowledge, 16, 40
Raymond Katzell, ix, 5
Realistic practice, 36, 41, 95, 97, 98, 99, 176
Remembering, 16, 21, 25, 31, 32, 38, 39, 41, 43, 52, 53, 56, 73, 95, 96, 97, 101, 103, 116, 122, 124, 130, 168, 186, 190, 221, 222, 223, 231, 233, 237
Repetition, 16, 19, 36, 37, 38, 41, 95, 101, 103, 207, 255
Resilience, 107, 112
Response rates, xi, x, 202, 203, 204, 205, 206, 207, 208, 209, 213, 214, 239, 253, 255, 256
Richard Clark, 13
Robert O. Brinkerhoff, v, xv, 5, 240
Roy Pollock, vi, xv
Ruth Clark, v, xv, xvi, 249, 251
Scenario questions, 5, 14, 97
Self-efficacy, 41, 107, 109, 110, 111, 114
Sharon Shrock, 10, 18
Smile sheets, vi, vii, ix, xvii, xviii, 4, 7, 8, 11, 12, 13, 14, 15, 17, 24, 25, 27, 29, 30, 31, 40, 41, 43, 52, 56, 73, 75, 139, 192, 215, 229, 231, 232, 237, 247
Spacing effect, 38, 41, 95, 101, 253, 254, 255, 256
Stakeholder management, xviii, 6, 7, 25, 30, 49, 51, 52, 55, 56, 57, 58, 84, 87, 89, 103, 125, 130, 139, 142, 175, 187, 192, 198, 215, 218, 227, 234, 244, 248
Standards, 49, 50, 51, 52, 53, 75, 83, 84, 85, 89, 99, 109, 111, 131, 217, 218, 224, 227
Stealth messages, 6, 52, 56, 57, 58, 89, 95, 103, 105, 112, 114, 118, 130, 145, 162, 199
Structured interviews, 239
Subjective inputs, 15, 16, 17, 27, 241

Supervisors/Managers, vii, xiii, 2, 25, 33, 34, 42, 56, 58, 59, 63, 125, 126, 128, 161, 190, 191, 198, 199, 200, 210, 240, 241, 246, 247

Thalheimer, 4, 58, 101, 126, 193, 240, 243, 252, 256, 259

TiER1 Performance, 251, 252, 259

Timing of learner surveys, 19, 20, 21

Top of mind, 9, 19, 20, 189, 190, 200

Training design, 19, 30, 31, 39, 49, 227

Transmortify, 23, 24

Triangulating, 241

Triggering, 22, 26, 38, 41, 55, 95, 97, 103, 104, 105, 122, 168, 223

Work performance, 30, 32, 62, 82, 84, 130, 243, 247

Working memory, 20, 122, 218

Work-Learning Research, vii, 37, 248, 251, 259

Made in the USA
Columbia, SC
07 June 2022